THE BIBLE AS DRAMA

THE BIBLE AS DRAMA

by
Lawrence Waddy

PAULIST PRESS
New York / Paramus / Toronto

Library of Congress
Catalog Card Number: 74-34527

ISBN: 0-8091-1875-0

Published by Paulist Press
Editorial Office: 1865 Broadway, N.Y., N.Y. 10023
Business Office: 400 Sette Drive, Paramus, N.J. 07652

Printed and bound in the
United States of America

CONTENTS

INTRODUCTION

In this course you are going to be asked to take an active part. Instead of reading about people in the Bible, or hearing explanations from a teacher, or watching films, you will be asked to put yourself in the place of Bible characters.

Drama is an old Greek word. It means "doing" something. Twenty-five hundred years ago, the Greeks were pioneers in the idea that stories come alive when they are acted out. That is the object of this course. You do not need an elaborate stage, or properties, or costumes, to bring a story to life in dramatic form. You only need a simple text, a little imagination, and the willingness to experiment together.

For many people, this is the best possible way to enjoy learning. It is hard to forget a story, once you have been a part of it. And so we invite you to do just that: find out about King Solomon, St. Peter, the characters in Jesus' parables, and Jesus himself, by taking part in scenes from their lives. Make up your own scenes also. Above all, treat them as real people, and get inside them.

In fact, *do it yourself!*

LEADER'S HANDBOOK

This handbook is designed to help the leaders of groups, or teachers of classes, who are using any of the three Parts of the series: *The Bible As Drama: Do It Yourself.*

Part I is devoted to the Old Testament.

Part II is devoted to the Life and Teaching of Jesus.

Part III is devoted to the Young Church, as portrayed in the Acts of the Apostles.

In the handbook, dramatic examples are given for each of the three Parts. Ideally, they fit together as a unified course of Bible study through drama. But if you are using any single Part, you should still find all of the examples helpful.

The Bible is a unity, containing an infinite variety of situations and people. Whatever casts light on one aspect of it helps you to appreciate the whole better.

1. The use of religious drama

During World War II, a cartoon appeared in *Punch* in England. The first drawing showed an entertainer singing to a hall full of soldiers. A look of blank boredom was on all of their faces. In the second drawing, she was appealing to them to join in singing. In the third, they were all letting themselves go with obvious enthusiasm. In the fourth and last, they were applauding her—or rather themselves.

It was not only funny, but plausible. It put in a simple form the truth known to many teachers, that a class begins to learn when it begins to be involved. And the principle of this book is that students of all ages will love the Bible, and learn what it says, by involvement rather than by listening. Once you have *been* Noah steering the Ark, or Isaac waiting for the knife to descend, or Boaz falling in love with Ruth, or David waiting to fight Goliath, or Solomon weighing economics against religion, or a Jewish girl being dragged away into exile; once you have *acted out*, rather than read, the story of the Good Samaritan or the Rich Farmer, you cannot easily forget them. And you do not need to be a good actor, far less a trained one, to feel the involvement and remember the meaning.

The method of teaching put forward in this book is that of drama and discussion. It would be my hope and belief that a student who worked his way through these scenes, reading the kindred Bible passages and taking part in discussion of the importance of

3

each, would end up with a love of the Bible and a very fair knowledge of its highlights. Hopefully also he would have a desire to
know more. All of us who are involved in Church School teaching
know that we are up against a barrier of ignorance, and that it is
very hard to make a straight teaching course, similar to the School
lessons of the week, inspiring. Yet the Bible, quite apart from its
religious content, is also the source of so many thrilling stories that
it is tragic if students only learn to associate it with boredom. The
conventional courses are indeed excellently taught by many teachers; but it is surely right to make available every type of approach
which may suit a particular teacher's abilities and tastes.

A drama course is not a gimmick. It demands much of the
teacher or leader, but its rewards are great. If your experience is
the same as mine, you will end up with new flashes of insight and
understanding, often provided by the way in which the students interpret their parts. I can never forget one of the first rehearsals of
my first Bible play, a musical version of "The Prodigal Son." It
was written for an intelligent, talented group of seventeen- and
eighteen-year-old boys, just about to leave their boarding school in
England. We added to the text, and worked out the interpretation,
as rehearsals proceeded. One day the Prodigal was rehearsing his
return home. Dragging his steps, tired and in rags, he was coming
from the back of the hall. He sang, in a broken voice and with no
accompaniment:

> I will rise, and go to my Father,
>   And tell him of all my sin.
> I will knock at the door, and entreat him
>   To open and let me in.

The boy taking the part of the Devil came to me. "Can't I do
something to try to stop him, sir?" I told him to go ahead and try
whatever seemed natural. So the Devil went and knelt in the aisle,
praying in dumb show to the Prodigal not to go home. It must
surely be the first time the Devil has prayed on a stage! I waited
to see what the Prodigal would do—kick him aside, speak angrily,
or what. He did nothing like that. He simply never saw him. With
his eyes on home, he had broken the power which the Devil had
exercised over him. The contrast with the earlier scene, in which he
had been an easy victim of the Devil's persuasion, was overwhelming. Two boys, by their own identification with their parts, had
transformed the scene in a few seconds.

I could give many other examples, after more than ten years of numerous productions in schools and churches. During the first production of a musical version of "Noah," all of us who were involved in it realized for the first time the power and beauty of the *end* of the story, after the waters had receded. The rainbow covenant, symbol of the bridge between God and man; and the humility and courage of Noah's sons, as they go out on their separate ways to rebuild a dead world; these, acted out by young actors with sincerity and simplicity, had a very big impact. On a different level, my first use of the parable contained in Part II, "Guests From Out of Town," was with fourth grade boys; and it immediately made them interested in discussing Jesus' other teaching about prayer.

The scenes composed for this book are deliberately left flexible. It would have been quite easy to make all of them into set plays, with definite and complete parts written for each actor. But it seemed to me, from my use of them with classes, that this would be a mistake. The need to improvise part of the scene should sharpen the interest of the actors. However, it adds to the responsibility of the leader—and, I believe, to the interest of the challenge. You will never quite know, at the beginning of a session, how much guidance you will need to give. The acting out may just "happen," with spontaneous skill and insight; or it may take a good deal of nursing before it becomes significant. If you, as the leader, are steeped in the story, you will know how much discussion it is right to have before acting out begins. In my experience, it is a good thing to begin to act as soon as possible. Discussion arises through the situations which the actors meet.

It must not be thought that drama is an easy option for the students. They should be asked to learn the facts and lessons taught by the acted stories. As a simple test, I recently asked two groups of well-educated adults how much they could remember of the Book of Ruth. They were ashamed of the results, I think. We then went over the scenes as they appear in Part I, and they agreed that if they had ever taken part in acting these out, it would have been very hard to miss the beauty of the story and the lessons which it teaches. If you will think out for yourself how to make the most use of the course, your class should gain from it a basis of clear knowledge.

Modern parallels for the situations encountered in the scenes are often easy to find, and help to bring them alive. With the parables, which are timeless, an actual modern situation seems to be the appropriate setting; hence the judge on the golf course and the farmer building his silo, in Part II. And for parallels with Old Testament stories, it is usually all too easy to point to modern examples of forced labor, exile or deportation of subject peoples. I remember that I was studying for an examination on the Book of Jeremiah when the Vichy Government was being formed in France, and the book seemed to be a truly contemporary document. However you treat the stories, never let your students feel that the Bible is something which happened a long time ago, and is being dragged up out of the past as a burden to be dutifully endured.

The scenes in this book cover only a small selection of the Bible stories. You and your class may wish to write or improvise many more. If you do receive this impulse from the use of the book, it will be a proof of its success. For it is offered to you as a springboard, not as a solid platform.

2. The leader's role

Only a few notes and suggestions are needed to enable you to make the most of the course. I have not called this a "Teacher's Manual", because the teacher-pupil formula does not apply to all of the many ways in which the course can be used. Within my own experience, parts of it have been successfully shared with fourth, fifth and sixth grade groups, junior high and high school, adult study groups, and—best of all—with groups in which both adults and younger members took part.

Your role is going to vary according to the circumstances in which you use the course. But the class members can safely be called "students", since we are all in that category, I hope, whatever our age or status.

Every study group needs a leader; or, to use a now popular term, a facilitator. It may seem that a course called *Do It Yourself* will make fewer demands on its leader. This is both true and untrue. It is true that, from the start, the students take over an active role. It is also true that the course will be a failure unless the leader has worked hard to be ready for his job.

Above all, the leader needs the quality of enthusiasm.

Do not use the course unless, after you have looked at it carefully, you believe in it. I sincerely believe that it can be a wonderful success, if it is entered into with confidence and zest. But it will easily fail, if the approach is half-hearted.

Next after enthusiasm, and closely akin to it, are two other qualities which you will need: enterprise and adaptability. In a drama course, you and your students must do what Jesus told Peter to do: "Launch out into the deep!" Encourage your readers and actors to try bold experiments. Let them overplay their roles at first. You can easily pull them back later, if you need to do so. But try to avoid a dull, tentative beginning to the course.

The next requirement is careful preparation. The need for this, and the ways to achieve it, will be made clear later.

If you come equipped with these things, you will not need great skill or experience to make the course a success. Previous experience of drama will help you; but you can make the course successful and enjoyable, for yourself and your students, without it.

3. Preparing to read

Play reading is a very different thing from play production. More will be said about productions later in this Handbook; but for readings, and simple presentations, common sense will carry you a long way. Here are a few general guidelines.

a) *SETTING.* Before you begin to read, make sure that the students are comfortable. This means that they have good light, and are sitting in a formation which will encourage effective reading and full involvement. There are always some people who love to sit at the back. The obvious answer is a circle, and as small a circle as you can comfortably manage. For this reason, it sometimes makes good sense for some of the group to sit on the floor.

b) *COPIES.* If possible, provide each reader with a copy. Sharing copies for a play reading is very difficult. It reduces concentration, and affects the quality and enjoyment of the performance. Each reader should also have a Bible, so as to be able to look up the references in the text.

c) *READING TECHNIQUE.* You will begin with a group who do not know how to read. Some of them will be nervous, and they need your help in order to prove to themselves that reading is enjoyable. Not all of them will learn to be very fluent or skillful, but they can all achieve clear and confident reading.

To do this, they must breathe properly. Why not begin by asking them all to take a number of deep breaths? Point out that a great deal of poor, inaudible reading is the result of inadequate supplies of breath. Hopefully they will enjoy taking some good gulps of air, and filling their lungs.

It is also necessary to open your mouth in order to read. Organize an informal contest in clear diction. (It is fun, which is always a help!) Who can say correctly *"six mixed lipsticks"* most times in fifteen seconds? The winner deserves a good part when the reading starts! Think up other phrases which involve moving your lips and tongue and teeth. And perhaps you might read this paragraph to the students with your mouth almost closed, as a parody of the way in which so many people speak. Reading like that is like running a race without stretching your legs or lifting your arms.

d) *PACE AND EXPRESSION*. Tell the students not to hurry their lines when they begin to read. They should come in quickly on cues, as slow cues make a scene drag. But gobbling the words spoils their effect. Point out to them that many people trail off into inaudibility at the end of each sentence. Read a passage, deliberately doing this, and get them to practice reading short sentences. Then take a short piece of dialogue from one of the scenes, and practice quick entries on cues. Change the readers around, so that everyone has a chance to try this out.

Here is a specimen of dialogue, which requires overlapping entry on the cues.

JOHN: I've got to go. Don't you realize—
MARY: You can't leave us now, just when we need you most.
JOHN: Can't you understand that I have no choice? I'm not doing this because I wanted it this way.
MARY: All right then, go! It's obvious that I mean nothing to you.
JOHN: Oh, Mary! Don't make things more difficult than they are.
MARY: I'm sorry, John. I really am sorry.

Practice the pace and expression required for this passage. Mary must break in on John's first line, and John must be ready to go on: "Don't you realize that I . . . ." if she has not taken up her cue. John must break in on Mary's line; and Mary on John's second line; and John on Mary's second line. But the last line is an exception to this rule. It would be effective for Mary to wait a full three seconds before her line: "I'm sorry, John." However, if the cues were slow in the preceding lines, the effect of the pause would be ruined.

Discuss the expression in these lines. You do not know what has been happening; and it makes a great deal of difference what John is going to do, what the relationship between John and Mary is, and so on. Get the students to expand on this, and to practice ways of saying the lines.

Then take this line:

"You mean he's dead? Oh, no! What am I going to do?"

Discuss, and practice, different ways of saying these words. Invent some other short speeches, with different kinds of dramatic impact: comic, violent, sentimental. Try them out with different members of the group.

Then go back to the basics: take some more breaths, and do another jaw-moving exercise.

If you think this out carefully, it should be stimulating and relaxing. And it will emphasize to the students that reading is an art and a skill, in its own way as subtle as singing or painting.

4. Reading

Having set the scene, you are ready to open the book and begin.

Every scene opens with a Bible reference. As leader, you must make yourself completely familiar with the Bible text and background of the scene. When questions arise in discussion, you should know where to look for relevant material in the Bible, to help to answer them. Needless to say, this is a hard challenge. It does not mean that you have to be a learned scholar; but you must convey to your students the fact that you care about the meaning and origin of the scenes, and have taken trouble over them.

Some people like to read the Bible passages first, before the reading of the scene. This is up to you. I prefer to read the scene, and go back to the Bible later.

You now come to the list of characters. Here at once you have a problem. In all parts of the Bible you will meet difficult names: Elimelech, Abinadab, Caiaphas, Manaen, Dionysius, and many more. You can, if you wish, substitute simple modern names, like Mel, Ben, Don. Suggest this plan to your students, and ask them whether they think it would be helpful. They may prefer to try to master the Jewish and Greek names.

For some of the scenes, a family tree set out on a chalkboard will be very helpful. This applies mainly to the Old Testament.

Good maps are also needed, for each part of the book. Understanding the context makes so much difference; and the relationship between Egypt and Israel, Galilee and Judaea, "Asia" and Macedonia, for example, is important for the full enjoyment of some of the scenes.

a) *CASTING*. Having read the scene carefully yourself, you will know what types of characters it contains. Point out to the students that any of them can attempt any part. You are not aiming for type casting, or looking for the stars in your group at the expense of the rank and file readers. At the same time, you do not want to put off a nervous reader by asking him to do too much all at once. If you have a predominance of boys or girls, men or

women, point out to them that they can do very well taking parts
of the opposite sex. (The first Lady Macbeth was a choir-boy, remember?) Emphasize that this is a reading, not a stage performance.

b) *HOW MUCH DISCUSSION?* A short discussion will help
to prepare the students for the reading. There are often some short
notes printed before the scene. Read these, and then give each
reader a brief idea of the character whom he will represent. It will
help Peninnah to know that she is spiteful and mean, in contrast to
the quiet Hannah (p. 57). The Pharisee needs to know how to point
up the contrast with the Tax-Collector (p. 150). The Philosophers at
Athens must be superior and academic, as opposed to the bluntness
of Paul (p. 257).

But do not drag out the preliminary discussion. Readers will
want to get their teeth into the text. They will soon find out what
is expected of them, and will interpret their parts in their own
ways.

c) *STAGE DIRECTIONS.* These are important in many of the
scenes. I suggest that you should make yourself responsible for
them during the first reading. It is a difficult job to do this without
holding up the scene. It needs preparation and adaptability.

d) *FIRST READING.* The quality of the first reading will depend upon the readers' experience and ability. It may go smoothly
all the way through. But it may also be better to stop and repeat a
section, if the readers have had problems. The confidence achieved
during a successful second attempt will add value to later scenes.

After the first reading, encourage discussion. Ask each of the characters how he felt in his part. On pages 73-80, what did Solomon think
about himself? Did Zadok experience torn loyalties, his love for God
overriding his affection for Solomon? What were the feelings of
Adoniram and Ben-Hur, as they tried to get through to the King?

On pages 144-47, how did the women in the different scenes interpret their attitude toward Jesus? What were Jairus and Simon
the Pharisee really like?

On pages 260-63, what were Sosthenes' feelings about Gallio and
Paul? And how would Gallio have later described the Jews and
Christians who appeared in his Court?

e) *SECOND READING.* Some scenes call for less analysis and
discussion than others. With many of them, the best background
for discussion is the Bible passage given as a reference. If discussion is animated, be prepared nevertheless to break into it, and
suggest a second reading. Change at least some of the casting. Ask

for a volunteer to read the stage directions, and arrange how he will fit them in, so that the readers will be assisted and not held up. You can dispense with many of the directions, now that the situation is clear.

Did the readers bring out their characters strongly enough in the first reading? Probably not. Urge them to do this, even to over-do it, on the second reading. Do not be content with a flat performance! Much better to have a little overacting, which can later be toned down.

After two readings, you will probably all want to go on to the next scene. If you do push ahead quickly, work out with the students how you can be sure to keep in close touch with the Bible text. And let me repeat that the more you know about the Bible setting, the more fruitful and enjoyable their use of the Bible will be. Building this bridge between the scenes and the Bible is the leader's most important task in this whole course.

f) *FROM READING TO ACTION.* Some scenes will catch the imagination of the students. After two readings, they will still be full of interest in the action and the characters. If so, this is the opportunity to introduce the technique of a "walk-through" presentation. Set up a stage, with a few simple props, and act out the scene, with the characters reading from their copies as they go through simple movements. It will not be a very good performance, but it can be exciting for students who have not done it before. Putting actions with words, even in a rudimentary way, makes the words come alive through a different dimension.

You may have a battle about priorities. Your students may well enjoy their first taste of action so much that they will clamor to "put on a play" without further delay. If so, I suggest that you encourage them to study a whole section of the book first (I,II or III). Keep an eye out for the most actable and effective scenes, with a view to performing them later. Emphasize that they will play their parts with greater discernment when they have a clear picture of the place which the chosen scenes have in the scheme of the Bible.

5. Improvisation

In many of the scenes, you will find that the actors are invited to improvise part of the dialogue. Even when this is not indicated in the text, there is no reason why you should not introduce the technique of improvisation. For example, I have not included improvisation in the scenes from Jesus' life (Part II). This is because they are written for presentation as a whole, with a set text. However, why should not Peter, Andrew, James and John discuss the fishing conditions before the call of Peter (p. 141)? Or the opponents of Jesus talk more about their reasons for being shocked at his teaching and actions (p. 151)?

At first, your students will not know what to do when they are asked to improvise. There is no need to hurry them into it. You can leave some of these scenes and sections out, and return to them later. However, as they grow more accustomed to reading, and more confident in their portrayal of characters; as the situations become more vivid to them, improvisation should become not only possible but almost essential. They will feel confined by the text, and want to step beyond it and breathe new life into it—their own interpretation of the character from inside.

In order to improvise, they must truly be inside the characters which they represent. Until a group of fourth graders improvised the scene, I had never thought about Isaac's response to Abraham's command that he prepare to be sacrificed. Did he protest, weep, struggle? Or did he acquiesce quietly? And what would the Priest and Levite answer, when the Innkeeper asked them the awkward question, "You came down the road from Jerusalem too, didn't you" (p. 194)? Or, to take a more challenging scene, how can a group of students get inside the atmosphere of Pentecost (p. 225)? Not, surely, by reading a text with a set dialogue, but by building their own reactions to the mounting tension in the Upper Room.

Improvisation can be exciting and very meaningful. It will not happen at once, unless your students are exceptionally flexible. But, given time and encouragement and enterprise, it will greatly enrich their Bible knowledge.

6. Classroom presentations

"Classroom" could equally mean "home." It implies any small-scale performance, without the complications of staging and lighting.

Choose a comparatively simple scene as a beginning. Examples are: The Justice of Solomon, p. 75; Jericho, p. 153; The Rich Farmer, p. 187; or In the House of Judas, p. 239.

Hold readings to determine the casting. Find small jobs for the students who have no speaking parts in the first presentation. An announcer can introduce the scene. The stage needs to be prepared. If other classes are to attend, some people can prepare and reproduce a program.

Keep the scenery simple. At this stage you are not thinking in terms of a curtain, and the props are minimal. The simplest of these scenes requires no scenery at all. Present the scenes in everyday dress, as though they were happening now. However, girls often feel more convincing in their parts if they wear long dresses.

Prepare a few simple diagrams of movements during the scene. You may find that these are modified as rehearsals proceed. Make sure that the actor who is speaking does not turn away from the audience. (And how about a repeat of those breathing and mouth-moving exercises at this point?)

Restrict movements at first, avoiding whatever is unnecessary. Make the speakers keep their feet still during their lines, and experiment with a few movements of the hands. A restless, foot shuffling actor loses the force of his words! It is by expression and emphasis that the words of these scenes will be made most effective. The actors who are not speaking should remain still. When a movement is made, it should be decisive. Frequent small moves only lead to a confused, uncoordinated performance.

Do not rehearse for too long. It is hard to lay down rules, because ability varies so much; but not more than four rehearsals should be needed for one of these scenes. After the first rehearsal, insist that the actors learn their parts, which are after all very short in most scenes. Have a prompter at the remaining rehearsals, who will supply the lines when necessary. (It is a difficult, unselfish job, to be given to a responsible person.) The actors will try to cling to their scripts. But until they act without a book in their hands they will have no real feeling for their parts.

7. Moving on from classroom presentations

Your students are almost sure to be discussing something more ambitious in the way of a performance. Bear in mind that "performing" can mean any of a number of things: classroom presentation without an audience; presentation with other classes present; a skit at a parish supper; a simple insertion in the liturgy of a Church; or a full-scale stage performance of one or more plays.

Let us suppose that you have successfully rehearsed and acted one or more scenes in a simple setting—a classroom or a home. You then have the choice of continuing to present scenes in this way, or attempting something on a bigger scale. There is nothing wrong with repeated classroom-type presentations. They increase confidence and fellowship, and for many groups they offer the right level.

But if you belong to an active Church community, you will find plenty of opportunities to use your students' skills and enthusiasms in the service of other people; and this must surely be one of your objectives.

Here are some suggestions.

a) You could offer the same kind of informal presentation to larger audiences, without changing the demands upon your actors. If your students are part of a Church School, invite more classes. Then include the parents, still within the Church School setting.

b) Make your presentation available for other groups. Guilds, convalescent homes, pot-luck suppers: these are only some examples of the opportunities for service to groups which are constantly looking for programs. If it is known that you have a presentation, which does not need elaborate staging or involve expensive, complicated arrangements, you will be very popular! The fun involved, the challenge to do a good job and to witness to your faith, are stimulating to you and your students.

c) Find out from your priest or minister whether you can make a contribution to the liturgy of your Church. This will be discussed in the next section.

But—do not hurry! Setting the right pace will be one of your important decisions. Only you and your group can tell what is right for them; and they may contain some impatient people. You must find a level somewhere between sloppy improvisation and fussy perfectionism. You are not trying to produce professionally drilled stars. On the other hand, you are making an offering to God, and it must be an efficient, worthy offering.

8. Drama and worship

In the text of all three parts of this book you will find suggestions about the use of scenes in Church worship.

The medieval Church used drama extensively. We still possess, and sometimes revive, the plays which were used then. Only a few of the people could read, and their knowledge of God and of their faith came from sermons, hymns, painted walls and windows, and drama.

For various reasons, this use of Church drama withered away. In England, the Puritan influence, especially in the time of Cromwell, was a prime cause.

However, in the last few years the chance for a thrilling revival of drama within the liturgy has arisen. Many new doors are opening, and it is of the utmost importance that what is introduced shall be of high quality. Participation by lay people of all ages has grown out of all recognition; and Bible drama offers one of the most fruitful opportunities for it.

You will therefore want to keep in close touch with your priest or minister. When the right moment comes, be ready to make your group's contribution available, in whatever way he approves.

Here again are some suggestions.

a) In place of a Scripture reading, present a scene. My recommendation would be that you do not attempt period costumes. There is real merit in acting Bible scenes in a contemporary setting. The important thing is that your presentation should be audible, and should bring out clearly the meaning of the Bible scene.

The change from classroom to Church is a big one, and it is essential that you not start off with a poor performance. The congregation will not be looking for a high level of technical skill; but they must be able to hear and see clearly.

In the book you will find suggestions for fitting some of the scenes into the calendar of the Church Year. This does not apply to the Old Testament Scenes in Part I. These scenes are in many cases excellent for presentation in Church; but they have no special application to the seasons. Parts II and III contain many scenes which do fit in with saints' days and other festivals. For example, what could be more appropriate to the Sunday nearest Saint Andrew's day than the presentation of the scene in which Andrew accepts the five loaves and two fishes, and offers them to Jesus (p. 148)? And how can the Epiphany season be better pointed up than by presenting scenes in which Paul is shown taking the Gospel to the Gentile congregations?

A Church using carefully chosen drama extracts in place of some Scripture readings would be teaching the participants and the congregation in a vivid manner, consistent with dignity. It is not difficult to work out a harmonious program, by which to blend drama into the scheme of Scripture teaching. If the manner of presentation is simple, direct and sincere, there should be no jarring note or cause for offense. You should constantly remind yourself, and all those for whom and with whom you work, that drama in the liturgy is a time-honored tradition, not a gimmicky invention of modern times.

b) In the case of the scenes from the life of Jesus (pp. 136-154) you will see that they are written to be used together. They form a program lasting forty-five minutes to one hour, according to the amount of music added to the text. A group of students who have studied the scenes, and the notes which accompany them, could make a significant contribution to the congregation's understanding of Jesus' life by presenting these scenes. If they are given in the "radio" manner suggested in the text, they do not require lengthy rehearsal.

9. Verse plays

In Part I and Part II you will find some Verse Plays. I have referred to them briefly already. It is now time to consider how they fit into the needs of your students.

The first difference between them and the Scenes is that they give opportunities to many more people. The Scenes have an average cast of four to six: the Verse Plays can keep thirty people active, as the Chorus can be of any size.

They are quite simple to read, but a production of one of them is quite different from the classroom presentation of the Scenes. I suggest that at an early stage in your reading you try out a small part of a Verse Play. Take the opening of "Joseph and His Brothers" or "The Prodigal Son," and see how your students react to Chorus speaking. If they are enthusiastic, fit the Verse Plays into their place in the course. It depends a good deal on the size of your group. If you have more than twenty, there is a great deal to be said for an early start on a play which will keep them all busy.

Choral reading should be a stimulating experience. See that the choruses are read with plenty of rhythm and vigor. If you can find a drum to beat out the rhythm, it will help. If anything, overemphasize the rhythm of lines like these, from "Joseph and His Brothers" and "The Prodigal Son":

> Then from FAR and WIDE came the FOLK of every
> LAND,
> There was CORN in E-GYPT.

> He was BURNing to Go, but he DIDn't know WHERE.

You can read the Verse Plays in the same way as the shorter scenes. The first reading will follow after a discussion of roles, including the role of the Chorus. Then read the Bible reference. After the second reading, try a walk-through performance among yourselves. And if this leads to the desire for a real performance, involve everyone in the group in the planning process.

10. Stage performances

If you take the decision to perform a Verse Play, you are facing quite a new challenge. The staging is still not very complicated, but there are a whole series of new problems: changes of scene, however simple the scenery may be; the collections of props; costume. Even if you stick to modern dress you will need to plan the costumes to some extent. Any attempt at "Bible" dress is a big undertaking.

Moreover, as soon as you move onto a stage, in a hall of some size, you enter a new world technically. There is a curtain, and there is lighting. Stage teams are needed, and the movements and audibility of actors take on a fresh dimension.

Before you decide to take this considerable step, make sure that you are ready. I suggest that you ask yourself and your students some of the following questions.

a) Are we planning something which will really help the Church's program, or the community's? For whom is the production going to be most useful and significant? Is the play well-fitted to the audience?

b) Are the actors and stage assistants ready to undertake the hard work and discipline necessary for success? Do they fully realize that this is quite a different thing from putting on short scenes?

c) Do we have the leadership? The Director of a play must have some experience, and a good rapport with the rest of the group. Lighting must be properly understood. Microphones, if they are used, must be fitted up and tested by an expert: they are tricky to control. Seating, tickets, programs, publicity, and perhaps refreshments will have to be coordinated.

In fact, look up Luke 14, verse 31: "Or what King, going to make war against another King, sitteth not down first, and consulteth whether he be able with ten thousand to meet him that cometh against him with twenty thousand?"

I do not mean that you should be frightened of the task of producing a play; only that you should take a practical view. When Jesus told Peter to "Launch out into the deep," he knew that he had a boat that would not leak, and nets which he had used many times.

PLANNING THE PERFORMANCE. Let us assume that you have thought out all these things, and have decided that you are equipped to go ahead. What kind of program should you plan?

Sometimes a single play is appropriate. I have produced "The Prodigal Son" (Part II) many times as an after-dinner skit. Either "Joseph and His Brothers" or "Job" could fit into this design perfectly (Part I).

However, if you are inviting an audience specifically for an evening of entertainment, any one of these plays is too short by itself. Therefore consider these possibilities.

You can fit your play into an evening of all-round entertainment: Solos, instrumental music, community singing, etc.

Or, you can put on more than one play. A combination of an Old and a New Testament play has many advantages. "Job" and "Good Friday" combine to make an impressive Lent and Easter program. "Joseph" and "The Prodigal Son" go well together. Allow about half an hour for each play.

I have often chosen two plays, and inserted a shorter play after the first, and before an intermission. To give an example from each Part of the book: "Prosperity and Moral Decline" (p. 77); "The Talents" (p. 179); "In the House of Judas" (p. 239).

An evening of Bible plays is a great tonic for a Church. It unites many people in a deeply moving and worthwhile experience. It provides entertainment and enjoyment; and some people at least come out of it with a new appreciation of the meaning of the Gospel.

MUSICALS. It is worth adding that all of these Verse Plays were written as Musicals. If you feel like tackling my music, which is bright and easy to sing, write to: Religious Drama Productions, 5910 Camino de la Costa, La Jolla, California 92037. Musical scores for each of the plays can be supplied, for $1.50.

11. Writing projects

So far I have discussed a number of ways in which scenes can be read, presented or acted. In this section I shall give some suggestions for a different kind of project, which you may or may not wish to undertake.

Why not write your own scenes? Not you, for your class, but your class, with you as guide.

Let me give some examples of scenes which could be developed, arising out of each part of the book.

Part I. Genesis 25, verses 27-34: Jacob, Esau and the Birthright. Judges 13-16: The Story of Samson. The Book of Jonah.

Part II. Mark 2, verses 1-12: The Healing of the Paralytic. Matthew 25, verses 1-13: The Parable of the Virgins. John 4, verses 1-30: The Woman of Samaria.

Part III. Acts 12, verses 1-17: Peter Escapes from Prison. Acts 13, verses 14-52: The Expulsion of Paul from Antioch.

These examples vary greatly in complexity. The Jacob and Esau scene contains only four characters; whereas Samson and Jonah require careful division into scenes, and a large cast.

The healing of the paralytic cannot very well be acted realistically, because of the roof incident. However, it is an excellent test for the writing of vigorous dialogue, because of the sharp contrasts in characters. The parable of the Virgins is one of the few New Testament stories in which women far outnumber men! It is also certain to provoke strong argument about the character of the "good" girls. As for the woman at the well in Samaria, she can become a very lovable and distinctive character; and this scene can bring in Jesus' disciples, as well as other Samaritans. What kind of questions would the woman's friends ask Jesus, when she brings them back to see him?

In the two passages from Acts, you have to pinpoint where to place your scene. The courtyard of Mary's house is the best setting for the Peter scene. There he can describe his release from the prison to Mary, Mark, Rhoda and others. They can talk about Herod's cruelty, and the dangers which face the Church. In chapter 13, set the scene in verses 44 to 52, and refer back to the earlier events in your dialogue.

The Bible is full of writing opportunities like this. If you are to use them, and your students to enjoy them, you must soak yourself in the stories. Think them through from the point of view of each character. Then read the Bible text with the class, and find out their opinions about the reactions of the characters. Divide them up into small groups (perhaps into pairs) to write and prepare their scenes. As soon as members of one group are ready to share what has been written, let them do so. The others can then contribute their criticisms and ideas. New approaches will become apparent, and this will give a fresh impulse to write more.

I suggest that you should start them writing, without putting too much emphasis on accurate research. They will want to find out more about the background when it becomes necessary for their writing. Let us suppose that they are writing about Samson. To make their scenes convincing, they will want to know who the Philistines were, and why there was so much border fighting. They will find some notes in the Jerusalem Bible (269-271); in Peake (92, the notes on Judges 13-16, and 278h—a fascinating sidelight about the suppression of blacksmiths in Israel); and also in Keller,

Part IV; especially chapters 3 and 4. What started out as a writing project would turn into an exciting search for the context of the story.

In writing about the Paralytic, they will wish to know more about these "Scribes," who watch Jesus to catch him out. What was the reason for the steady opposition to Jesus' teaching and healing? And what kind of house was it that could be taken apart so easily?

To write about Peter's escape, they will need information about Herod; and to set a scene in Antioch they will have to answer questions about Roman government in the Provinces, and the status of Jews. Notes in the Jerusalem Bible and Peake are always helpful; and the more enterprising students will discover how to find further information in libraries.

It is impossible to forecast how successful your writing venture will be. It could lead to more ambitious projects. At the very least it should make the students realize what goes into the creation of a scene, however short. They will understand that the characters in Bible stories are real people, whose thoughts, actions and reactions we need to understand through something more than superficial reading.

12. Bibliography

In each Part of the book, a short list of recommendations for the students' reading and reference is included.

In your own background reading, I recommend that you keep at hand more than one translation of the Bible. Comparison often brings out the meaning more clearly. The beauty of an older version like the King James (or Authorized) can be balanced by the simpler, more modern, language of the Jerusalem Bible or the New English Bible. As an individual translator, J.B. Phillips is outstanding.

You will need access to a good commentary. There are many of these available in libraries. You should try them out, and find the level of detail, and the type of interpretation, which suits your tastes and needs. I have given references to the Jerusalem Bible (JB: numbers refer to pages), which contains short, clear introductions to the Books and notes on the text. I have also referred to Peake's *Commentary on the Bible* (1962 revised edition: numbers refer to paragraphs). This is a much more detailed commentary, reliable and scholarly. For references to archaeology, I have used

Werner Keller's popular and easily readable book, *The Bible as History*.

For quick biographical reference, two excellent books are available: *Who's Who in the Old Testament*, edited by Joan Comay; and *Who's Who in the New Testament*, edited by Ronald Brownrigg.

For the life of Jesus, Daniel-Rops' *Jesus In His Time* is full of interesting background material, given in a readable form. A fine Gospel commentary, to which I have sometimes referred, is Vincent Taylor's *The Gospel According to Saint Mark*.

Then there are the biographies of Peter and Paul, recommended in Part III; written respectively by Oscar Cullmann and Edgar J Goodspeed.

There is no end to the list of books which you could read, and enjoy, in order to equip yourself for this course. But, I repeat, from beginning to end your real strength lies in your knowledge of the Bible. The writing of these scenes has taught me more about the people of the Bible than all my previous study, because it presents a challenge in depth. You can preach a sermon, or write a paper, about Moses or Peter or Paul, a correct, well researched, capable piece of work, without ever passing from accurate words to a flesh-and-blood appreciation. Drama forces you to ask questions. Who were these men? How did they feel when a challenge came? When they were hungry, lonely, excited, inspired? Drama may not get all the answers right, but it demands that you look for them. It moves you on from factual accuracy to emotional comprehension.

13. The Devil's view

Let me indulge in fantasy for a few paragraphs. Or is it fantasy?

My question is, what is the Devil thinking, and saying, and doing about the revival of Religious Drama? The answer can partly be found in these extracts from the report on a recent Conference of the C.C.P. ("Corruption of Church Programs") Department, held at Belial College, Satanville.

After discussing the revival of Religious Drama, and pointing out that it offers to Devils both a threat and an opportunity, the report goes on to list measures which are to be taken by those Devils responsible for a Wrecking Project. These include the following:

a) Since it is recognized that we cannot totally suppress this movement, it is our duty to direct it away from harmful consequences.

b) It is your responsibility to see that your Church acquires books favorable to our purpose. This means that they must on no account tell the *real* story of Our Enemy's so-called "Bible." Most of his followers know nothing about what the Bible really says, and find it unspeakably boring and incomprehensible, while pretending to treat it with great reverence. Keep it that way. Hollywood is very helpful to us in this respect; and by judicious use of the right films and books you will be able to convince the average human that when the Bible is intelligible it is a sordid mixture of sex, violence, and sentimentality. Burn on sight any drama texts which might lead them actually to think about the stories in that deplorable book.

c) If a dangerous book does find its way into a teacher's hands, you must sabotage its use. Your main weapons will be Vanity, Jealousy and Incompetence.

d) Drama brings out the worst in humans. They all think, either that they have outstanding talents, and should hold the center of the stage, or that the people who do hold the center of the stage are intolerably conceited. Often they are quite right. See to it that your teachers indulge their vanity, and offend the remainder of their colleagues by showing off the superiority of their classes; and that the students squabble over the limelight. In no time you can have a Church full of offended, and offensive, prima donnas, from the priest downward.

e) Luckily, the bubble of vanity is likely to be pricked by incompetence. Make the would-be "Director" choose plays that are far beyond the capabilities and understanding of the actors. We strongly recommend that you introduce musical drama, as this allows for the maximum combination of incompetence: nothing is better for us than the squeaky flute and the ill-played guitar, as preludes to the inaudible, shifty presentation of stilted dialogues. Old, badly-tuned pianos, with notes that stick, are also excellent weapons in our armory.

f) It is your responsibility. You have a choice before you. Either this revival of drama is going to undermine our whole Church program, by making the humans enjoy themselves, think harder, and apply the lessons of their terrible Book to their lives (a thought too frightful to contemplate); or we must wreck it here and now, rendering it at least harmless, or if possible positively advantageous to our cause.

So it might go on. There is much to be said for looking at our work from the Devil's corner, so to speak. You should recognize that there are many ways in which a drama course can be wasted or misused. But if you see them clearly, and recognize over against them the opportunities for genuine success, you can hope to avoid many of the pitfalls.

14. Launch out . . .

If this course is a success, it will be because you and your students put more of yourselves into it than into other types of Bible study. The more they put in, the more they will take out. The more they are involved, the more they will be fulfilled. Not only they, but you, the leader.

This is so true, that I would even call drama a powerful means of conversion to living Christian faith.

Which leads me to a true story, told to me as I was writing these notes.

In 1964, I produced "The Prodigal Son" at a Church in California. The actors came from the high school group. Late in the rehearsals, the boy playing the Father had to withdraw, and Jim came in as a substitute.

Jim learned the part, and was all ready to perform. There was one snag. He disliked—almost hated—the boy who was taking the part of the Prodigal. He felt no conviction at all about welcoming him home! He could sing the words, "Come home to me!", but he could not mean them.

The performance began. The Prodigal left the pig-sty, and dragged himself toward home. Jim stood waiting to go out and pick him up from the floor. As he waited, he had an overwhelming experience. Suddenly, he loved the boy who was his son in the play. He went and raised him up, and the dislike was wiped away.

Jim took over his own Church a few weeks ago. On his first Sunday there, the appointed Gospel was the story of the Prodigal Son. He told his own story of the play in that sermon.

If the drama of involvement has that kind of power, we cannot afford to waste it.

Work hard. Experiment. Let your imagination range freely. Use the imaginative riches of your students' talents. And may God bless your efforts, and bring you and your class to a closer, warmer understanding of the Book of Books!

PART I
THE OLD TESTAMENT

These scenes contain some of the most important stories of the 1500-year period from the age of Abraham to the end of the Jewish exile in Babylon.

We begin with Abraham's call to leave Haran and to look for a new country which he believed God to have promised to him and his people. This was the true beginning of Jewish history. It is not possible for us to know how far the details of the Book of Genesis are historical; but there is no doubt that the main characters, and the most important things preserved in Jewish tradition, have a real foundation. With Abraham's choice of the Judaean hills as a home, and the testing of his faith through the challenge to sacrifice his son, the story of this small, God-fearing people began (pp. 28-30).

For the three hundred years which separated Abraham from Joseph, the oral tradition of the Jews preserved only a few stories. The exciting career of Joseph is here described in a Verse Play. Then follows the story of the Jews at the time of Moses, who is usually assumed to have lived in the 13th century before Christ. In many ways Moses is the most important figure in the Old Testament. He led part of the Jewish people out of their serfdom in Egypt, kept them together during their journey through the wilderness, gave them laws which they never forgot, and stood firmly for his belief in one God, who would not forsake his people (pp. 31-56).

Under Moses' successor, Joshua, the Jews who had come from Egypt entered Canaan, and settled in tribal groups. Local leaders, whom the Bible calls Judges, led different tribes during this period, and there was no united action of all twelve tribes.

The prophet Samuel was called by God to find a King, at a time when strength and unity were absolutely necessary if the Jews were to survive the pressure from their neighbors to the Southwest, the Philistines. Samuel first chose Saul, a strong and brave military leader, and then David. David became King about 1000 B.C. (pp. 57-64).

For a short time, Israel was strong and prosperous. David was a man of many gifts, and in spite of his faults he was remembered as a national leader without equal. His son, Solomon, was brilliant and successful, but his search for more and more material prosperity weakened the religious stability of the people (pp. 65-80).

Solomon's son, Rehoboam, was quite unable to keep the Kingdom together. Ten of the twelve tribes broke away to form a fresh Kingdom, called Israel, while a smaller Kingdom of Judah remained in Rehoboam's hands, centered on Jerusalem. In these two Kingdoms a succession of Prophets arose, who gave to mankind a new vision of the majesty and love of God. Judah and Israel were insignificant countries, but they produced far more that was of long-term value to the human race than their more powerful neighbors, the Egyptians, Assyrians and Babylonians. This period is represented by one scene from the life of Isaiah, and a more detailed treatment of Jeremiah's life and teaching (pp. 82-108).

The Kingdom of Israel was crushed by the Assyrians after it had existed for 200 years. Judan retained its independence until 597 B.C., when it was captured by the Babylonians. Many of the young Jews were taken away into exile at Babylon, and some of the greatest of the Prophets arose there, to keep the courage of the people alive. The overwhelming joy of the exiles, when they were granted permission to return to Jerusalem if they wished to go, is shown in our last scene (pp. 109-115).

Jerusalem was now rebuilt, and the Jews enjoyed greater peace and stability. Although great books of the Bible, such as Job, Jonah and Daniel, were written after the Exile, the most memorable and productive part of Jewish history was now at an end. This part of the Old Testament is represented by a Verse Play, "Job" (pp. 116-131).

USEFUL BOOKS. The only essential book for you to use with this course is the Bible.

There are many translations from which to choose. The *Jerusalem Bible* has useful introductions and short notes, to which I have referred in the notes to some scenes. (JB, followed by a number, means the pages in the Old Testament of the Jerusalem Bible.)

The *King James* (or *Authorized*) *Version* remains the most beautiful translation of the Bible; but it should be used in conjunction with a more modern version. The *New English Bible* has been an excellent source for our purpose.

A very good selection of the most important parts of the Old Testament can be found in the Clarendon Press's *Shorter Oxford Bible*, with good introductory notes.

An exciting companion to the stories, giving the historical and archaeological background in a readable form, is Werner Keller's *The Bible as History.* I have given many references to this book.

The two Verse Plays, "Joseph" and "Job," were both written as musicals. If you wish to order the music ($1.50 for each play), write to Religious Drama Productions, 5910 Camino de la Costa, La Jolla, California 92037.

NOTE. Names marked with an asterisk (*) in the lists of characters have been made up to add vividness to the stories. They are all, however, genuine ancient names.

1. ABRAHAM

SCENE: THE CALL OF ABRAHAM

Bible reference: Genesis 12, 1-3

CHARACTERS: ABRAHAM
               LOT
               SARAH
               VOICE OF GOD

NOTE: Start with a good map, and show the extent of Abraham's journey from Haran to Canaan. Explain the names of Abraham and Sarah, by referring to Genesis 17, verses 5 and 15. In other parts of the Bible name changes for religious reasons are recorded: Jacob became Israel; Simon was named Peter ("the Rock"); and Saul assumed his Roman name, Paul.

The setting is ABRAHAM's *farm hear Haran. He and* LOT *are inspecting the land.*

LOT: This wheat crop is wonderful, Uncle.

ABRAHAM: Yes. It looks like being a great harvest.

LOT: But we will need better irrigation in the eastern fields. Is there any news from the contractor?

ABRAHAM: He thinks the work can be done late in the fall; but—

LOT: That's wonderful! It will mean we can almost double what we are producing now.

ABRAHAM: (*Hesitantly*) Yes.

LOT: What's the matter, Uncle Abraham? Is there something on your mind?

ABRAHAM: I don't know, Lot. It's nothing that I can put into words. We have been blessed here, and we are growing rich. And you have worked for me like a son.

LOT: But I am not your son. I know, Uncle. I understand your sorrow at having no heir of your own family.

ABRAHAM: But it's not only that I—how can I say it? This land is my home; and yet I feel I seek another home. I have spent my life here—but I still long for a new life, and the fulfillment of my dreams. Ah, Well! We have no time to waste on thoughts like that. Is Nahun coming to report on the cattle?

LOT: He's down at the hut. I was just going to meet him.

ABRAHAM: Walk on ahead! I will join you in a minute.

(LOT *goes out.* ABRAHAM *stands silent for a minute.*)

ABRAHAM: Yes, this is a good land; and all my kinsfolk are round me. Why am I restless and dissatisfied? Why? Why?

VOICE OF GOD: Abraham!

ABRAHAM: (*falling to his knees*) Who is it?

VOICE OF GOD: I am the Lord your God, Abraham. I know that you are waiting to hear my voice; and I have work for you to do. Will you put your faith in me, and do what I ask?

ABRAHAM: Oh, Lord God! I long to know you and worship you. I have waited so long! Tell me your will, and if I am worthy I will do it.

VOICE OF GOD: You are worthy, Abraham. Now leave this place. Leave your kindred, and take your own family with you. Go toward the South! I will show you the way. And I will make you the Father of a great nation.

ABRAHAM: Yes, Lord. But—(*He waits silently, but no more words come*) Did I really hear the voice of God?

(*After another silence,* SARAH *comes in.*)

SARAH: I brought you your lunch, and—why, what are you doing, Abraham? Are you sick?

ABRAHAM: (*laughing*) No, Sarah, I am not sick. I have heard the voice of God, after waiting so long. Lot! (*louder*) Lot! Come back here quickly!

SARAH: Oh, husband! You mean you saw a vision?

ABRAHAM: It was his voice I heard, as clearly as I hear yours now.

LOT: (*running in*) What is it, Uncle?

ABRAHAM: The message for which I have waited and waited has come. Now I will what God wills for us.

SARAH: What message did he give?

ABRAHAM: We are to pack everything up, and leave at once.

LOT: Leave? But where are we to go?

ABRAHAM: To the South. I know no more than that—except that he will be with us.

SARAH: Sell the farm?

LOT: Can you be serious?

ABRAHAM: There will be no trouble about selling this land. We have no shortage of anything. It is a clear purpose that I have been lacking.

SARAH: But Abraham . . .

ABRAHAM: There are no "but's," Sarah! When God speaks, he
speaks clearly. We shall leave as soon as we can make everything ready. Come back to the house, and we will make our
plans!

2. JOSEPH AND HIS BROTHERS

Bible reference: Genesis 37-50
Read Keller, Part II, chapters 1-2

CHARACTERS:

NARRATOR	PHARAOH OF EGYPT
JACOB	CHIEF BUTLER TO PHARAOH
RACHEL, *his wife*	CHIEF BAKER TO PHARAOH
JOSEPH, *their son*	A JAILER
BENJAMIN, *their youngest son*	A SOLDIER
JOSEPH'S BROTHERS (*ten*)	A TRAVELLER

CHORUS, *including* PHARAOH'S *Wise Men; Midianite merchants, Guards and Soldiers; Egyptians and Foreigners begging for food.*

NOTE: Although the death of Rachel is recorded in Genesis 35, 19, Jacob refers to Joseph's mother in 37, 10. The balance of the play is improved by making her a living character.

There is no need for ancient dress or complicated scenery. The BROTHERS wear jeans and open shirts. PHARAOH may wear a dictator's uniform. JOSEPH wears a shirt "of many colors" at the beginning, and his ceremonial dress in Egypt can be a uniform or a tailcoat.

SCENE ONE	Jacob's house
SCENE TWO	Dothan
SCENE THREE	Jacob's house
SCENE FOUR	Potiphar's house
SCENE FIVE	A prison
SCENE SIX	Pharaoh's palace
SCENE SEVEN	Jacob's house
SCENE EIGHT	Joseph's house in Egypt
SCENE NINE	The same

SCENE ONE: JACOB'S HOUSE

During the opening verses the family move about the stage.
RACHEL *is sitting, sewing* JOSEPH's *coat.* JOSEPH, *a boy of 17, and*
BENJAMIN, *10, are at a table eating.* JACOB *is talking to them. The*
other BROTHERS *come in and out, talking.*

NARRATOR

In the land of Canaan,
Ages long ago,
Jacob, son of Isaac,
Watched his children grow.
Some were born of Zilpah,
Or fed at Leah's breast;
But the sons of Rachel
Jacob loved the best.

CHORUS

Now she took rich wool and the hair of a goat,
And she made for Joseph a many-colored coat.
It was dyed all shades with many-colored dyes,
And it made him hateful in his brothers' eyes.

> (RACHEL *is now trying the coat on* JOSEPH. *The* BROTHERS, *in*
> *a group, are watching with obvious scorn and dislike.*)

For his brothers used to see their Father dote
On Joseph in his many-colored coat;
And his Father's doting and his Mother's sighs
Made Joseph hateful in his brothers' eyes.

It was sad to see those elder brothers gloat
At the boy who had the many-colored coat.
For his Father and Mother never could realize
That it made him hateful in his brothers' eyes.

JOSEPH: Are you coming to have your supper now, Reuben?
REUBEN: No, thank you, brother. I shall wait. I might be in the
way.
JOSEPH: Are you angry with me?
SIMEON: Angry? Why should we be angry?

> (*The* BROTHERS *stand in a close group in one corner.*)

REUBEN: A coat of many colors   On his back!
SIMEON: A coat of many colors,   While I wear black!
LEVI: A coat of many colors,   To flaunt all day!
JUDAH: A coat of many colors,   While I wear gray!
ZEBULUN: A coat of many colors!   I call it mean!
ISSACHAR: A coat of many colors,   While I wear green!
DAN: A coat of many colors,   Bright and new!
GAD: A coat of many colors!   Mine is faded blue!
ASHER: A coat of many colors!   What a sight!
NAPHTALI: A coat of many colors!   Mine is old and white!
JOSEPH: I dreamed a dream last night. Perhaps, if I tell it to all of
   you, one of you can explain to me what it means.
SIMEON: Perhaps!
JUDAH: Tell us your dream, brother!
JOSEPH: Last night I dreamed a dream,
            For the Lord sent a sign.
            All your sheaves in the field
            Bowed down before mine.
BROTHERS: Joseph is a dreamer!
            Dreams that he is King!
            We are all his slaves,
            and must obey in everything!
JOSEPH: Last night I dreamed a dream;
            It was clear to see.
            The sun and moon and stars
            Bowed down before me.
BROTHERS: Joseph is a dreamer!
            Dreams that he is best
            We must be his servants,
            who will bow at his behest!

SCENE TWO: DOTHAN

NARRATOR

So his brothers envied Joseph. But his Father remembered the
dreams, and wondered what they meant. And Joseph's brothers
went to feed their Father's flocks. Jacob sent Joseph to join them.
And Joseph met a traveller, who told him: "They are gone to
Dothan." So Joseph followed them. And when they saw him afar
off, they conspired against him to kill him.

(*The* BROTHERS *are sitting around a fire.*)

BROTHERS

Behold! This dreamer cometh
Wearing his colored gown!
Behold! This dreamer cometh!
Come! Let us strike him down!

He is the cause of envy;
He is the cause of strife.
Why should we serve this dreamer?
Come! Let us take his life!

SIMEON: Come here, dreamer! (JOSEPH *comes in slowly.*)
JUDAH: Welcome, brother!
LEVI: Come nearer, so that we can bow down to you!
SIMEON: Tie him up, and throw him into the pit!
REUBEN: Don't hurt the boy!
JUDAH: Oh, no! We shan't hurt him!
LEVI: Take the coat, and smear it with goat's blood!
SIMEON: Yes, and we can tell Father that an evil beast devoured him.

(*They strip* JOSEPH, *and tie his hands. Then they push him off stage.*)

LEVI: There you go, Mother's darling!
JUDAH: Go to sleep down there, and dream!

CHORUS

So they tied his hands, and mocked him with their wit,
And they threw him down a deep and rocky pit.
For they would not dare to strike a brother dead;
But they left him there, and sat them down to bread.

(*The* BROTHERS *sit round the fire again, eating and drinking.*)

Then they stripped him of his many-colored coat,
And they dipped it in the blood of a goat;
And they took that coat, now stained a crimson red,
And they told their Father that his son was dead.

(*During the next reading we see the* MIDIANITE MERCHANTS *come on. The* BROTHERS *bring back* JOSEPH, *his hands tied, and sell him. The* BROTHERS *receive the money and count it. All this is mimed in silence.*)

NARRATOR

Then there passed by Midianites, merchantmen; and they drew and lifted up Joseph out of the pit, and sold him for twenty pieces of silver. And they brought Joseph down to Egypt.

BROTHERS

(*together, or each taking two lines*)

Twenty pieces of silver,
 To be rid of this pest!
Twenty pieces of silver
 And my conscience at rest!

Twenty pieces of silver!
 Modest payment indeed!
Twenty pieces of silver!
 Don't accuse me of greed!

Twenty pieces of silver!
 They could take him for ten!
Twenty pieces of silver,
 Not to see him again!

SCENE THREE: JACOB'S HOUSE

During the next chorus reading, we see the BROTHERS *bring the coat to* JACOB. *He sits numb and broken-hearted.* RACHEL *and* BENJAMIN *try to comfort him.*

CHORUS

(*slowly*)

Jacob mourned for his son,
Mourned for his son, and refused to be comforted.
Jacob mourned for his son,
Mourned for his son, and refused to be comforted.
"For I will go down into the grave mourning.
"I will go down into the grave, to my son, mourning."
Jacob mourned for his son,
Mourned for his son, and refused to be comforted.

SCENE FOUR: IN EGYPT—POTIPHAR'S HOUSE

During the next Chorus *reading we see the* Merchants *sell* Joseph *to* Potiphar. *Then* Joseph *is left alone on stage.*

Chorus

Midianites, merchantmen,
Took Joseph down to Egypt.
Midianites, merchantmen,
Sold Joseph there in Egypt.
In the house of Potiphar
The boy was bought and sold.
Merchantmen of Midian
They traded him for gold.
Midianites, merchantmen,
Sold Joseph there in Egypt.
Midianites, merchantmen.

(Joseph *sits alone, his hands still tied.*)

Joseph

I'm eating my heart away
For love of my fatherland.
I'm eating my heart away.
O wind, that blows on land and sea,
Be bearer of my word.
O wind, that blows on land and sea,
When will my cry be heard? When will my cry be heard?

I'm eating my heart away
For love of my fatherland.
I'm eating my heart away.
O Lord, who rules in earth and sky,
When will you turn and heed?
O Lord, who rules in earth and sky,
Pity me now in my need! Pity me now in my need!

I'm eating my heart away
For love of my fatherland.
I'm eating my heart away.
O birds, that fly by land and sea,
Be mindful of my plight!
O birds, that fly by land and sea,

Bend to my Father your flight! Bend to my Father your flight!

I'm eating my heart away
For love of my fatherland.
I'm eating my heart away.

SCENE FIVE: A PRISON

The stage is empty at the beginning of the narration. Then JOSEPH, *the* BUTLER *and the* BAKER *are pushed in by the* JAILER. *They sit on the floor, bound with chains.*

NARRATOR

When Potiphar, an Officer of Pharaoh, brought Joseph from the Midianites, Joseph found favor in his sight. Potiphar made him overseer of all that he possessed. But Potiphar's wife cast her eyes upon Joseph, and sought to make him her lover. Joseph would not betray his master, but she accused him of doing her violence. So Potiphar threw Joseph into prison.

And after this Pharaoh was angry with his chief Butler and his chief Baker; they were put into prison with Joseph.

The Butler and the Baker each dreamed a dream. The Butler dreamed of a vine with three branches, which bore fruit; and he took juice from the grapes and set it before Pharaoh. But the Baker dreamed that he had three baskets on his head; and the top-most basket contained the bakemeats for Pharaoh. But the birds came and ate them from the basket.

(*During the latter part of the narration, they have mimed sleep, awakened and told* JOSEPH *their dreams, and he has interpreted them.*)

NARRATOR

Pharaoh's Butler dreamed a dream
  In his prison cell.
Joseph told him what it meant,
  The son of Israel:
Told him he would soon be back
  Serving Pharaoh's wine:

Told him, in his darkest day,
    The sun would surely shine.

Pharaoh's Baker, when he dreamed,
    Also wondered why.
Joseph's heart was sad for him,
    For he must surely die.
Pharaoh on his birthday feast
    Had the Baker slain;
But the Butler was restored
    To his place again.

(*The* JAILER *and* GUARDS *enter. The* BUTLER *is freed, but the* BAKER *is dragged away with a halter round his neck.* JOSEPH *is left alone.*)

SCENE SIX: PHARAOH'S PALACE

During the narration and chorus, mime of PHARAOH *seeking an interpretation of his dreams. He calls in* PRIESTS, *who cannot tell him the answer. He shows great anger, and everyone else is frightened.*

NARRATOR

    And while Joseph was in the prison Pharaoh also had two dreams. He dreamed that seven lean cattle came after seven fat cattle, and devoured them; and seven thin ears of corn devoured seven fat ears. None of his wise men could interpret his dreams.

CHORUS
(different voices each line)

Pharaoh's dreaming, dreaming, dreaming!
What shall we do?
Call the interpreters! Call the necromancers!
Call the Priests of Osiris and Isis!
Pharaoh's dreaming, dreaming, dreaming!
What does it mean?
Seven fat kine, seven lean kine,
Seven rich ears, seven thin ears.
Pharaoh's dreaming! Pharaoh's dreaming! Pharaoh's dream-
    ing!
What shall we do?

PHARAOH: Can nobody tell me what my dreams mean?

BUTLER: Your Majesty, I have thought of a man who might tell you the truth; one whom, to my shame, I have forgotten and used ungratefully.

PHARAOH: Who is he? Where is he to be found?

BUTLER: I remember, in the prison,
>
> There was a man in chains with me.
> When I dreamed, he told me the meaning,
> Turned it, and made it plain to see.
>
> His name—ah, yes! His name was Joseph.
> I will go and fetch him here.
> He may tell this dream for Pharaoh.
> He may make its meaning clear.

(*During the next narration* JOSEPH *is brought on, his hands freed. He kneels in front of* PHARAOH. *Mime his explaining of the dreams.* PHARAOH *jumps up from his throne, and puts his ring on* JOSEPH's *finger. The* BUTLER *brings a gold chain, which* PHARAOH *puts round* JOSEPH's *neck. Then* PHARAOH *goes out, and* JOSEPH *sits on the throne.*)

NARRATOR

And so Joseph was brought from the prison, and he told Pharaoh the meaning of his dreams. So great was Pharaoh's joy, that he set Joseph over all the land of Egypt. And Joseph built storehouses, and set aside corn in the seven fat years; so that when the years of famine came all the people begged him to sell them food.

(*A great crowd of* EGYPTIANS *gathers in front of the stage*).

CHORUS

> All the men of Egypt came to him, Joseph, Joseph.
> You could hear them cry his name to him, Joseph! Joseph!
> > Give us barley, give us wheat!
> > Give us grain, or give us meat!
> We are starving! We must eat! Joseph! Joseph!
>
> All the people came and sighed to him, Joseph, Joseph.
>
> Rich men, poor men, came and cried to him, Joseph, Joseph.
> > Give us barley, give us wheat!
> > Give us grain, or give us meat!
> We are starving! We must eat! Joseph! Joseph!

We will pledge our lands and lives to you, Joseph! Joseph!
All our children and our wives to you, Joseph! Joseph!
    Give us barley, give us wheat!
    Give us grain, or give us meat!
We are starving! We must eat! Joseph! Joseph!

NARRATOR

And men came from other lands also, to buy from Joseph, because there was corn in Egypt. Jacob also said to his sons, "Go to Egypt, and buy corn, so that we may live, and not die!"

(*A crowd of people of all colors and races come before* JOSEPH *during the next chorus. Toward the end his* BROTHERS *come, and kneel on the stage.*)

CHORUS

Then from far and wide came the folk of every land.
    There was corn in Egypt!
They came by the mountains, and they came by the sand.
    There was corn in Egypt!
They came by the rivers, and they came by the seas,
They came with their money, and they came with their
    pleas,
They came there to Joseph, and they fell on their knees.
    There was corn in Egypt!

From the North and the South, from the West and the
    East.
    There was corn in Egypt!
All the rich and the poor, all the greatest and the least.
    There was corn in Egypt!
They came by the rivers, and they came by the seas,
They came with their money, and they came with their
    pleas,
They came there to Joseph, and they fell on their knees.
    There was corn in Egypt!

Then the sons of Jacob set their beasts in the way.
    There was corn in Egypt!
They journeyed from Canaan both by night and by day.
    There was corn in Egypt!
They came by the rivers, and they came by the seas,

They came with their money, and they came with their
    pleas,
They came there to Joseph, and they fell on their knees.
    There was corn in Egypt!

(*All go off except* JOSEPH *and his* BROTHERS.)

JOSEPH: What men are you, and what is your country?

REUBEN: My Lord, we are from Canaan, sons of Jacob. We were
twelve brothers; but one is dead, and the youngest is at home.

JOSEPH: How do I know that you are not spies, come to see the
nakedness of the land?

SIMEON: No, my Lord! We are not spies. We have come only to
buy food.

JOSEPH: Then if your story is true, prove it! Send and fetch this
youngest brother to me! And one of you shall stay as hostage
here in prison.

(*While the narrator continues,* JOSEPH *calls* GUARDS, *who bind*
SIMEON *and take him off. The other* BROTHERS *bow, and go
out.*)

NARRATOR

So Joseph sent his brothers home with sacks of corn, and put
back in the sacks the money which they had paid. But when Jacob
heard what had been done, he would not let them take Benjamin
to Egypt.

SCENE SEVEN: JACOB'S HOUSE

JACOB *sits at a table, with* RACHEL *and* BENJAMIN. THE BROTHERS
stand in a group.

JACOB: No, I tell you—no! I will not let Benjamin go!

REUBEN: Not let him go? He must go!

JACOB: I have lost one of the two sons on whom my heart was set,
because he went with you. Must the other also be lost?

REUBEN: (*angrily*) You have other sons, Father! Do you care nothing for them?

LEVI: Must Simeon rot in an Egyptian jail?

ISSACHAR: And the rest of us starve to death?

LEVI: Give us your favorite, and let us fetch food!
REUBEN: (*more gently*) Let him go, Father! It is for the best.

JACOB

> I'm eating my heart away
> For one who has left my side.
> I'm eating my heart away.
>
> O Lord, who rules in earth and sky,
> Shine on us with your light!
> O Lord, who rules in earth and sky,
> Show me the path that is right!
> Show me the path that is right!

RACHEL

> I'm eating my heart away
> For one who has left my side.
> I'm eating my heart away.
> O Lord, who rules in earth and sky,
> When will you turn and heed?
> O Lord, who rules in earth and sky,
> Pity me now in my need!
> Pity me now in my need!

JACOB

> I'm eating my heart away
> For one who has left my side.
> I'm eating my heart away.

RACHEL: We must let him go, Jacob.
JACOB: Yes, wife. He must go. Journey with them, Benjamin; and may God's blessing be with you all!

(THE BROTHERS *go off, with* BENJAMIN. JACOB *and* RACHEL *watch them.*)

NARRATOR

But when the famine grew sore again, at length Jacob let Benjamin go. Nevertheless, his heart was heavy, and so was the heart of Rachel, Benjamin's mother.

SCENE EIGHT: JOSEPH'S PALACE IN EGYPT

JOSEPH *sits on his throne. A table is laid for a feast. Guards bring in* THE BROTHERS, *who bow before* JOSEPH.

JOSEPH: You are welcome back, my friends. Peace be with you!

REUBEN: We have brought our brother Benjamin, sir, as you commanded us.

JOSEPH: So you are Benjamin! Geeetings! Bring the prisoner Simeon out to join us at our feast! Sit down at my table, and let us eat and drink!

> (*As they sit down,* SIMEON *is brought on, and greets his* BROTHERS. *Lights should be lowered slowly to a black-out during the narration.*)

NARRATOR

So Joseph welcomed his brothers. And again he sent them on their way home with sacks of corn, and put their money inside the sacks. But he told his Steward to put in Benjamin's sack the golden cup from which he used to drink, and which he used in his prophecies. Then Joseph sent his servants after the brothers to stop them, and to threaten that the one in whose sack the cup was found should become his slave. They found the cup in Benjamin's sack. Then the brothers were brought back into Joseph's presence.

SCENE NINE: JOSEPH'S PALACE

When the lights come up, BENJAMIN *is held by the guards. The other* BROTHERS *stand in a group before* JOSEPH.)

GUARD: This is the one, my Lord! The cup was in his sack.

JOSEPH: Then he must be my slave for the rest of his life.

JUDAH: (*kneeling*) My Lord, will you listen to me, if I make a plea to you?

JOSEPH: You may speak.

JUDAH: My Lord, this is our youngest brother. Since our other brother was lost to us, this youngest boy has been our Father's favorite. That was why he did not come with us on our first journey.

REUBEN: Our Father Jacob could scarcely bear to let him come this second time, my Lord. I do not know how to face him, if we leave Benjamin here.

JUDAH: And so I beg of you, sir, to be merciful, and to let me take his place! I will be your slave, if that must be. But, in God's name, let the boy go home to his Father!

LEVI: Yes, my Lord! If you have ever known what the bond between Father and son can mean, I beg you to grant this prayer of ours! Take any of us, but not our youngest brother!

JOSEPH: (*to the guards*) Free the boy, and leave us alone! (*the guards go out*) Reuben, Judah, Benjamin—all of you, my brothers! I am Joseph! Yes, you may well stare at me! But it is true. I am Joseph, whom you meant to kill; and whom you then sold into slavery. But God sent me before you, to prepare the way—to save your lives, and the lives of my Father and my Mother.

REUBEN: Joseph!

JUDAH: O God, forgive me!

LEVI: I cannot face you! It makes me afraid!

(THE BROTHERS *speak individual lines, while* JOSEPH *goes and greets each of them. They kneel throughout these verses.*)

BROTHERS

I'm afraid of Joseph! What is he going to do?
I'm afraid of Joseph, and it scares me through and through.
I have earned his hatred. I have earned his scorn.
And my mind is fearful, and my heart is torn.
I'm afraid of Joseph! What is he going to do?
I'm afraid of Joseph, and it scares me through and through.
If he seeks for justice, he can strike me dead;
For my guilt is heavy on a brother's head.
I'm afraid of Joseph! What is he going to do?
I'm afraid of Joseph, and it scares me through and through.
If he seeks for vengeance, that is in his hand.
Then my life is forfeit, for the deed I planned.
I'm afraid of Joseph! What is he going to do?
I'm afraid of Joseph, and it scares me through and through.

JOSEPH: Do not be afraid! Stand up, all of you, please! God has brought good out of evil, a blessing out of violence and hatred. Soon you shall go to Canaan, and fetch my Father and Mother to live here, on good land which I shall give you. Then I shall see them again, after my years of loneliness and exile.

REUBEN: We will bring them, Joseph. But can you truly forgive us?
BROTHERS: Yes, Joseph. Forgive us, if you can!
JOSEPH: Forgive you? It is for God to forgive, and for God to
punish. It was his hand that guided us to see this hour.

> You meant to do me evil.
> You tried to take my life.
> But God can bring a blessing
> From man's most bitter strife.
>
> You cursed me for a dreamer,
> And envy filled your breast.
> But God can take our passions,
> And turn them for the best.
>
> For he has brought me riches,
> And he has brought me fame.
> He chose me out to serve him,
> And to exalt his name.
>
> I have come safe through danger,
> I have come safe through pain.
> At last my God has brought me
> To my loved ones again!

(*During the final narration,* JACOB *and* RACHEL *enter, and embrace* JOSEPH. *They all join in the chorus, which is a version of psalm 150.*)

NARRATOR

So they rejoiced together. And Joseph's brothers fetched their
Father Jacob, and Rachel his wife, to Egypt. They were overcome
with joy when they found their son alive. Jacob settled in Egypt,
and he and his sons prospered, until the time of his death. And his
sons became the Fathers of the Tribes of Israel.

(*All* CHORUS MEMBERS *should return, on or below the
stage, during the final chorus.*)

CHORUS

> O praise God in his holiness!
> Praise him in the firmament of his power!
> Praise him in the high notes!
> Praise him in the low notes!
> Praise him on the trumpet and the psaltery and harp!

Praise him with the timbrels!
Praise him with dances!
Praise him with the strings and the wind and the organ!
Praise him! Praise him!
With the clash of the loud, high-sounding cymbals!
Let everything that hath breath
Praise the Lord!

3. MOSES:

LEADER AND LAWGIVER

BIBLE REFERENCE: The story of Moses is the longest in the Bible, covering the Books of Exodus, Leviticus, Numbers and Deuteronomy. Parts of these books have no interest for the general modern reader, and the essentials of the story are hard to pick out, except in a book of selections like the "Shorter Oxford Bible." Nor is it easy to treat the stories dramatically. But Moses is of such fundamental importance in the development of Jewish history and religious ideas that the student must understand him to read intelligently about those who follow him. Therefore his life is portrayed here in a series of short scenes. If these are supplemented by discussion and Bible reading, the character of Moses, and his greatness, should become clear. (Read Keller, Part II, chapter 3, and Part III.)

SCENE ONE: THE BURNING BUSH

Bible reference: Exodus 3, 1-15

CHARACTERS: MOSES
              ZIPPORAH, his wife (carrying their baby son Gershom)
              VOICE OF GOD

MOSES *is sitting among his flocks of sheep in Mount Horeb.* ZIPPORAH *enters.*

MOSES: Greetings, wife! What brings you so far from home?
ZIPPORAH: I came to bring you more food, and also news from Egypt.
MOSES: News? First sit down here and rest. You must be tired, with the baby to carry.
ZIPPORAH: My father came with me. Our mule is at the foot of the path, and he went to see the other flock.

MOSES: Well, and how is my son Gershom? How are you, stranger?

ZIPPORAH: He is a strong man, like his father.

(*They laugh. Improvise more dialogue about the baby.*)

MOSES: You said you had news from Egypt?

ZIPPORAH: A message from your brother Aaron. The boy who brought it arrived yesterday.

MOSES: What did he say?

ZIPPORAH: That things grow worse and worse since the old Pharaoh died. The work is always being increased, and the people are near to the breaking point. And—

MOSES: Yes? What else?

ZIPPORAH: Oh, Moses, I'm frightened! Are you going to leave me, and risk your life down there?

MOSES: What was the rest of the message?

ZIPPORAH: That every Jew with a strong right arm is needed to fight the battle of his people. But, Moses, we are so happy here! Must you go? What good can one man do?

MOSES: If we always asked that question, Zipporah, and shrank from risking our lives for what is right, nothing would ever be done. Go home now! Thank you for bringing the food, and for making this long journey to tell me news which you would rather have hidden. You are a good wife to me. Whatever happens, we shall face it together, and Gershom will grow up to be our helper.

ZIPPORAH: I will leave you then, Moses. My father will want to go on to visit the other shepherds. Come home to us as soon as you can!

(*She goes out.* MOSES *sits silently, then kneels and prays.*)

MOSES: O God, when will you show mercy to our people? When shall we see any hope of relief? I feel within me that you have called me to be a leader; but how can we break away from this bondage?

(*After another period of silence, he suddenly turns to one side, and shades his eyes with his hands.*)

What is that light? O God! Is it a sign? The mountain burns, but not the bushes. I must go nearer, and see. (*He rises*)

VOICE OF GOD: Moses!

MOSES: Yes, Lord?

VOICE OF GOD: I am here, Moses. Take off your shoes, for you are standing on holy ground. (*Moses takes off his shoes*) I am the God of Abraham and Isaac and Jacob. I have seen my people's affliction, and I shall deliver them from the Egyptians. They shall go to a good land, a land flowing with milk and honey, the country of the Canaanites.

MOSES: (*kneeling, with his face covered*) Lord, why do you tell me this?

VOICE OF GOD: Because you must lead them. You must go to Pharaoh, and you must lead the people out of Egypt.

MOSES: Who am I, Lord, to go to Pharaoh? How will he or the people listen to me?

VOICE OF GOD: Say that the God of their Fathers, the only true God, the God "I AM," has sent you. That is my name; and you shall serve me faithfully, and have no other God.

MOSES: Yes, Lord. (*He looks toward the fire.*) The fire is out. Oh, give me strength to make it all come true!

SCENE TWO: MOSES AND PHARAOH

NOTE: The following four Scenes cover the confrontations of Moses and Pharaoh, the plagues wrought upon Egypt and the eventual departure of the Jews across the Red Sea. They are perhaps best treated as a unit.

Bible reference: Exodus 5-14

CHARACTERS: PHARAOH
OFFICERS OF PHARAOH
MOSES
AARON

PHAROAH *is sitting in his palace, surrounded by* OFFICERS. MOSES *and* AARON *are brought in.*

PHARAOH: Bring them here, and let us have done with this.

OFFICER: Kneel before the King, you dogs! (*they bow*) Down on the floor! (*He pushes them down on their knees*) That's better! I don't know why you waste your time on these scum, Your Majesty.

PHAROAH: I wish them to take a message to their people.

MOSES: Your Majesty—

OFFICER: Silence! Don't interrupt the King!

MOSES: I bring a message to Pharaoh, and to all of you.

PHARAOH: Oh, really! A message from whom?

MOSES: From the one true God.

PHARAOH: The one true God! Is he an acquaintance of yours, Jew?

MOSES: He sends his word to you through me, sir. Listen to it, if you value your life and the good of your people!

OFFICER: Do you want me to throw these two out, sir, or have them whipped for insolence?

PHARAOH: No. Let us hear this so-called message.

MOSES: Speak, Aaron! Tell the King the message of the Lord!

AARON: Thus saith the Lord God of Israel: "Let my people go, that they may hold a feast unto me in the wilderness." Let us go three days' journey into the desert, sir. That is the bidding of God.

PHARAOH: The bidding of God? Thank you! He seems to be the God of scroungers and work-shy idlers. I have heard about you two. That is why I called you here today. If you want to be leaders of your people, you do as I say. Otherwise, we shall deal with you. Now go and tell your Jews that I am not satisfied with the work that they are doing. I expect more work, and better work. My Officers will see to it that idleness and waste are punished severely. Is that understood?

MOSES: Then you refuse to listen?

PHARAOH: Me? Pharaoh of Egypt listen to a common laborer? Go and tell your God that this is Egypt, and the person who lays down the laws here is the Pharaoh. If I so much as hear one word more—

MOSES: Then I warn you, Pharaoh of Egypt—

OFFICER: Silence!

MOSES: I warn you that I shall do the Lord's bidding. I shall smite the Nile with my rod, and the water will turn to blood—

OFFICER: Get them out of here! (*Several officers surround them.*)

PHARAOH: Stop! So, Jew, you will turn the Nile to blood. All right! You do that, and meanwhile I will tell my taskmasters to double the work in your camps and cut down the ration of food. Let us see who is God! Let them go, Officer! I think they are madmen, not dangerous criminals.

SCENE THREE: MOSES AND PHARAOH— A SECOND CONFRONTATION

The same setting as Scene Two, some months later. PHARAOH *now looks haggard and angry, and his* OFFICERS *frightened.* MOSES *and* AARON *come in.*

MOSES: You would not listen, Pharaoh!

PHARAOH: No, Moses. I would not listen, and I will not listen! I demand an end to your magic and your threats, or I will have you flayed alive!

MOSES: No, Pharaoh. You dare not harm me. You are too much afraid.

PHARAOH: Look, Moses, and you, Aaron. I have tried to be reasonable. I wish you no harm.

AARON: We have heard that many times, Pharaoh. Broken promises, soft words. You have seen what they have brought upon you and your people: plagues and disasters.

PHARAOH: Coincidences, you mean.

MOSES: Do the Egyptian people think that they are coincidences, Your Majesty?

PHARAOH: The Egyptian people are not there to think. They do as I tell them.

MOSES: Then there is no room for further discussion. Goodbye!

PHARAOH: Wait! Can we not make some compromise? I cannot let the whole of your people leave their work.

MOSES: There can be no compromise. It is too late. Up to now, the Lord has struck the land and the water, the crops and the animals. By this time tomorrow he will have struck the people of Egypt. Your son shall die, Pharaoh, and so will the first-born sons of all the Egyptians. Come, Aaron!

(*They go out. Nobody tries to prevent them.*)

PHARAOH: It cannot be true! Their God cannot have this power!

OFFICER: But what if he does, Your Majesty? Must our sons die?

PHARAOH: (*shouting*) I tell you I will not yield! Set extra guards over the Jews, so that they cannot plan any trick! I will not yield!

SCENE FOUR: PHARAOH'S BEDROOM

This is to be improvised by two actors. Pharaoh is asleep in his bedroom. An Officer comes in, hesitates, then shakes him, and kneels by the bed. Pharaoh wakes suddenly, and sits up.

The Officer tells him that his son is dead, from a sudden plague.

Pharaoh jumps out of bed, calls his other Officers, and sends one with a message to Moses, that the Jews may go and sacrifice. The messenger is to plead with Moses to stop the plague which has struck the first-born sons.

Improvise dialogue with the Officers about the plague—what they have seen and heard.

SCENE FIVE: FLIGHT FROM EGYPT

This is also to be improvised. The scene is a hill, just beyond the place where the Jews have crossed the Red Sea. Moses, Aaron and other Jewish leaders are looking back toward Egypt. They see the cloud of dust formed by the advancing Egyptian Army. All of them, except Moses, are in despair. He remains certain that their flight was the will of God.

Suddenly Moses notices that the wind has changed; and that the waters, which had been blown apart and left a dry passage, are flowing back and closing the gap.

They watch the Army grow nearer, not realizing its danger. Then they see the disaster happen. The song in Exodus 15 shows the wild joy which the Jews felt at the destruction of the men who had treated them so cruelly. The women, led by Miriam, played timbrels and danced.

SCENE SIX: THE GOLDEN CALF

Bible reference: Exodus 32

CHARACTERS: Aaron
             Aholiab
             Moses
             Joshua
             Crowd of Jews

AARON *is standing beside two large baskets.* JEWISH MEN *and* WOMEN *file by, putting gifts into the baskets.*

AARON: Please put your gifts in the baskets. Thank you. Thank you.

FIRST WOMAN: This is my wedding ring, sir.

AARON: You are all generous. Tomorrow Aholiab will have made the Golden Calf, and you will be able to worship it.

SECOND WOMAN: My earrings. An Egyptian lady gave them to me.

AARON: Thank you. Your gold is much better offered to God than worn as an ornament to your body.

AHOLIAB: That is enough, Aaron. Let us take it to the furnace.

AARON: Very well. My people, we have enough gifts. Keep what you still have. We shall assemble tomorrow for the evening sacrifice, and worship the Golden Calf.

(*The people disperse.*)

AHOLIAB: Aaron, are you sure that Moses will understand why we are doing this?

AARON: I cannot be sure, Aholiab. But—Moses has been on the mountain so long! And the people need something to worship. They are all afraid that Moses is dead, or has abandoned us—

AHOLIAB: Very well. I will make the calf. It will be beautiful: I promise you that.

AARON: I know it, Aholiab. You are a fine craftsman. And it will be so much easier for the people to pray to an image of gold—something that they can see. Moses talks of God as a spirit, but are we ready for that? Yet I am afraid—

(*It is the next evening. The calf is set up on an altar.* AARON *stands by the altar, and a* CROWD OF JEWS *kneels in front of it.*)

AARON: O God, we have made our offerings to you, of all that was most precious among our possessions. We pray to you through this image of gold. We give you thanks for our deliverance from the land of Egypt. And now, in our suffering and our need, we pray for strength and help. As we have offered our gold to fashion your image, so reward us with precious gifts, with food and drink and victory, until we come to our promised land. O calf of gold, symbol of richness and fertility, give us your blessing, and lead us to a land of plenty and of peace. (*He turns to the people.*) Now, men of Israel, dance and sing before the image of our God! Strip off your robes, and dance!

(*The people rise, and begin to shout "Long live Aaron!" As they strip off their outer garments, musicians prepare to lead the singing and dancing. Then* MOSES *runs in, shouting.*)

MOSES: In the name of God, stop! (*There is complete silence.*) What is this madness? My brother, what sacrilege have you committed?

AARON: You were away from us so long, Moses! We thought that perhaps you were dead.

MOSES: I should rather be dead than see my people wallowing in idol worship, and betraying their God.

AARON: We are not betraying God! We are only trying to worship him through an image, as our masters in Egypt did. It is so hard—

MOSES: Stop! Some evil spirit must have struck you with madness. I came from the very presence of God on Mount Sinai. I came bringing from him the tables of Laws and Commandments for us to observe, the symbol of our covenant with the one true God. When I heard what was happening in the camp, I broke the tables of the Laws, and ran to save you from abomination.

AARON: Is what we have done so wrong?

MOSES: You have denied the very essence of our faith, Aaron. You have lowered your people to the level of barbarians and pagans, bowing before wood and metal, and mouthing superstitions and spells. Where is Joshua?

JOSHUA: I am here, Moses.

MOSES: Take all the men you can trust, and kill the leaders of this madness! Not my brother, for I truly believe that he was struck with a frenzy which was not of his own making. But kill those who have danced naked before this image! And you, Aaron, and Aholiab: take this evil thing to the furnace! Grind it to powder before my eyes, and we shall mix it with the water which our people drink. They shall be made to taste and swallow their sin!

AARON: They begged me to make them new Gods, Moses! They offered their gold freely—

MOSES: Be silent, Aaron! Do not try to excuse what you have done. Pray with me that, if it be possible, God may forgive this crime! Pray that I may be allowed to return to him in penitence, and bring back from the mountain the Laws which he has written for us! And, if this cannot be, may I be blotted out, and our people forgotten here in the wilderness! Come, bring the calf to the furnace! And Joshua, do your work!

NOTE: You could complete this Scene by making Moses read the Ten Commandments (Exodus 20, 1-17) to the people, after his second ascent to Sinai. Then discuss the relevance of the Commandments today. For example:

1) How do you show in your life that you give God priority?

2) A "graven image" is anything which you worship, and so upset the balance of your life: a TV set, a baseball bat, a relationship, drugs, money.

3) Perfunctory, insincere worship is the chief example of taking God's name in vain. What others are there?

4) Do you use Sunday to "charge your batteries" for the week? Is it a day of joy, and refreshment of the spirit?

5) Do you combine a right use of freedom and responsibility with a loyal regard for authority?

6,7,8) Jesus goes beyond these negative commandments, to question ultimate motives in our hearts: love, purity, honesty. Failure in these deep-seated motives will result in outward actions.

9) Gossip and malice are "false witness," a negation of love. All the time you are "witnessing," one way or the other, without being in a court of law.

10) The cure for envy is thankfulness for what we have and enjoy.

SCENE SEVEN: MOSES AND JOSHUA

Bible reference: Numbers 13; Numbers 27, 18-23. Deuteronomy 30, 11-20; Deuteronomy 34.

CHARACTERS: MOSES
JOSHUA

The setting is the top of Mount Pisgah, overlooking the Jordan Valley and Jericho.

JOSHUA: (*Approaching* MOSES, *who is sitting and gazing at the valley.*) You asked me to come to you, Moses?
MOSES: Yes, Joshua. I asked you to come, so that I could give you my last words of counsel and farewell.

JOSHUA: Farewell? Why—

MOSES: I know from the Lord that I shall go no further than this. He has let me see the Promised Land, but I cannot set foot in it. You must lead the people across Jordan.

JOSHUA: If it is God's will.

MOSES: We have come a long way together, Joshua. We have seen victory and defeat, faith and betrayal. And now, there lies our country—promised by God to Abraham, to Isaac, and to Jacob. My part is done; but yours is only beginning. You have fought by my side; and you went to spy on the land of Canaan. Now you are the leader whom the Lord has chosen. Will you keep his commandments faithfully?

JOSHUA: I will, Moses, as far as in me lies.

MOSES: His commandment is not hidden, or far away. It is not in the sky, or beyond the sea; but in your mouth and in your heart. You must choose between life and good, and death and evil. Walk in the ways of God, and keep his word, and you will live and multiply, in the land which you go to possess. But if your heart turns away, and you serve other Gods, you will die, Joshua, and so will all the people. There is life, and there is death; a blessing, or a curse. Choose life, for yourself and all the people! And now, leave me to make my peace with God before I die. May God bless you and keep you always!

4. SAMUEL:

PROPHET AND KING-MAKER

NOTE: The story of Samuel is found in the First Book of Samuel, 1-25. References for the scenes are given at the beginning of each. Read JB 229-230. Keller, Part IV, Chapter 4.

Samuel ushers in a new period in the history of the Jews. He is the first of the great Prophets. Under God's guidance, he chose and anointed (we should say crowned or consecrated) the first two Kings of the Jewish tribes.

SCENE ONE: HANNAH'S PRAYER

Bible reference: I Samuel 1, 1-18

CHARACTERS: ELKANAH
HANNAH
PENINNAH
ELI
PENINNAH'S TWO CHILDREN

The setting is Shiloh, a sacred place, where ELI *is Priest.* ELKANAH, *his two wives and the children are in the place of worship at Shiloh.*

ELKANAH: Now that I have made our offering to God, let me give each of you your gifts.
PENINNAH: Come here, children! Sit down quietly! Your father has presents for you.
FIRST CHILD: Oh! I wonder what I shall get.
SECOND CHILD: Not as much as I shall. I'm the eldest!
PENINNAH: Be quiet!
ELKANAH: Hannah, come and sit with us.
SECOND CHILD: Does she get a present too?
ELKANAH: My child, if you ever grow up to deserve a present as much as Hannah does, you will be a wonderful woman.
PENINNAH: Oh yes! She can't do anything wrong. It's just a pity God doesn't think so too!
ELKANAH: Be silent, Peninnah!
PENINNAH: Why should I be silent? You always prefer her to me,

and give her a bigger portion. Why does she have no children?
Tell me that! If she's so wonderful, why does God—
ELKANAH: Peninnah, I told you to be silent! Hannah, where are
you going?
HANNAH: Leave me alone! Please, leave me alone! I want to go
and pray. I can't bear to be with you when she talks like that.

(*She runs to the other side of the room.*)

ELKANAH: Peninnah, why can't you learn to control your tongue?
Because of what you said, I shall double Hannah's portion, and
put it aside for the children who may yet be born to her; and
your portion and those of your children will be less.
FIRST CHILD: That's not fair!
SECOND CHILD: No. Why—
ELKANAH: Be quiet! Now go back to the carriage, and wait for
me. I shall come soon.
PENINNAH: Come on, children! We're not wanted here. Leave her
to her prayers. A lot of use they will be to her!

(ELKANAH *walks over to* HANNAH, *as* PENINNAH *and the*
CHILDREN *go out.* HANNAH *is kneeling and praying silently,
her lips moving.*)

ELKANAH: Why are you crying, my dear?
HANNAH: How do you think I can bear any more of that? The insults and mockery of that woman, and her greedy, vulgar little
children? Oh, Elkanah! I try to love them, but I am weak. I
want a child of my own!
ELKANAH: I know, I know. I try to be better to you than sons and
daughters, but I know that you long to have them.
HANNAH: Leave me for just a few minutes, Elkanah, and I will
come to the carriage and join you.
ELKANAH: Very well, Hannah. Surely God will listen to your
prayers!

(ELKANAH *goes out. As* HANNAH *prays silently,* ELI *comes in.*)

ELI: What is it that you are praying for?
HANNAH: Oh, sir! I did not see you.
ELI: I saw your lips moving, and no words came. I thought per-
haps you were drunk. But I can see that you are praying deeply,
and there are tears on your cheeks. Can I help you?
HANNAH: I begin to lose hope that anybody can help me, even
God.

ELI: What is it that you want?

HANNAH: A son, sir! I love my husband so much, and he loves me; but we have no child. If I could only have a son, I swear that I would bring him to the shrine and let him serve you and the Lord.

ELI: Go in peace, Hannah! I will pray for you also; and perhaps God will hear our prayers and grant you your wish.

HANNAH: Thank you, sir. Thank you for your kindness.

SCENE TWO: A COAT FOR SAMUEL

Bible reference: I Samuel 1, 19—2, 11.

CHARACTERS: HANNAH
                 SAMUEL
                 ELI

(*This setting is the same as Scene One. It is about ten years later,* SAMUEL *is sweeping the floor of the temple, when* HANNAH *enters.*)

HANNAH: Samuel!

SAMUEL: Why, Mother! I knew you would come soon.

HANNAH: My child! You've grown so tall! It was time I did come, wasn't it, with your new coat? Look!

(*She holds out a new jacket, and he tries it on.*)

SAMUEL: Thank you, Mother. It's beautiful!

HANNAN: I'll take the old one, and pass it on to one of the poor children in our village.

ELI: (*as he enters*) Welcome, Hannah! What do think of your son?

HANNAH: Greetings, sir! My husband Elkanah sends you greetings, and I have offerings for you outside. The boy has grown so much!

ELI: I see you brought his new coat. Samuel, go out and ask your Mother's servant to bring in the offerings. (SAMUEL *runs out.*) He is a very fine boy, Hannah. God did more than answer your prayers.

HANNAH: I know, sir. Each year I come to give thanks more and more.

ELI: I believe that he has a special kind of faith, a close relationship with God. One day he will do great things. Now I know that you want to pray. I will go and speak with your servant.

(ELI *goes out.* HANNAH *kneels and prays.*)

HANNAH: O Lord, my heart rejoices in you. You are the only God, the rock of our lives. You weigh all our actions and our needs. You raise the poor out of the dust, and give children to the childless. You are the judge of all the world. Make me worthy of the happiness which you have given to me in my husband and in my son!

SCENE THREE: THE CALL OF SAMUEL

Bible reference: I Samuel 3.

CHARACTERS: VOICE OF GOD
                SAMUEL
                ELI

SAMUEL *lies asleep on the floor of the shrine.* ELI *sleeps on a bed.*

VOICE OF GOD: Samuel!
SAMUEL: (*Sitting up.*) Yes? Here I am. (*He waits a minute, then gets up and runs over to* ELI) Here I am, sir.
ELI: (*Sleepily.*) What is it, my son?
SAMUEL: I heard you call, sir; so I came to see what you wanted.
ELI: No, Samuel. I didn't call. Go back to sleep.
SAMUEL: Yes, sir. I must have had a dream. (*He goes back and lies down. There is a pause, and he is again sleeping.*)
VOICE OF GOD: Samuel, wake up!
SAMUEL: What? (*He goes to* ELI.) Here I am, sir.
ELI: What is it? Again, Samuel? I never called you. Now go to sleep!
SAMUEL: I was sure that a voice woke me up. I am sorry, sir.

(*He returns to his rug and goes back to sleep.*)

VOICE OF GOD: Samuel!
SAMUEL: Yes? (*He goes to* ELI.) It happened again, sir. I swear you called me.
ELI: No, Samuel, I did not call; but I believe that there is a voice calling you. Lie down! And if the voice comes again, just say,

"Speak, Lord, for thy servant heareth." Can you remember that?

SAMUEL: Yes, sir. "Speak, Lord, for thy servant heareth."

ELI: That's right. Now go back to sleep!

(SAMUEL *again returns to his rug and goes to sleep.*)

VOICE OF GOD: Samuel, wake up!

SAMUEL: Speak, Lord, for thy servant heareth.

VOICE OF GOD: Eli is right, Samuel. It is I, the Lord, who am calling you. I want you to be my servant and messenger. Men's ears will tingle at the things that I shall do through you. There are hard days ahead for Eli and for the Jewish people; but you must listen for my words, and follow what I say. For I have chosen you to be a prophet to my people, the mouthpiece of my commands. Now sleep, Samuel, son of a noble father and of a blessed mother!

(*After a pause,* SAMUEL *slowly lies down again and goes to sleep.*)

SCENE FOUR: SAMUEL AND SAUL

Bible reference: I Samuel 9—10

CHARACTERS: SAUL, *a young man of huge physique*
SAUL'S SERVANT
SAMUEL
CROWD OF JEWISH MEN AND WOMEN

The setting is a village in Israel, where SAUL *and his* SERVANT *are looking for his father's lost donkeys. They enter, very tired.*)

SAUL: We are going to have to give up. It's no use.

SERVANT: Yes, sir. I'm afraid the donkeys are lost. Look, here's a village!

SAUL: Good! We can find somewhere to eat and sleep, and then return to my father.

(*They meet several people in the street.* SAUL *approaches them.*)

SAUL: Excuse me! Have any of you seen a herd of donkeys? My

father, Kish, of the tribe of Benjamin, has lost them, and he sent
me to look for them.

MAN: No, I haven't seen them. (*Improvise dialogue, with several
of the crowd making suggestions: "Have you tried down by the
river?" etc.*)

SAUL: Isn't there a prophet who lives here?

MAN: You mean Samuel? Yes, he is here.

SERVANT: Let us go and ask him, sir!

SAUL: But we have no food or money left for a gift to him.

MAN: Here he comes! He won't worry about a gift.

    (SAMUEL *enters. When he sees* SAUL, *he stops and looks at
him intently.*)

SAUL: Sir, are you Samuel the prophet?

SAMUEL: I am. Walk with me, Saul, son of Kish! I was expecting
you. (SAMUEL *and* SAUL *walk aside from the others.*) You can
forget about your father's donkeys, Saul. They have been found.

SAUL: How did you know—? And you say you are expecting me?

SAMUEL: I have heard the word of the Lord, Saul. You know that
our people are divided, and that our enemies always defeat our
tribes because we have no unity. What do you think Israel needs
most? A King, Saul: a strong man, to enforce unity. And whom
do you think God has chosen? You!

SAUL: Me? A Benjamite, from an unknown family? Don't mock
me, sir!

SAMUEL: This is no mockery. It is God's will, shown to me clearly. We shall go on now to my home, and eat dinner, and you
shall rest. Tomorrow I am going to anoint you King of all the
tribes of the Jews; and we shall go to Mizpeh, and proclaim
God's will to all our people.

SAUL: But how will they accept me, an unknown man?

SAMUEL: They will accept God's choice, at the bidding of God's
prophet. He has chosen me to be his spokesman, and you, with
all your strength, to be his warrior. Do not be afraid! The Spirit
of the Lord will come into your heart, and you will fight with
his strength, not only with your own. Now, let us call your servant and go to my house.

SCENE FIVE: SAMUEL ANOINTS DAVID KING

Bible reference: I Samuel 16, 1-13

CHARACTERS: SAMUEL
              VOICE OF GOD
              JESSE
              SEVEN SONS OF JESSE, *David's elder brothers*
              DAVID

The setting is Bethlehem, where David's father Jesse lived. SAMUEL *is standing in front of an altar.*

VOICE OF GOD: You have listened to my command, Samuel, and come to Bethlehem to sacrifice.

SAMUEL: Yes, Lord; but I do not know what you mean me to do here.

VOICE OF GOD: Call Jesse to bring his gifts, with his family. Look at his sons; for one of them is the King whom you must anoint.

SAMUEL: While Saul is still the anointed King, Lord?

VOICE OF GOD: Yes, for Saul has proved unworthy. He served me well, but now he has turned to disobedience and selfishness. You must do as I command you.

SAMUEL: Yes, Lord. I will call Jesse. (*He walks to one side, and calls.*) Let Jesse of Bethlehem bring his gifts to the altar!

JESSE: (*Approaching.*) Sir? Did you call me?

SAMUEL: You are Jesse?

JESSE: Yes. What do you want with me?

SAMUEL: Bring all your sons to me: first the eldest, and then each of the others.

JESSE: But, sir—what is the matter? Have we done something wrong in God's sight?

SAMUEL: No, nothing wrong. I will tell you the will of God when I have seen your sons. Call them one by one!

JESSE: Very well. (*He calls.*) Eliab!

    (ELIAB *enters. He is tall and good-looking.*)

SAMUEL: (*Softly, to himself.*) Surely this must be the man!

VOICE OF GOD: (*Heard only by* SAMUEL.) No, Samuel, Do not look on his face or his stature. I have rejected him. You must look into the heart of men, as I do.

SAMUEL: Call your second son!

(JESSE *calls, in turn,* ABINADAB, SHAMMAH, *and four others. Improvise dialogue, as he says something about each: their age, skills, etc. "Abinadab is a Cavalry Officer," "Shammah is the best swordsman in the family," for example. At length all seven have come and gone.*)

SAMUEL: Have you no more sons?

JESSE: Only my youngest boy, David. I didn't call him in, because—

SAMUEL: Call him! The Lord commands me to see all of your sons.

JESSE: Very well. Eliab! Call David in from the sheepfold! He is only sixteen, and spends his time looking after our sheep. I didn't think—

SAMUEL: It is for us to do as God commands, Jesse. Has the boy fought with the Army yet?

JESSE: No. He stays here on the farm when the others go away. Just a country boy, a good singer too; and he makes up his own songs to the guitar. But—

DAVID: (*Running in, breathless.*) You wanted me, Father?

JESSE: Yes, David. The prophet Samuel wishes—

VOICE OF GOD: You see, Samuel? There is your king!

SAMUEL: God be praised! I have found him! Leave us alone, Jesse.

JESSE: What? David? What can God want with him?

SAMUEL: Leave us alone! (JESSE *goes out slowly.*) David, I am the prophet of the Lord. I do not speak or act for myself, but for him. Kneel down!

DAVID: Yes, sir.

SAMUEL: David, neither you nor I can fully understand the will of God in this. It will be shown to you later. I anoint you in the name of God, as the chosen future King of all Israel. Make yourself ready, by prayer, and by the training of your mind and body and heart! He will reveal to you how you are to serve him. Do you accept this responsibility?

DAVID: Yes, sir. If you say that it is his will, I accept. I will do my best to serve King Saul, and to follow wherever God leads me.

SAMUEL: Then go back to your sheep, my boy. And may the blessing of God always go with you!

5. DAVID

The portrait of King David in the Bible is wonderfully honest. He was remembered as the most lovable of all the Kings, but no attempt is made to idealize his character. His sin in betraying Uriah, and the weakness which he showed in old age, are truthfully described. But the things remembered about him most were his courage, his love of God and of his people, and his wonderful versatility as ruler, soldier, poet and singer.

SCENE ONE: DAVID AND GOLIATH

Bible reference: I Samuel 17

PURPOSE: To show David's courage, and the fact that he was well trained to meet the crisis when it came. Courage without proper training is wasted, whether we are faced by a physical or a spiritual danger. Discuss the kind of training that a Christian needs for spiritual crises. Read the description of the "armor of God" in Ephesians 6, 1-10

CHARACTERS: KING SAUL
                ELIAB
                ABINADAB
                SHAMMAH
                DAVID
                GOLIATH
                CROWD OF JEWISH AND PHILISTINE SOLDIERS

The setting is the camp of KING SAUL's *army, opposite the Philistines.* DAVID's BROTHERS *are sitting around a fire in the camp. They are depressed, and are talking about the defeats that the army has suffered. Improvise this dialogue.*

ELIAB: It's no use. Nobody can fight Goliath.
ABINADAB: So we shall just have to surrender, and be humiliated?
ELIAB: What else can we do?
SHAMMAH: Look who's coming!

    (DAVID *enters.*)

ABINADAB: David! What in the world are you doing here?

DAVID: Brothers! I bring messages from Father and Mother.

ELIAB: Are they well?

DAVID: Yes. Everybody is well. And they sent these. Look! Bread, and parched corn.

SHAMMAH: Ten of Mother's loaves! That's wonderful.

ABINADAB: And cheeses!

DAVID: Wait a minute! Those are for your Colonel.

ELIAB: Not that any of it will help us, as things are now.

DAVID: Why? What's the trouble?

(*Improvise the dialogue in which they discuss the bad news.*)

DAVID: Is that Goliath, out there on the hill?

SHAMMAH: That's right. Nobody can fight a freak like him.

DAVID: He looks tough all right. But he looks clumsy too.

ELIAB: Not too clumsy to carve up anybody who gets within reach.

DAVID: Within reach—yes. Eliab, would they let me try to fight him?

ELIAB: You? Don't be crazy!

DAVID: I'm not being crazy. You say nobody else will try?

ELIAB: I tell you, it's impossible. We're not cowards, but—

DAVID: It isn't impossible. Difficult, yes. But I think I could do it.

ABINADAB: But how? Wait a minute! He's calling out the challenge again.

GOLIATH: (*Shouting, from a distance.*) This is your last chance, Jewish dogs. Will none of you be a man and face death? You have fifteen minutes to send a champion, or else surrender. My sword is thirsty for a Jew's blood.

SHAMMAH: Curse him! Here comes the King.

(*They all stand, as* SAUL *walks past.*)

DAVID: Your Majesty!

SAUL: Yes, boy? Who are you?

DAVID: David, sir, son of Jesse of Bethlehem. Your Majesty, may I fight Goliath?

ELIAB: We've told him not to be silly, Your Majesty, but—

SAUL: My son, nobody can help us now.

DAVID: But I think I can, sir, I really do. Look, he's far too strong for anybody who fights at close quarters. I know that; and if he gets near me I shall die. At least I shall die for the Lord and for my country then—but I think I can kill him before he reaches me.

SAUL: Kill him before—but how? What weapons can a boy have?

DAVID: This. (*He brings out his sling.*) You see, sir, I'm in charge of the sheep back on our farm. We have a lot of foxes, and sometimes a wolf, out to get at the flock. I have had to learn to hit them with a sling-stone before they can reach the sheep.

ABINADAB: That's true, too. He can hit anything.

SAUL: But a wolf has no armor, David. You cannot pierce a bronze breastplate.

DAVID: I know that. It will be difficult. But even Goliath has to see. Look at his helmet. It leaves his eyes and nose and part of his forehead exposed.

SAUL: You mean you can aim for that? It's impossible!

DAVID: Not after all the practice I have had, sir. I just hope I'm not too frightened to remember to aim straight. There won't be a second chance. I shall need to come as close as I dare before shooting.

SAUL: David, do you feel in your heart that God wants you to do this?

DAVID: Yes, Your Majesty. I do.

SAUL: Very well. Wear my armor. At least you shall have the best protection.

(*He begins to strip off his breastplate, shin-greaves and helmet. They dress* DAVID *in them.*)

DAVID: It's no use. I can't use these.

SAUL: But you must have some protection.

DAVID: My protection has to be my sling. If I hit him with a stone, I need no armor; and if I miss him, no armor will help me. These would only cramp me. I have never worn them before.

SAUL: Then go, David, and may the Lord protect and bless you!

(GOLIATH *calls out his challenge again.* DAVID *stands a long way from him and shouts his reply.*)

DAVID: I am coming, Philistine! I will fight you in the name of the Lord God of Israel.

GOLIATH: What? A boy? And no sword or armor? What kind of joke is this? Send me a man to kill!

DAVID: You will find out which of us is a man, Goliath.

GOLIAH: Very well, boy. Come over here, and I will give the dogs and the vultures something to eat. You crazy little hero!

(DAVID *stoops down to pick up stones, then whirls his sling round to take aim at* GOLIATH.)

GOLIATH: What's that you've got? Do the Jews fight with pieces of string as weapons?

DAVID *walks closer, and slings a stone.* GOLIATH *cries out, and falls.* DAVID *runs to him, draws an imaginary sword, and beheads him. The two armies cry out in joy and despair.*)

SCENE TWO: THE SIN OF DAVID

Bible reference: 2 Samuel 11, and 12, 1-25. For the background of David's reign, read Keller, Part V, Chapter 1.

CHARACTERS: KING DAVID
BATHSHEBA, *his wife*
NATHAN, *the prophet*
A SERVANT

The setting is DAVID's *house at Jerusalem.* HE AND BATHSHEBA *are sitting together, and she is holding their baby son. A* SERVANT *enters.*

SERVANT: Your Majesty, the Prophet Nathan is here.
DAVID: Now? At this hour of the evening? Tell him to come to-morrow.
SERVANT: He is insistent on seeing you, sir.
DAVID: All right. Let him come! (*The* SERVANT *goes out.*) I have not seen Nathan since—since we were married.
BATHSHEBA: What is the matter, David? You look frightened!
DAVID: I? Frightened of Nathan? Why should I fear him?
SERVANT: (*Showing* NATHAN *in.*) The prophet Nathan, Your Majesty.

(*He goes out.*)

DAVID: Nathan, you have come at a late hour.
NATHAN: I am sorry to disturb you, Your Majesty, and your Queen. And this is the new-born Prince!
DAVID: You have been away from our Court, Nathan. What brings you back?
NATHAN: A case of injustice, sir. I should like you to hear it, and give your judgment.
DAVID: Surely it could have waited—

NATHAN: I come at the bidding of the Lord God, sir. When he gives me his word, I do not wait.

DAVID: Very well. (*To* BATHSHEBA) Will you take the child, and go to your room?

BATHSHEBA: As you wish, David.

NATHAN: No, sir. I should like the lady Bathsheba to wait and hear what I say.

DAVID: You are taking a great deal on yourself, Nathan. Very well. Stay, Bathsheba, and listen!

NATHAN: This is the story of two men in one of our cities, sir. One was rich, and had everything he could wish for. The other was poor, and had only one ewe lamb, in comparison with all the rich man's flocks. This lamb was like a daughter to him, they say. It grew up with his children, and ate and drank at his table. You understand, my lady?

BATHSHEBA: What is it to me?

NATHAN: Just a story. Now hear the end! A traveller came to visit the rich man. He was unwilling to kill one of his own sheep; and so he took the poor man's lamb, killed it, and served it as a meal for his guest.

DAVID: But that is unforgivable! Tell me who he is, and I will see that justice is done. He must be made to—Why do you look at me, Nathan?

NATHAN: Why do I look at you, David, King of Israel, conqueror of Jerusalem, rich and mighty ruler? I look at you because you are the man who did this thing! There beside you sits the wife of the faithful soldier whom you killed—oh, not with your own hand, but by cunning and cowardice. And there is the son born of your sinful marriage!

DAVID: Stop! If you must say these things to me, do not say them to her! She had no guilt. I have sinned, I know it—

NATHAN: You have sinned, and you have brought shame and suffering on her. For the child will die, David. This son of yours will die, and there will be violence and discord among your other sons, because you despised the Lord's law. God is merciful, and will give you and the Queen other sons when this child is dead. But hear his word, and do justice in his eyes!

BATHSHEBA: Oh, David, stop him, stop him! I do not want my child to die!

DAVID: I cannot silence the word of a prophet. I have sinned, Bathsheba, towards Uriah, whom I killed, and towards you, whom I stole from him. May God forgive me!

NATHAN: I will leave you now. When the child dies, mourn for

him, and then turn to the work of God and pray that you may
sin no more!

SCENE THREE: THE ANOINTING OF SOLOMON

Bible reference: I Kings 1, 1-40

CHARACTERS: DAVID, now an old man
                ABISHAG, a young girl
                BATHSHEBA
                ZADOK
                BENAIAH
                NATHAN

The setting is a room in DAVID's *house.* BATHSHEBA *sits at a table.*
NATHAN *is standing.*

NATHAN: My Lady, we all know that the King no longer understands clearly what is happening outside.
BATHSHEBA: I know it, Nathan. His mind is wandering, and Abishag
is the only person whom he wants near him.
NATHAN: Somehow you must reach him, and make him understand. Adonijah has virtually proclaimed himself King. Solomon's
throne—and his life—are in grave danger. Which means your
life too, and the lives of all of us who are faithful to the true cause
of the people.
BATHSHEBA: I will go to him, and do what I can. Please wait here!
NATHAN: I will, my Lady. God bless you!

    (BATHSHEBA *goes to the next room, where* DAVID *sits wrapped
    in rugs.* ABISHAG *sits at his feet, chafing his hands.*)

BATHSHEBA: May I speak to you, David?
DAVID: Who is it, Abishag? My eyes and ears are dim.
ABISHAG: It is Queen Bathsheba, my Lord.
BATHSHEBA: Let me come close to him, Abishag. I have news to
give, and I must make him understand.

    (ABISHAG *gets up and stands aside.* BATHSHEBA *kneels by the
    king.*)

DAVID: Don't leave me, girl! Where are you?

BATHSHEBA: David, my Lord, it is I, Bathsheba. You must listen, and help us!

DAVID: (*Slowly.*) Bathsheba. Yes, yes.

BATHSHEBA: My Lord, you swore that your son and mine, Solomon, should be King after you. Do you remember?

DAVID: Solomon. Yes, I remember. But Absalom—

BATHSHEBA: Absalom is dead, David.

DAVID: Dead?

BATHSHEBA: And Adonijah has proclaimed himself King. He has sacrificed sheep and oxen at the Serpent's Stone at En-Rogel, and—

NATHAN: (*Who has entered the room quietly.*) May I speak to my Lord the King?

BATHSHEBA: It is Nathan the Prophet, David. He has come to tell you more.

DAVID: I am tired! Where is Abishag?

NATHAN: She is here with you, David. But first you must listen. You gave your oath to Queen Bathsheba, and to all of us who are your loyal servants, that Solomon should be King. This is the hour to make it come true, sir—now, or never!

BATHSHEBA: Adonijah will be King, and you will be murdered or a prisoner, unless Solomon is proclaimed by you, David.

DAVID: (*Suddenly sitting up, and showing some of his old fire.*) Adonijah King? You are right, Bathsheba. It is hard for me to turn my mind to the things that must be done, now that I have grown old. What is it that you want from me?

NATHAN: Zadok the Priest is outside, sir, and Benaiah, Chief of your Army. Let me call them, and bring the document proclaiming Solomon your true heir. Seal it, and give us your command!

DAVID: Call them in! (NATHAN *hurries out.*)

BATHSHEBA: You will never regret this day, my Lord! When Solomon is proclaimed, you can rest in peace.

DAVID: Yes—in my grave, Bathsheba. My limbs are cold, and I shall not have the warmth of life in me for many days. I have tried to serve my God—

BATHSHEBA: You have served him well, my dear Lord and husband! Your people love you, and will never forget you!

(NATHAN *re-enters, with* ZADOK *and* BENAIAH.)

ZADOK: Greetings, Your Majesty!

BENAIAH: Your Majesty! (*They kneel before* DAVID.)

DAVID: That is Zadok's voice. And who is with him?

BENAIAH: It is Benaiah, sir.

DAVID: Ah, yes, Benaiah. You were with me in the old days—

NATHAN: Here is the decree, sir. Make your mark, and I will seal it with your seal.

(*He holds a paper on* DAVID's *knee.* DAVID *makes a mark with a pen, and* NATHAN *seals the paper.*)

DAVID: Now go to Solomon! Take my own mule, and set him on it. Bring him to Gihon, and let Zadok the Priest and Nathan the Prophet there anoint him King over Israel! Blow the trumpet, and cry, "Long live King Solomon!" Then set him on my throne, for all the people to see.

BENAIAH: Amen! Let us waste no time. May God bless us this day! And may he be to King Solomon as he has been to you, and make his throne greater even than yours!

ZADOK: Goodbye, Your Majesty! We will bring you back news when it is done.

(*They go out.* BATHSHEBA *again kneels by* DAVID.)

BATHSHEBA: Blessings be upon you, David!

DAVID: I am tired and cold. Where is Abishag?

ABISHAG: Here, my Lord.

BATHSHEBA: She shall look after you, and warm you.

(ABISHAG *kneels by* DAVID, *and takes his hands.*)

DAVID: That is better. I think I shall sleep now.

BATHSHEBA: Tonight we shall all sleep, without fear. Thanks be to God!

6. SOLOMON:

THE DANGERS OF SUCCESS

In the three following scenes, which deal with Solomon's reign, we see an historic example of the effect of power and wealth on a man. Solomon's wisdom turned into worldly wisdom, and he found it too hard a task to retain the sense of proportion, and the priorities, which he shows in the first Scene. His reign provides the most vivid of all links between archaeology and the Bible story, and your class would certainly be interested to hear how the huge stables at Megiddo, and the copper smelting works near Ezion-Geber have revealed the geniuneness of the Bible's account of his enterprise and success. (Keller, Part V, chapters 2-3). One of the class might write a short scene about the visit of the Queen of Sheba to Solomon, I Kings 10.

SCENE ONE: THE NEW KING

Bible reference: I Kings 2; 3, 1-15

CHARACTERS: KING SOLOMON, *a very young man*
*QUEEN MERRIS, *daughter of Pharaoh of Egypt*
BENAIAH, *an Officer in Solomon's army*
VOICE OF GOD

The setting is SOLOMON'*s bedroom, in his house at Jerusalem; later it shifts to a shrine nearby, where he goes to pray. At the opening,* SOLOMON *is pacing up and down the room, while the* QUEEN *sits on her bed.*

MERRIS: Why don't you rest, Solomon?
SOLOMON: I cannot rest until I hear from Benaiah.
MERRIS: Do you have to kill your enemies? Must your reign begin with bloodshed?
SOLOMON: Only the blood of those whom I swore to my Father to kill. I cannot be safe on my throne while Joab lives. He tried to make my brother Adonijah King. With those two dead—Wait! I think I hear somebody coming. (*A knock at the door.*) Who is it?

BENAIAH: (*From outside.*) It is I, Benaiah, Your Majesty.

SOLOMON: (*Opening the door and letting him in.*) Well?

BENAIAH: Joab is dead, sir. He would not leave the sanctuary of the altar. I killed him there, and we buried him secretly.

SOLOMON: Thank God! Benaiah, you have served me as loyally as you served my Father, David. From now on you are Commander of my Army.

BENAIAH: Thank you, sir. I shall not fail you, I promise; nor you, my Lady. Now you can rest in peace.

SOLOMON: In the morning, after the sacrifice, we will meet with Zadok the Priest and Nathan the Prophet. Thank you, Benaiah! You too can rest peacefully now.

>   (BENAIAH *bows and goes out.*)

SOLOMON: Merris, now we shall have peace. I want no more bloodshed, I promise you. I want to give my people comfort and justice, and to have happy relations with our neighbors on every side.

MERRIS: I will help you, Solomon, as much as I can.

SOLOMON: We shall make our Kingdom the envy of the world, if God is with us.

MERRIS: Yes, Solomon.

SOLOMON: Tonight I shall sleep at the shrine, and say my prayers in preparation for the sacrifice. Sleep well, Merris! You have come a long way from home to be my wife and Queen. I want to make you happy, and proud of our country.

MERRIS: I shall be happy, if you succeed.

SOLOMON: One day we will build a Temple for God—the finest in the whole world. And then a Palace for ourselves. There is no limit to what I can do, now that I am truly King. Good night, Merris. I will return in the morning.

>   (*He goes out, to the shrine next door. All that is needed is a couch on which he can lie. First he kneels and prays.*)

SOLOMON: O God, I thank you for the victory which you have granted me, over the enemies of my Father. Strengthen me now and always, that I may lead my people in justice and righteousness, and preserve them from all that may do them harm!

>   (*More of the prayer may be improvised. Then* SOLOMON *lies down and sleeps.*)

VOICE OF GOD: I have heard your prayer, Solomon.

SOLOMON: (*Still lying as though asleep, and speaking in his dream.*) Lord, is it really your voice that I hear?

VOICE OF GOD: Yes, Solomon. I am glad that you came to the shrine to ask for my guidance. I have come to offer you a gift in return: whatever you ask to have.

SOLOMON: Whatever I ask?

VOICE OF GOD: Yes. You are little more than a boy, and called to be King. Ask what you think will help you most.

SOLOMON: Lord, you made my Father King, and you loved him because he served you faithfully. Now you have called me to be King, over a people too great to number; and I am young. Give me an understanding heart! Give me wisdom to govern your people, and to see the difference between good and evil!

VOICE OF GOD: You shall have your prayer answered, Solomon. And because you did not ask for victory in war, or for riches, but for wisdom, you shall indeed have the gift of wisdom to discern what is right; and you shall be rich also, and shall increase the greatness of your Kingdom, so long as you remain humble and serve me faithfully. Now sleep in peace! Tomorrow your task begins.

SCENE TWO: THE JUSTICE OF SOLOMON

Bible reference: I Kings 3, 16-28

CHARACTERS: KING SOLOMON
                 GEBER, *an officer under Solomon*
                 *MIRIAM ⎱ *two women who have come to court*
                 *ESTHER ⎰

The setting is a courtroom in SOLOMON's *house in Jerusalem.* SOLOMON *is sitting at a table writing.* GEBER *enters, and bows.*

SOLOMON: What is the next case?

GEBER: Two women, Your Majesty. A dispute over a baby.

SOLOMON: Very well. Bring them in.

GEBER: Yes, sir. (*He goes to the door, and ushers in the women.*) Stand in front of the King. That's right. Now kneel.

SOLOMON: You may rise, both of you. Which is the petitioner?

MIRIAM: I am, Your Majesty. You see—

SOLOMON: Your name?

MIRIAM: Miriam, Your Majesty.

SOLOMON: And yours?

ESTHER: Esther, Your Majesty. This woman is lying—

SOLOMON: Be quiet! Miriam, make your petition.

MIRIAM: We live in the same house, you see, Your Majesty—

GEBER: Call the King "Sir," Miriam. You need not say "Your Majesty" each time.

MIRIAM: Yes, my Lord—sir. Well, each of us had a baby last week, sir. Hers was born three days after mine. And it died, sir. She must have lain on it in the night. It was terrible, I know—

ESTHER: It was her child that died.

MIRIAM: No, sir. She's lying! She got up in the night, and took my son, while I was asleep, and put the dead baby in my bed. I woke up, sir, and got ready to feed my son, and—oh, sir, it was so awful! There was this baby, cold and dead. And then I saw it wasn't my baby at all, but hers.

ESTHER: Yes, that's what you said when you woke up, after crushing your child. She went half crazy, sir, and tried to tear my baby away from me—

MIRIAM: I tell you it is my baby. You can't lie to the King!

GEBER: Be quiet, both of you!

SOLOMON: That's enough, Geber. I've heard all I need to know.

GEBER: I don't see how we can tell which of them is lying, sir. It's an impossible case.

SOLOMON: You think so? I think it is one of the simplest cases we have ever had to decide.

GEBER: Simple? I don't understand, sir.

SOLOMON: Yes, simple. Where is the baby, by the way?

GEBER: Outside, sir, with one of the servants. I didn't want it squalling in here during the trial.

SOLOMON: Quite right, Geber. Well, fetch the baby in here.

GEBER: Yes, sir. But—

SOLOMON: And fetch my sword.

GEBER: Your—what, sir?

SOLOMON: My sword, You're very slow this morning, Geber. Here is a case in which two women claim one baby. We can't give each of them a whole baby; so the only fair thing to do is to give them half a baby each.

GEBER: Half a baby? Your Majesty, are you saying that you are going to cut this baby in half—kill it?

SOLOMON: You can't cut it in half without killing it, Geber.

MIRIAM: Oh, no! Oh, God, you can't! My baby!

SOLOMON: Fetch the baby, Geber. And fetch the sword.

GEBER: Yes, sir. (*He walks toward the door.*)

MIRIAM: Wait! I—oh, Your Majesty, don't kill the child!

SOLOMON: It is the only way to give you both justice, isn't it, Esther?

ESTHER: Yes, sir. It's better than allowing her to have my child.

MIRIAM: Then give her the child, sir. If it has to be so, give her the baby!

SOLOMON: Give the baby to his mother, Geber.

GEBER: Yes, sir; but we don't know which his mother is.

SOLOMON: Yes, we do, Geber. Miriam is his mother. She would not let her child die, even if it meant losing him.

ESTHER: You tricked me—

SOLOMON: It was you who tried to trick us, Esther. You have lied in this court, and you deserve to be punished. But God has already given you the heavy punishment of your baby's death. Go now, and from now on speak the truth! And, Geber, see that Miriam is rewarded for her honesty.

SCENE THREE: PROSPERITY AND MORAL DECLINE

Bible reference: I Kings 4-11

CHARACTERS: KING SOLOMON, *twenty years older*
*BEN-HUR, *his Secretary*
ADONIRAM, *Officer in charge of the labor force*
*BAANA, *Officer in charge of new building projects*
ZADOK, *the Priest*
VOICE OF GOD

The setting is a luxurious room in SOLOMON'*s palace. He is walking up and down, talking to* BEN-HUR, *who sits writing at a desk.*)

SOLOMON: Make a note that I need a report from Ezion-Geber about the fleet.

BEN-HUR: Yes, sir.

SOLOMON: And are those returns in yet, from the copper mines?

BEN-HUR: Not yet, sir. The accountants—

SOLOMON: Tell the accountants from me that they are fired unless they produce the full figures within two days. Now fetch Adoniram!

BEN-HUR: Yes, sir. (*He goes out, and shows in* ADONIRAM.)

SOLOMON: You wanted to see me, Adoniram?

ADONIRAM: Not so much that, Your Majesty. I thought it was my duty to report to you.

SOLOMON: Oh? You sound very stiff and formal today.

ADONIRAM: Look, sir—you have always told me to speak frankly.

SOLOMON: And I meant it. Come on, Adoniram! Sit down. There's something on your mind. Let's have it!

ADONIRAM: Thank you sir. Ever since you became King, you've had just one motto: Expand, Expand, Expand. You're a genius, and it has worked out—so far. We all recognize that. You have given us peace, and a standard of living beyond anything this country had ever dreamed of. But—

SOLOMON: But it's hard to keep people grateful.

ADONIRAM: Grateful? The people you see are grateful, sir. They may complain of the taxes, but they know when they are well off. I'm talking about the people whose lives have been uprooted without any desire of their own—

SOLOMON: Your laborers? They get double the wages—

ADONIRAM: Sir, you must listen! I've done the job you told me to do. I've recruited labor for the mines and the building program and the fleet and the timber industry. But I'm warning you, some of the new projects are going to cause big trouble.

SOLOMON: Oh? And why should the new projects be any different from the others?

ADONIRAM: Because, to be blunt, the ordinary people, the people I have to shift from one job to another, don't think you are building up the nation any more. They think that your head is turned, and that you just want more and more and more for yourself—

SOLOMON: That's enough, Adoniram! I suggest that you stick to your job, and leave mine to me.

ADONIRAM: Yes, sir. Well, at least I've said what I came to say.

(*He bows, and goes quickly out.* SOLOMON *again paces up and down.*)

SOLOMON: Ben-Hur!

BEN-HUR: (*Entering.*) Yes, Your Majesty?

SOLOMON: Fetch Baana in here!

BEN-HUR: Certainly, sir. He's outside. (*He goes out, and shows* BAANA *in.*)

(*Improvise this dialogue, based on I Kings 9-10.* BAANA *answers questions about new buildings: towns, office blocks, stables, or the new homes for* SOLOMON'*s many wives. Other officers can come in and give reports.* SOLOMON *must show great intelligence and efficiency; but he has become a hard man, restless and greedy.*)

BEN-HUR: (*Entering.*) Excuse me, Your Majesty. Zadok is here, asking to see you.

SOLOMON: Oh, he is, is he? Well, I suppose he had better come in. (BEN-HUR *shows* ZADOK *in.*) Trouble as usual, Your Holiness?

ZADOK: Greetings, Your Majesty! In the old days you would not have expected trouble when the Lord's Priest visited you.

SOLOMON: No, Zadok. You're right. Those were good days, and you are a loyal servant of God. What is it?

ZADOK: I have just been shown the plans for the new shrines—that is what the architect calls them—which you have ordered to be built on the hill, behind the homes of your—ladies. A shrine to Milcom, a shrine to Chemosh, a shrine to Ashtoreth. And space left for others to come, no doubt. Is this true, Solomon?

SOLOMON: Yes, it is true. It is no business of yours.

ZADOK: No business of the Lord's chosen High Priest? Are you mad? Is this the son of David whom I anointed King—

SOLOMON: It is no business of yours, because these shrines are not for our people. To strengthen our foreign ties, I have been obliged to make many political marriages. If my wives wish to be faithful to their own Gods, am I to refuse?

ZADOK: Being 'faithful' to Chemosh, sir, happens to involve the regular sacrifice of children, to be burned alive in his brazen image.

SOLOMON: (*Shouting.*) Get out of this room! I have made this Kingdom great! Everything you eat, every offering in the Temple, is due to me, Zadok. Do you think I shall let a snivelling Priest tell me what to do? Now go! (ZADOK *bows, and goes out silently. Enter* BEN-HUR.) What do you want?

BEN-HUR: There are four more of your Officers waiting—

SOLOMON: Send them away! I don't want to see anybody.

BEN-HUR: Excuse me, Your Majesty. I think you ought to know that there's bad news about Jeroboam.

SOLOMON: I gave orders that he was to be caught and put to death.

BEN-HUR: He got away, sir. He went toward Egypt. They say he is in league with Hadad the Edomite. And you know that Rezon is in Damascus—

SOLOMON: Go away! Leave me in peace, all of you! (BEN-HUR *goes out*.) Nothing can touch me! God is with me. (*He kneels*.) O God of my Fathers, God of Abraham and Moses and David, what have I done? What have I done? Are you forsaking me now?

VOICE OF GOD: It is you who have forsaken me, Solomon.

SOLOMON: (*Still kneeling*.) Forsaken you, Lord?

VOICE OF GOD: I told you that if you deserted your faith you and the people would be destroyed. Zadok is right, Solomon. It is not only for your women that you build these abominations. I have tried to warn you and to turn your heart, but you would not listen.

SOLOMON: But I have made you great in the eyes of the world!

VOICE OF GOD: I do not need greatness, Solomon. I told you, when you were a boy, that faithfulness and humility were all that I asked of you. Where is your humility? And with all your fine clothes, are you as rich in beauty as the flowers in the fields?

SOLOMON: Give me another chance! I will repent—I swear it!

VOICE OF GOD: I cannot give you any more chances. The time has come for you to die, Solomon; and you cannot take any of your gold or your copper, your peacocks, or your women, with you. You have done great things for good, and great things for evil. Now your son must fight his own battles.

SOLOMON: My son? Rehoboam? But—he isn't ready. He will throw everything away!

VOICE OF GOD: If he is not ready, whose fault is it but yours? You were too busy making new fortunes to teach your son to follow me.

SOLOMON: O God! (*He falls to the ground*. BEN-HUR *runs in*.)

BEN-HUR: Your Majesty! (*He kneels by* SOLOMON, *then runs toward the door*.) Send for a Doctor quickly! The King has fainted. A Doctor! (*He comes back, and feels* SOLOMON's *pulse*.) He is dying!

THE PROPHETS OF ISRAEL
AND JUDAH

The name "Prophet" means, in Greek, one who "speaks forth." It does not necessarily imply the foretelling of future events, though that was part of the task which the Prophets received from God.

There were great Prophets all through Jewish history; but the age specially associated with prophecy was the two-century span from Amos (about 750 B.C.) to Ezekiel and the second part of the Book of Isaiah (6th century B.C., during the Exile).

You could find many other scenes to write, if you studied the prophetic books. I have taken Jeremiah as an example of the Prophets, for several reasons. We know more about his life than about any of the others. It is an exciting story, full of variety. The time in which he lived was very important, and full of interest. Finally, his own character, and the brilliance and sincerity of his message, make the setting complete.

A single scene has been chosen to introduce Isaiah.

7. ISAIAH

ISAIAH AND THE SIEGE OF JERUSALEM

Bible reference: II Kings 18, 13-19. Read JB 969-970. Keller, Part VI, chapter 3.

CHARACTERS: Inside Jerusalem: ISAIAH THE PROPHET
KING HEZEKIAH
ELIAKIM, MAYOR OF
JERUSALEM
SHEBNA, THE SCRIBE (*a religious leader*)
MESSENGER
CROWD OF JEWS

Below the wall: RABSHAKEH *General of the Assyrian Army*
RABSARIS
A JEWISH PRISONER
ASSYRIAN SOLDIERS

The setting is the city of Jerusalem, during the siege of 701 B.C. The Assyrians, who had already crushed the Northern Kingdom of Israel, were now ravaging Judah. The other cities of Judah could not resist and were being brutally destroyed. It now seemed certain that Jerusalem would also fall. Ideally, this scene should be acted in a hall or church with a gallery, or outside under a balcony. Failing this, some chairs in a classroom can represent the wall. In the city, the KING is sitting near the wall, with ISAIAH and courtiers around him. They have just heard that an exhausted MESSENGER has arrived and is on his way up. Improvise dialogue before he enters. He kneels at the KING's feet.

MESSENGER: Sir, I bring terrible news.
KING: What is it?
MESSENGER: The Assyrians are coming—the whole of Sennacherib's Army. They have burned Lachish. I only just escaped. It was horrible!

(Improvise dialogue, with the KING *and others asking him questions, and the* MESSENGER *describing the cruelty of the conquerors.)*

KING: Oh, God! What are we to do? We have paid tribute to Sennacherib. I even stripped the gold off Solomon's Temple to give to him. Are we to lose Jerusalem and become slaves?

ISAIAH: No, Your Majesty. I know in my heart that God does not mean to let Jerusalem fall. You must have faith, however hard it seems, and keep the gates barred against the Assyrians.

(Shouts from those near the wall: "They are coming! Look, you can see the dust rising. God protect us!" Different voices should join in.)

KING: You know what happens to cities that resist their army. Fire, and murder, and slavery—

ISAIAH: I know it, sir. I still say that God will protect Jerusalem. That is the message he has told me to proclaim to you.

KING: Shebna, and you, Eliakim, be ready to talk to the Assyrians when they come. Let us see if we cannot make some kind of agreement.

ELIAKIM: There is no kind of agreement possible with Sennacherib's men. You give them everything, or you have your throat cut. Even if we surrender we shall be lucky to stay alive.

(A shout is heard from below the wall, where the two GENER-ALS *are now standing, with the* PRISONER *held by soldiers.)*

RABSHAKEH: You up there! You Jews! Fetch your King to the wall!

RABSARIS: *(After a pause)* No answer. We shall have to burn the place down, I suppose.

RABSHAKEH: Oh, he'll come in a minute. These Jews are a lot of cowards.

RABSARIS: Try another summons.

RABSHAKEH: Jews! For the last time—bring out your King and open your gates!

*(*ELIAKIM *and* SHEBNA *appear on the wall.)*

SHEBNA: King Hezekiah has sent us to answer you. What do you want with him?

RABSHAKEH: I don't talk to underlings.

ELIAKIM: I am Mayor of Jerusalem, and this—

RABSHAKEH: If you interrupt me, I shall have your tongue pulled out before I skewer you on a stake. You have five minutes to fetch your King.

ELIAKIM: What message do you wish us to take to him?

RABSARIS: What message? Well, you just guess, Jewish rat! Or better still, hear what your own countryman has to say. (*He strikes the* PRISONER.) Speak up, dog! Tell them what happens to the enemies of Assyria!

PRISONER: Shebna! Lord Eliakim! Don't try to resist! Open the gates, please! We are crushed, and the other cities are in ruins; but the Assyrians will spare your lives if you open the gates at once.

RABSHAKEH: You see? Now fetch your King!

SHEBNA: Sir, could we confer with you in your language? We un-derstand it—

RABSHAKEH: So that your own people can't understand you? No, dog, you can not. I am about to give the order to burn Jerusa-lem in the morning. And you, Mr. Mayor, will be roasted. You have five minutes!

(ELIAKIM *and* SHEBNA *go back to* HEZEKIAH.)

HEZEKIAH: It's no use. We have to give way. How can Judah fight the whole Assyrian Empire?

ISAIAH: We cannot fight Assyria. But I still say that God wants us to trust him to save our city. I know in my heart that his mes-sage is: "Shut the gates and have faith!"

ELIAKIM: It is now or never, Your Majesty.

HEZEKIAH: (*After a pause.*) I shall trust in the Lord. We shall not open the gates.

(*The scene returns to the Assyrians below the walls.*)

RABSARIS: Five minutes. They haven't opened the gates.

RABSHAKEH: Very well. Take this man, and put him to death. He is no more use to us. (*The prisoner is dragged away, shouting.*) Set sentries, and tell the rest of the Army to camp. Tomorrow they shall have all the spoils that we do not burn.

(*Now it is night-time. The Assyrians are asleep.* ISAIAH *is praying on the wall.*)

ISAIAH: Oh, God, I did as I knew you meant me to do. I cannot see how you can deliver us from this danger, Lord; yet I believe that you will, for your message was clear in my heart. Keep faith with us! We have sinned, but we are your people, and this is your holy city. Save us, Lord!

HEZEKIAH: (*Approaching him.*) Do you really think that your prayers can save us, Isaiah? The dawn is coming, and at dawn we must all die by fire or by the Assyrians' swords.

ISAIAH: I still believe. I still know what the will of God is.

HEZEKIAH: They seem all asleep. I can't even see their sentries patrolling. That's strange!

ISAIAH: Yes. No movement. Oh, God! I think I understand. Don't you see? The angel of the Lord has struck them! They are not asleep—they are dead!

(*Below,* RABSARIS *runs in and wakes* RABSHAKEH.)

RABSARIS: General Rabshakeh! For God's sake, sir, wake up! Wake up!

RABSHAKEH: What is it? What in Heaven's name has come over you, Rabsaris? You're trembling like a leaf.

RABSARIS: They're stone dead, my Lord! Thousands of the men are stone dead, with their tongues blackened and their eyes staring. The plague struck in the night—or the God of these cursed Jews destroyed us. You have no Army left.

RABSHAKEH: In the name of the Gods! Plague! (*He goes from corpse to corpse.*)

RABSARIS: Don't touch them! You'll die of the plague yourself!

RABSHAKEH: Let's get out of this place! Muster all the men who can walk. Leave the sick behind. Put an arrow through any of them who try to follow us. We will go home before this curse destroys us all.

(*They hurry away. On the walls, the people gather, and kneel.*)

HEZEKIAH: Oh, God of Abraham, Lord of our people, we have seen the deliverance which your hand has wrought. Make us worthy of it! I, who have sinned in the weakness of my faith, swear that I will use this victory for your glory and your service, O Lord. (*He turns to* ISAIAH.) Speak to the people, Isaiah, faithful and true prophet. We owe our deliverance, under God, to you.

ISAIAH: Not to me, Your Majesty. I only speak what the Lord puts into my heart and into my mouth. Listen to me, all you citizens of Jerusalem!

(*Use the parable of the vineyard, in Isaiah, 5. It can be read, or paraphrased by the actor portraying* ISAIAH.)

Now let us sing together the triumph song of God; and then we will bury the dead.

(*Read or sing Psalm 150.*)

Points for discussion: The prophet Isaiah, author of the first 39 chapters of the book named after him, was the greatest figure among the prophets whose books survive. Other prophets excel in a particular side of their message: Amos in describing the justice of God, Hosea in describing his tenderness, Ezekiel in the vividness of his spiritual visions. Isaiah seems to have every gift of a prophet in rich measure: courage, vision, tenderness, and above all a grasp of the majesty of God.

His courage during the scene of Jerusalem is an undoubted historical fact. Archaeology has shown what happened to Lachish when the Assyrians destroyed it. There must have seemed to be little or no hope for Jerusalem. The context of the parable of the Vineyard is not known, but it fits this scene well.

The call of Isaiah, chapter 6, is not suitable for a written scene; but this would be a good time to discuss it.

8. JEREMIAH:

COURAGE IN ADVERSITY

The story of Jeremiah is complicated. There has to be some guesswork, and some filling in of missing details, to make the scenes coherent. However, they remain close to the original text.

These two tables of dates will help to clarify the background of the scenes. The dates are approximate.

EVENTS IN THE LIFE OF JEREMIAH

646 B.C.	Jeremiah born at Anathoth
626	The call of Jeremiah
621	The discovery of the Law Book in the Temple
612	Nineveh (Assyrian capital) falls to the Babylonians
609	King Josiah of Judah killed at Megiddo
605	The Egyptians defeated by the Babylonians at Carchemish
597	King Jehoiakim of Judah rebels against Babylon. Jerusalem captured. Many Jews taken away to Babylon.
586	King Zedekiah of Judah rebels and is defeated. More Jews deported to Babylon. Gedaliah appointed Governor of Judah by Babylon, but murdered after a few months. Johanan flees to Egypt with many of the Jews, forcing Jeremiah to accompany him.

Date unknown; Jeremiah dies in Egypt.

KINGS OF JUDAH

687-642	MANASSEH
642-640	AMON, son of Manasseh. Killed in a Palace conspiracy.
640-609	JOSIAH, son of Amon. An important reign, in which reforms of religion and administration took place. Killed in battle against Egypt.
609-608	JEHOAHAZ, son of Josiah, for three months. Sent to exile in Egypt by Pharaoh Necho.

608-598	JEHOIAKIM, son of Josiah. Set on the throne by Egypt, but became subject to Babylon after 605. Died during his revolt against Babylon.
598-597	JEHOIACHIN, son of Jehoiakim, ruled for three months until the City fell. Taken into exile to Babylon.
597-586	ZEDEKIAH, son of Josiah and Uncle of Jehoiachin, was set on the throne by Babylon. He led another revolt, and was deposed and taken to Babylon (blinded) in 586.

If you wish to simplify the names, substitute your own modern, shorter names for Ebed-Melech, Shephatiah, etc.

SCENE ONE: THE PROPHET AT HOME

Bible reference: Jeremiah 1; 11, 1-23; 16, 1-9

CHARACTERS: HILKIAH, *a priest, father of Jeremiah*
              *LEAH, *his wife*
              *MICHAL, *their daughter, younger than Jeremiah*
              JEREMIAH
              SHALLUM, *Uncle of Jeremiah*
              HANAMEL, *son of Shallum*

The year is 625 B.C. It is one year after the call of JEREMIAH *to be a prophet. The setting is the home of his father,* HILKIAH, *in Anathoth, a village near Jerusalem.* HILKIAH *and* SHALLUM *are seated at a table.* JEREMIAH *sits alone in front of them.* LEAH, HANAMEL *and* MICHAL *sit in the background. For reasons which are not made clear in the book,* JEREMIAH'*s family opposed him violently, and even tried to kill him. A possible explanation of their hostility comes out in this scene.*

HILKIAH: My son, I have asked your Uncle Shallum to come and talk to you, because he can speak for our family, the house of Abiathar. He will tell you how you can best use your gifts to serve God.

JEREMIAH: I thank you, Father; and you, Uncle, for coming here. But—

SHALLUM: Let me speak, Jeremiah.

JEREMIAH: Yes, sir.

SHALLUM: I am told that you have been prophesying in the gate of the Lord's house in Jerusalem. Is that true?

JEREMIAH: Yes, sir. It was his bidding. I—

HANAMEL: His bidding! That is what we hear all the time. Nobody knows what the Lord wishes, except our household prophet!

LEAH: Be quiet, Hanamel! Let Jeremiah speak for himself.

HANAMEL: For himself? Oh no—he speaks for the Lord. Nothing that we say—

HILKIAH: Be silent! Let your father be our spokesman.

SHALLUM: It seems that your own kinsmen do not find you to be a prophet of great authority, Jeremiah.

JEREMIAH: I cannot help that, Uncle. I cannot help what any man thinks. God has called me, and I must do his will.

MICHAL: I understand, brother!

HILKIAH: Michal, be silent! This is man's work.

SHALLUM: So you were called, my boy? Are you sure that you could recognize the Lord's voice?

JEREMIAH: Yes. Yes, I knew his voice.

HILKIAH: He always sticks to this story. He is convinced that he saw a vision.

JEREMIAH: I saw no vision; but it was the Lord's voice. He told me that he had formed me in the womb to be a prophet to the nations. I didn't want to listen. I had no skill with which to proclaim his word. But he touched my mouth, and told me to have courage.

MICHAL: It is true, Uncle! Don't you understand? When he speaks in prophecies, it is not his own words—

HILKIAH: I told you to be quiet, girl!

LEAH: What she says is right, husband. He speaks with two voices: his own—

HILKIAH: I will not have this house ruled by women! If you wish to stay, hold your tongues!

SHALLUM: Let us not argue. Jeremiah, I am sure that you are sincere, and love God. But you have a loyalty to the house of Abiathar our ancestor. Don't you know that all of us who belong to his family must work together to restore our rightful position in the Priesthood of our land?

HILKIAH: Not only that, but you will bring us all into trouble with King Josiah, if you speak against the rulers and their policy.

JEREMIAH: How can I make you understand? Either I was called by God, or not. If not, then all that I say is worth nothing. But if he did call me—as I know he did—it is his word that I speak, and I cannot be silent.

HANAMEL: But we are to be silent, I suppose, when you stab your own kinsfolk in the back—traitor!

LEAH: My son is not a traitor, Hanamel.

HANAMEL: Yes, Aunt, he is! How else can he go whining around the streets that the Lord will not protect us? And that the people of the North will wash over us like a roaring sea? At least other cowards keep their views to themselves.

SHALLUM: Is that what you believe, Jeremiah?

JEREMIAH: In God's name, listen, Uncle! And all of you, listen! When God called me, he showed me signs. I saw the world around me through his eyes. He showed me the almond tree blossoming—the watchful tree—and I knew it was a symbol of his watchfulness. He showed me a boiling pot, facing away from the North, and told me to warn King Josiah not to resist the Northern enemy—

HILKIAH: Yet the same Lord told Isaiah the prophet to strengthen King Hezekiah's will, so that he would shut the gates against the Assyrians.

HANAMEL: That was only Isaiah, Uncle! Our great prophet sees more clearly—

MICHAL: When have you ever had the courage to stand up to a crowd, and say what you believe? You are the coward, Hanamel, and a blind, stupid—

SHALLUM: Please, my children! Be quiet! Jeremiah, we have not come here to argue with you, but to tell you our decision.

JEREMIAH: Your decision?

SHALLUM: That is what I said. In the name of Abiathar the High Priest, our ancestor, we bid you speak no more to the people, unless you first have the approval of your father and me.

HILKIAH: We have decided to arrange a marriage for you, and to give you land here in Anathoth—

JEREMIAH: Marriage? I tell you I cannot marry! The children of this place will rot away through disease and famine and the sword, and will die unwept. Haven't you read what Hosea said—how Israel in God's eyes was like his own unfaithful wife? I cannot marry, and I will not keep silent—

HILKIAH: You refuse obedience to your elders?

JEREMIAH: You have no right to ask me to disobey God. Do you think it is easy for me to stand against you? I tell you it is agony! But God has set me apart, and I cannot—

HANAMEL: Then go to Sheol, and prophesy there, traitor!

(*He jumps on* JEREMIAH, *and they struggle, until they are pulled apart.*)

SHALLUM: Violence brings no answers to our problems. But we must warn you, Jeremiah. Unless you work with us, and see the will of God through our eyes, you will be hated wherever you go, and your life will be worth very little.

JEREMIAH: I know that. I know that our people are blind, our prophets write with false pens, and boast of visions which are lies, our priests are stiff-necked and corrupt. I see idols spread like scarecrows in a field of cucumbers, and our spiritual leaders are like broken cisterns that cannot hold the truth. I can only pray that God will spare a remnant, in the hour of our disaster, before all Jerusalem becomes a thing to be hissed at, a lair for the jackals.

HILKIAH: This is the kind of wild talk we hear from him all the time.

SHALLUM: Surely you want to work with us to save your country, when you see those threats so clearly?

JEREMIAH: I will work as I must work, and speak as I must speak. If I go as a lamb to the slaughter, because I serve God, then that must be his will.

SHALLUM: He will not listen! Hilkiah, guard him carefully—and you, Leah! Perhaps even now he will learn wisdom. If not, I foresee that he will live to be hated and scorned by our friends and enemies alike. I pray God that it may not be so!

SCENE TWO: REFORMATION IN JERUSALEM

Bible reference: II Kings 22-23; Jeremiah 5, 30-31; 8, 8; 11, 1-8; 14, 11-18; 28

CHARACTERS: HILKIAH (*not to be confused with the other Hilkiah, the High Priest, II Kings 22*)
JEREMIAH
SHAPHAN, *temple secretary*
HULDAH, THE PROPHETESS

The year is 621. JEREMIAH *is about 25 years old. An ancient Law Book was discovered in the Temple, and King Josiah proclaimed a*

"Reformation," based on this Second Law ("Deuteronomy"). At first, JEREMIAH *seems to have welcomed this new development; but he probably lost faith in it, when he saw how it was exploited by different parties.*

The scene is imaginary, JEREMIAH *may not have been important enough for the authorities to worry about what he taught at this time. But by creating the scene we can bring out the different points of view which* JEREMIAH *must have known and criticized during this exciting period. The interpretation of the prophecies in chapters 8 and 11 is very uncertain. We can only say that* JEREMIAH'S *opinions were probably those which are expressed in the scene.*

The setting is again HILKIAH'S *house. The four men are seated. They are in the middle of their argument when the scene starts.*

SHAPHAN: Can't you see the importance of unity at a time like this?

JEREMIAH: How can you talk about unity? The only thing that unites the three of you is hostility toward me.

HILKIAH: We all love our country—

JEREMIAH: Do you? I know that you hate me, Father, because I don't side with the Priests of Anathoth against the Temple party —that means against you, Shaphan, and all that you stand for. Huldah hates me for being a rival prophet, and for exposing the emptiness and dishonesty of those who are cheating the King and his people. But you don't really love the Temple Priests, Huldah, any more than you love my father and the house of Abiathar. To make the circle complete, you don't trust the prophets, Shaphan. They may say something outside the party line, and people may listen. You both know what you want to suppress—the freedom of the people to worship in local shrines. Beyond that, you have nothing in common. You cry 'Peace! Peace!,' but if I walked out now you'd be at each other's throats in a minute.

HULDAH: You don't seem to see that there is a focal point for all of our loyalties. If we support the King, there will be peace, and unity. He has humbled himself before the Lord, and the Lord will hear his cry.

JEREMIAH: No, Huldah, no! It won't work! You can't patch up our nation like an old robe. Shaphan wants power—power for the Temple, and control of the King by—

SHAPHAN: Not control, no! But he must have a strong central organization—

JEREMIAH: Exactly! The Priests of Zadok! How about that, Father?

HILKIAH: The day must come when the house of Abiathar will return to its rightful place. But meanwhile—

JEREMIAH: Meanwhile forget our differences? And you, Huldah, do you think the Temple clique will allow prophets to speak freely? Of course they won't! They will have their own prophets, carefully coached to speak the official bulletins—men like Hananiah—

SHAPHAN: You're very free with your insults! What is your solution, I'd like to know? To leave every man free to preach defeatism, like you? At least Hananiah has the courage to believe in Judah.

JEREMIAH: Courage? I call it expediency. He says whatever he thinks the people above him will approve of. He licks their boots, so as to earn his pay!

HULDAH: So we are all hypocrites—all except you?

JEREMIAH: I don't know, Huldah. I don't want to believe that. I think you at least want to find the truth, and to speak out. But you are blind to the weaknesses of the King's policy. You might as well try to paint an Ethiopian white, or change a leopard's spots, as to unite the Priests of Zadok with the successors of Amos and Isaiah.

HILKIAH: Even if that is true, my son, you have not told us how you would advise the King to act.

JEREMIAH: Father, I have said it a thousand times in the streets— with stones flying past my head. We don't need reform of the Law, but a change of heart. God has told me to try to glean Judah like a vine; to refine the people like metal in a furnace. He has told me to warn Josiah and the rest of our rulers that the power from the North is unbreakable. We cannot resist, and we must not try.

SHAPHAN: I have heard enough.

HULDAH: No true prophet of the Lord could say that. The old prophets would turn in their graves to hear a coward claim to speak in God's name.

SHAPHAN: I came here hoping to protect your son, Hilkiah. I hoped to warn him, and make him see reason. But I find him eaten up with pride. He cannot be left free to spread this kind of poison!

HULDAH: Shut him up in your home, Hilkiah! If he comes to Jerusalem, he will end up dead or in prison.

HILKIAH: I am at my wits' end what to do. He takes no notice of our warnings. Some of my kinsmen have tried to kill him already—as though that could be the will of God. He has brought sorrow to my old age, and I know no way to turn him from his folly.

JEREMIAH: Oh, Judah, Judah! Truth is called folly now, and the face of oppression is harder than rock. Father, you see no way out—nor do I. We shall be drunk with the wine of wrath, till we stagger, and vomit, and fall, and die. Oh God! Must I always be hated and despised for speaking your word?

SCENE THREE: JEREMIAH PREACHES AT THE POTSHERD GATE

Bible reference: Jeremiah 19-20

CHARACTERS: JEREMIAH
PASSHUR
SHAPHAN
AHIKAM
BARUCH
CROWD AND ATTENDANTS

The year is about 606, and JEREMIAH *is 40 years old. Tragedy struck Judah when* JOSIAH *was killed by the Egyptians at the Battle of Megiddo (II Chronicles 35, 20-24).* PHAROAH NECHO *then forced upon Judah* JOSIAH's *eldest son,* JEHOIAKIM, *as King.* JEREMIAH's *opinion of this ambitious, selfish King is given in 22, 13-19.* SHAPHAN *and his son* AHIKAM *were at least partially in sympathy with* JEREMIAH *(26, 24).* BARUCH *was from this time on his faithful friend and secretary. The pun on* PASSHUR's *name is not a reproduction of what* JEREMIAH *said, but it is an example of the type of play on names frequently used in the Old Testament (see 20, 3).*

The setting for this scene is the street near the East Gate of Jerusalem. JEREMIAH *stands on some steps, raised above the large crowd, who surround him on three sides. Begin with an improvisation of the prophecies given in 19, 1-9 and 22, 13-19.* JEREMIAH *may read these from the Bible, but it would be better for him to prepare a speech based on them. Improvise interruptions and questions from the crowd, which is partly friendly to* JEREMIAH, *partly hostile.*

JEREMIAH: And now hear what the Lord has called me to do. I will break this people (*Here he breaks the bottle—see 19, verse 19.*), as this earthen bottle is broken—so that they shall never be mended. (*Cries from the crowd.*) And the body of your King shall be dragged out to burial, like the carcass of a donkey—

(PASSHUR *has entered, with his attendants.*)

JEREMIAH: There is still time to listen, and repent.
PASSHUR: Arrest him! Don't let him get away!

(JEREMIAH *is pulled down from the steps, and* PASSHUR *mounts them.*)

PASSHUR: Go home, good people! Don't listen to this traitor! We will deal with him. (*Shouts from the crowd: "Leave him alone! We want to hear him!" and "Beat the traitor! Put him in the stocks!"*) Officers, disperse this crowd!

(*Some of the* ATTENDANTS *push the* CROWD *away. Meanwhile others have beaten* JEREMIAH, *and put his feet in the stocks. He is badly hurt, and bleeding.* SHAPHAN *and* AHIKAM *push their way forward through the retreating crowd.* BARUCH *stands in the background, watching.*)

SHAPHAN: What is all this noise? Passhur! I might have known it would be you.
JEREMIAH: Is this Passhur? The one they call the Slasher? I hope you're satisfied with what your men have done to a defenseless man of God.
PASSHUR: Man of God! A fifth column Babylonian pacifist—that is all you are!
AHIKAM: Are you all right, Jeremiah?
JEREMIAH: I am hurt; but my cuts and bruises will mend.
SHAPHAN: There was no need for that, Passhur.
PASSHUR: Are you teaching me to do my job, Shaphan? I am Chief Officer of the Temple, and I intend to see that God is not insulted in our streets by a foreign spy!
AHIKAM: That's ridiculous!
PASSHUR: Is it? What do you think it does to the people to be told that the enemy will break us like a bottle? (*He kicks the fragments of the bottle which* JEREMIAH *had broken.*) That's what your Jeremiah thinks of Judah! And he also speaks open treason against the King.
JEREMIAH: Free speech is treason. That is what we have come to.

SHAPHAN: You're a hard man to help, Jeremiah. You know that.

JEREMIAH: Because the truth is hard. Our King tries to be another Solomon, when he is really no more than a puppet of Egypt.

PASSHUR: Not a puppet: an ally. And with Egypt on our side—

JEREMIAH: With or without Egypt on our side, we shall perish for our sins against God, Passhur.

AHIKAM: Surely there's no need to keep him here, Passhur, like a criminal.

PASSHUR: He is a criminal. Treason is a capital crime. Let him think about it through the night! And I advise you not to interfere.

SHAPHAN: There's nothing we can do today, Ahikam.

AHIKAM: We have to do something about those cuts. He'll bleed to death.

BARUCH: (*Coming forward.*) Don't worry, sir. I will attend to him.

SHAPHAN: Who are you?

BARUCH: My name is Baruch. I have heard the prophet speak many times. I want to serve you, Jeremiah.

JEREMIAH: Baruch? I have seen your face before, in the crowd.

PASSHUR: All right. You can bring him water and bandages, and patch him up. Give him something to eat, if you like. Even though he wouldn't be much loss, we don't want him dying in the street. But don't you try to set him free, or there'll be big trouble. Understand? My men will be keeping an eye on him.

SHAPHAN: Thank you, Baruch. We will return in the morning.

PASSHUR: I'd appreciate if you would keep out of this, Shaphan. Let me handle it! The King won't thank you for interfering.

AHIKAM: Let's go, Father!

(PASSHUR, SHAPHAN *and* AHIKAM *go out.*)

JEREMIAH: So you want to help me, Baruch?

BARUCH: Yes, Master. I want to serve God, and through you I have heard him speak.

JEREMIAH: Blessings be upon you! I need a friend. Sometimes it seems that even God is against me.

BARUCH: Whatever happens, I will be loyal to you. Let me go and fetch water now.

JEREMIAH: Where do you live?

BARUCH: Close by the Benjamin gate. You shall come there and rest, when they set you free.

JEREMIAH: It sounds as though the Lord has truly sent me a friend, Baruch.

BARUCH: He has sent me a teacher and guide. At home, I have parchment rolls. After you are well again, I will write down the prophecies that you speak in the Lord's name. But lie back now —here, on my cloak! I will return as soon as I can.

SCENE FOUR: JEREMIAH IN PRISON

Bible reference: Jeremiah 29; 37-39; II Kings 25, 1-12.

CHARACTERS: JEREMIAH
     BARUCH
     SHEPHATIAH
     JUCAL
     EBED-MELECH
     KING ZEDEKIAH

The year is 588. Jeremiah is about 58 years old. Rebellion against Babylon broke out again, under the weak King Zedekiah. Jeremiah knew that it was hopeless, and that dependence upon help from Egypt was a vain dream. Jerusalem held out for another two years, but in 586 it was captured and ravaged for the second time in eleven years.

The setting in this scene is the courtyard of the prison in Jerusalem. The opening of a cistern is in the middle of the yard. JEREMIAH *is lying on the ground, exhausted, emaciated, and covered with mud.* EBED-MELECH *and* BARUCH *have just lifted him out of the cistern with ropes.*

EBED-MELECH: Help me carry him into the shade. Gently! (*They carry him to one side.*) There! Watch over him, Baruch! I will fetch some wine.
JEREMIAH: (*Faintly.*) Water, please.
EBED-MELECH: Yes, of course. He looks bad. But I don't expect he could swallow wine or food yet. (*He goes out.*)
BARUCH: Master! Jeremiah, can you hear me?
JEREMIAH: My eyes ache. Where am I? The light hurts—
BARUCH: Here! I'll cover your eyes, until you're used to it. And we have to wash away the smell of that slime.
JEREMIAH: I never thought I should come out of it alive.
BARUCH: But for Ebed-Melech, I don't think you would have made it. He persuaded the King to see you again.

JEREMIAH: The King is coming? Poor Zedekiah! He can't make up his mind. He gives me a special ration of bread, and buries me alive in mud. He asks my advice, and does the opposite.

EBED-MELECH: (*Returning.*) Here, Jeremiah. Drink this!

JEREMIAH: Thank you. You're a brave man. Ah! That's wonderful!

EBED-MELECH: Are your arms all right? I was afraid the ropes would hurt them.

JEREMIAH: They are a little more sore than the rest of my body; but the rags you threw down made all the difference.

BARUCH: When the King comes, we'll tell him that you must have a Doctor. (*A gate is heard opening.*) There's someone now!

(SHEPHATIAH *and* JUCAL *hurry in.*)

SHEPHATIAH: What is this? Who gave orders for the removal of this man from the cistern?

EBED-MELECH: King Zedekiah gave the orders, Shephatiah—just in time to save you from the stain of murder.

JUCAL: I don't believe it!

EBED-MELECH: You'll be able to ask him yourself, Jucal. He is due here now, to talk to Jeremiah.

SHEPHATIAH: This is your doing, Ebed-Melech! We'll see that you pay for it. Shielding a traitor isn't a light charge, you know.

JEREMIAH: What exactly is the charge against me, Shephatiah? Since there has been no trial, I am still in the dark.

SHEPHATIAH: With a Babylonian army outside the walls, we don't have time for trials—and we don't need them. The charge is simple: you were caught trying to desert to the enemy.

BARUCH: You still say that? You know that I submitted complete evidence that Jeremiah was on the way to Anathoth to take up the land bought from his Uncle.

JUCAL: So you said! What Court would swallow an excuse like that?

JEREMIAH: No Court has had a chance to decide. It really is ironical. I bought the land to show my faith in the future of Judah, and to help morale in Anathoth. God knows they need it there, after what they have gone through in the occupation! And you arrested me for treason! Oh God! Why do I always have to preach to deaf ears and stony hearts?

JUCAL: So you say you didn't try to desert. All right, then. Answer me this! Did you or did you not encourage other people to do the same? We have witnesses who heard you say: "Anyone who stays in the city will die by the sword, or by famine or pestilence; but anyone who defects to the Babylonians will survive."

SHEPHATIAH: And another witness heard you say that there is no hope for the city—it is bound to fall soon—so get out while you can. Did you say that?

JEREMIAH: Yes, I said it. If facing reality is treachery, then—

(*The gate is heard opening, and* KING ZEDEKIAH *comes in.*)

EBED-MELECH: Now you can ask your question, Jucal!

(*All except* JEREMIAH *bow and say 'Greetings, Your Majesty!'*)

ZEDEKIAH: Are you safe, Jeremiah?

JEREMIAH: I shall live, sir. It takes more than the efforts of these gentlemen to silence me.

SHEPHATIAH: Let me remind you, sir, that it was by your order—

ZEDEKIAH: Yes, Shephatiah. You forced me to give you permission to work your will on Jeremiah. And how savagely you did it!

JUCAL: Can anything be too bad for him? He is like a poison to the city!

ZEDEKIAH: Oh, Jucal! Leave me! I am in torment, and I must ask the prophet for counsel. Leave me, all of you! And remember that you have not seen me here. I want nobody to know of this meeting. Is that understood?

SHEPHATIAH: Yes, sir.

EBED-MELECH: We understand, Your Majesty.

ZEDEKIAH: Who is this man?

EBED-MELECH: This is Baruch, sir, the prophet's friend. You can trust him.

ZEDEKIAH: Thank you, Baruch; and you, Ebed-Melech. You have done good service to your country. Now, please leave us alone.

(*All but* JEREMIAH *and* ZEDEKIAH *go out.*)

JEREMIAH: You want my advice?

ZEDEKIAH: I need you, Jeremiah. I am sorry—

JEREMIAH: You are sorry that I was near to death, buried in a dungeon by murderers? Thank you, sir. Before I say any more, can I have your assurance that I shall not be handed over to them again?

ZEDEKIAH: I promise that. For your own safety, and mine, you must stay here. But Ebed-Melech will be in charge of you, and Baruch may come and go freely. Now, tell me what to do! I am going mad with fear and uncertainty.

JEREMIAH: I have told you. God's word does not change. Surrender yourself and the city to the princes of the King of Babylon. Then you, and all of us, will be saved. Otherwise, Jerusalem will be burned and Judah wiped out.

ZEDEKIAH: Oh God! I can't do it, Jeremiah! I can see that you may be right, but I—What would happen to me? They would hand me over to the Jews who have already gone over to Babylon—

JEREMIAH: Zedekiah, don't think about the dangers! Think about what is right, and act like a King! Our exiles won't hurt you. Babylon despises them, even though she will use them as tools and puppets. I'm telling you to do what the Lord commands, however hard it is. Surrender! If not, you will hear your own wives cursing you, as they are dragged away into captivity.

ZEDEKIAH: But is there no hope that Egypt will—

JEREMIAH: I have told you, Pharaoh Hophra and his army are doomed. They will be bitten to death, like a heifer, when all the gadflies from the North assail them.

ZEDEKIAH: So you have no comfort for me?

JEREMIAH: Yes. The comfort of the truth. And that is one word: Surrender!

ZEDEKIAH: (*Walking up and down restlessly.*) Don't tell anyone what we have said, Jeremiah! Just say that you asked to be freed from the dungeon, and I—

JEREMIAH: You will do nothing. That is what I fear. You will know the Lord's will, and you won't do it—for fear of your false advisers. We shall all pay the price.

ZEDEKIAH: I—oh God! I must think! There are so many dangers, whichever way I turn.

JEREMIAH: I have said all I can. And I am tired. Please leave me, sir, and send my friend to me.

ZEDEKIAH: Yes. Yes, I will try to protect you, Jeremiah.

JEREMIAH: Think about your duty, not about me! May God bless you, and give you the strength to stand firm!

SCENE FIVE: HARVEST TIME AT MIZPAH

Bible reference: Jeremiah 40; 41, 1-10

CHARACTERS: GEDALIAH
JOHANAN
JEREMIAH
BARUCH
ATTENDANTS

The year is 586. JEREMIAH *is about 60 years old. King Zedekiah was blinded and led away to Babylon. His sons, and the "nobles of Judah," were executed (39, 6-7). But the Babylonians showed moderation and good sense in setting up a new Government, with a Jew of noble birth at its head,* GEDALIAH, *the son of Ahikam. This scene shows the tragic end of his short regime. He had, in a few short months, brought new hope to* JEREMIAH *and to the shattered people of Judah. The setting is Mizpah, a village a few miles North of Jerusalem, where* GEDALIAH *established himself. Servants are preparing an outdoor meal.* GEDALIAH *brings the other three in.*

GEDALIAH: Jeremiah, I want you to meet my chief adviser, Johanan, son of Kareah. And this is Baruch, the prophet's friend.

(They exchange greetings.)

GEDALIAH: Come and eat, my friends! I will give the blessing. Oh God of Abraham, Yahweh, Lord of all nations, we thank you for these fruits of the earth, given to us in such abundance. We pray for courage to overcome sufferings, and for your guidance in all things, that we may rebuild Israel according to your will. Amen.

ALL: Amen.

(They sit down, and the servants bring food.)

JOHANAN: Is it true that you expect a record harvest, Gedaliah?

GEDALIAH: So they say. It seems incredible, after all the destruction earlier in the year. But God has blessed us!

JOHANAN: I never thought we should have enough labor to get the work done, after the deportations.

JEREMIAH: Now that we have followed the way of the Lord, our exiles have returned from Moab and Ammon and Edom.

JOHANAN: I have wanted to meet you, Jeremiah, for a long time. Of course I have heard the story of your courage during the siege.

JEREMIAH: (*Laughing.*) Courage? Not many people called it courage then.

GEDALIAH: But it was, Jeremiah. You could not save us from disaster; but you can help us to restore the people's hopes.

JOHANAN: They say you were almost deported yourself after the siege.

JEREMIAH: That is quite true. Baruch and I were taken in chains to Ramah, with the rest of the men from Jerusalem.

JOHANAN: You have been friends for a long time?

BARUCH: For over twenty years. I have tried to write down the words of the prophet faithfully.

JEREMIAH: Far more than that! Baruch has been a true friend in all my needs and dangers.

GEDALIAH: And now we hope the dangers are over.

JEREMIAH: God grant it may all be true! We have seen the destroyer come at noonday, and anguish and terror fell suddenly upon us. Now it fills my heart with wonder and joy to watch the people gathering the harvest and treading the grapes.

JOHANAN: Yes. What Gedaliah has achieved is incredible. But I have tried to warn him that there are fresh dangers; and I hope you can help me to make him see it, Jeremiah. He has to take more precautions.

GEDALIAH: I cannot live in a fortress, Johanan! We are trying to give the people confidence. They won't trust me, unless I show trust in the people around me.

JEREMIAH: Whom do you fear, Johanan?

JOHANAN: To put it bluntly, I don't trust Baalis, the Ammonite King. Do you suppose he wants to see Judah back on its feet?

JEREMIAH: No. You are right to fear him.

JOHANAN: He's a treacherous rat. And now we have all these so-called exiles streaming back, unchecked. Only one of them has to be in his pay, to murder you.

GEDALIAH: And you think it may be Ishmael?

JOHANAN: I do. I can't be sure; but I find him too smooth to be true. I think Baalis has sent him. And the only way to stop him is to act first.

JEREMIAH: To kill him?

GEDALIAH: More killing? No, Johanan. I will be as careful as I can; but I will not have blood shed because of mere suspicions.

That would be betrayal of the new age we are trying to create.

JOHANAN: All I hope is that those fine words won't be choked off when they cut your throat.

GEDALIAH: I have Captain Sarsechim, and a company of Babylonian guards. I can't do more than that without turning myself into a tyrant. Why don't you take Jeremiah and Baruch, and show them the vineyards? I have work to do. We can meet here in the evening, and I promise that we will discuss it again, Johanan.

JOHANAN: Very well, sir. I have a plan to suggest, but it can wait until suppertime. Will you come with me, Jeremiah?

JEREMIAH: Thank you. We will. And thank you for your hospitality, Gedaliah. Our country is blessed in having you as guide. But Johanan is right—be careful!

(*They go out.*)

NOTE: An optional addition to the scene, which can be improvised, is the murder of Gedaliah. He is sitting at the table writing, after the servants have cleared away the meal and been dismissed. Ishmael comes in quietly, unannounced. He speaks in a friendly way, but Gedaliah is on his guard. Gedaliah moves to ring a bell on the table, but Ishmael draws a knife, and tells him not to move. He says that the house is surrounded, and if Gedaliah calls for help from the Babylonian guard he will be killed before they come. Ishmael then calls in some of his men, and tells Gedaliah that they are going to take him away as a prisoner. But when they have tied his hands, they smother him, and Ishmael stabs him. He can go on to trap the Babylonian Captain into coming in alone, and murdering him; and then make plans to slaughter the men from Shechem. Nothing can be too grim in depicting the despicable Ishmael. He marks the terrible contrast with the hopes which Gedaliah had aroused.

SCENE SIX: JOHANAN AND THE FLIGHT TO EGYPT

Bible reference: Jeremiah 41, 11-43, 7

CHARACTERS: JOHANAN
                   AZARIAH
                   JEREMIAH
                   BARUCH
                   SENTRY

The year is 586, soon after the last scene. Ishmael escaped JOHANAN's *revenge, and* JOHANAN *was left to try to rally the people. But confidence had vanished with Gedaliah's death.* JOHANAN *was terrified of Babylonian reprisals. And so once again* JEREMIAH *prophesied to frightened men, who would not listen. The setting for this scene is a village near Bethlehem, where* JOHANAN *had made his headquarters.* JOHANAN *and* AZARIAH *are armed and in uniform. The* SENTRY *brings* BARUCH *in.*

JOHANAN: Well? What news?

BARUCH: The prophet is coming to you in a minute.

AZARIAH: We've waited ten days! Does it take that long for a prophet to make up his mind?

BARUCH: Not to make up his own mind, Azariah—to know for certain what God wills. Do you find it easy to answer that question?

AZARIAH: No. You're right, and I'm sorry.

JOHANAN: Our nerves are all on edge. I haven't slept for three nights.

AZARIAH: Did you confirm the order to double the sentries?

JOHANAN: Yes. Though what good it will do—

   (*The sentry enters again.*)

SENTRY: The prophet Jeremiah, sir.

JOHANAN: Bring him in! (JEREMIAH *enters.*) Sit down, Jeremiah!

AZARIAH: Tell us quickly! (*They all sit.*)

JEREMIAH: You swore to listen to me, and to do whatever the Lord revealed to me.

AZARIAH: That was ten days ago. We—

JOHANAN: Be quiet, Azariah! Yes, we swore it. But things have changed since then—

JEREMIAH: Changed? That is what I fear, Johanan—that once again it will be my fate to speak to men whose hearts are blind with fear.

AZARIAH: Why don't you come right out and say it? You're telling us to stay!

JOHANAN: And to wait for another Babylonian army—more slaughter, more deportations. We let Gedaliah be killed—their own appointed Governor—and Sarsechim, and a whole troop of Babylonian soldiers. We didn't even catch the murderer—

BARUCH: Won't you even listen?

JOHANAN: I'm sorry. Tell us your message, Jeremiah!

JEREMIAH: It is plain and simple. I prayed and prayed, and I know that God spoke. Stay here! Don't be afraid of Babylon! And don't, above all, run away to Egypt!

AZARIAH: The same thing always! Trust Babylon!

JOHANAN: You're lying, Jeremiah! Baruch put you up to saying this. He's a spy for Babylon!

BARUCH: God forgive you, Johanan! I have said nothing, and Jeremiah would not listen if I did.

AZARIAH: Then who does put these lies into his mouth? Not God —you can be sure of that!

JOHANAN: Can't you see that Egypt means food, and rest, and an end to fear and violence?

JEREMIAH: No, Johanan. It means disgrace and suffering, and finally death. (*He rises.*) Come with me, Baruch! It is useless to stay here.

JOHANAN: Oh no, you don't! Not this time!

JEREMIAH: What do you mean?

JOHANAN: Sentry! (*The* SENTRY *runs in.*)

SENTRY: Sir?

JOHANAN: Tell Captain Nathan to assign four men to guard Jeremiah and Baruch. They are not to leave the compound. Is that clear?

SENTRY: Yes, sir. (*He goes out.*)

JEREMIAH: So I am a prisoner again?

AZARIAH: Yes, a traitor and a prisoner.

JOHANAN: I'm sorry. We can't afford to let you talk to the people. They are too much confused already, and we must speak with one voice. You will both start with us for Egypt in the morning.

JEREMIAH: So be it. We shall all die in Egypt, and Jerusalem will again be a place of desolation.

BARUCH: Johanan, think again! Listen—

JOHANAN: Shut your mouth, Baruch! Or I shall shut it with my sword. Azariah, go and give the final orders about moving out at dawn. I'll see that these two don't get away.

JEREMIAH: Don't worry, Johanan! I shall not run away. But I warn you that your name will become a curse and a horror and a taunt, because of what you are doing today. God's will be done! We shall never see Jerusalem again.

SCENE SEVEN: THE LAST DAYS

Bible reference: Jeremiah 44; 46; 23, 1-8; 31, 29-34; 33, 12-18

CHARACTERS: JEREMIAH
BARUCH
JOHANAN
*PRINCESS HAMMUTAL

The time is soon after the last scene, perhaps in 585. JEREMIAH *is about 61 years old. He died, as he lived, a brave but saddened man. The Jews in Egypt fell away from the exclusive worship of Yahweh, the women introducing the Babylonian cult of the Queen of Heaven.* JEREMIAH *was shocked and depressed by this. He also knew that their trust in Egypt as a safe refuge from Babylon was an illusion. In this scene he looks back over his life, and I have introduced some of the greatest passages in his teaching. The setting is a house at Pathros in Upper Egypt, near to a courtyard in which* JEREMIAH *has been addressing a large crowd of Jewish men and women.* BARUCH *and* JOHANAN *carry* JEREMIAH *in, and* HAMMUTAL *follows them.*

HAMMUTAL: Here, on the bed!

BARUCH: Will you fetch some water?

HAMMUTAL: Yes. (*She goes out.*)

JOHANAN: The old warrior prophet! God, I admire that man!

BARUCH: And you have killed him.

JOHANAN: Don't be bitter at me, Baruch! I did what I thought was right, bringing him here. Who can tell whether he would have been better off staying in Jerusalem?

BARUCH: The important thing is to save his life, if we can.

HAMMUTAL: (*Returning.*) Drink this! I will bathe your face.

JEREMIAH: Thank you, Princess. I feel better.

HAMMUTAL: You must rest. Don't try to move!

JEREMIAH: Is Baruch here?

BARUCH: Yes, Master.

JEREMIAH: I should like to be alone with Baruch. Thank you for your kindness.

JOHANAN: Come, Princess!

HAMMUTAL: We will bring you food later. Jeremiah—

JEREMIAH: Yes?

HAMMUTAL: I'm sorry that what we did—

JEREMIAH: That you made me ill? I am an old man, and it matters little how long I live. Go away, and pray to the Lord for a clear vision of his will. And give my blessing to all of the people.

HAMMUTAL: We will. God be with you!

(*She and* JOHANAN *go out.*)

JEREMIAH: Do you have a pen and paper, Baruch?

BARUCH: Yes. But rest now—don't try to talk!

JEREMIAH: If I don't talk now, what I say may never be written. Perhaps it would make no difference. I sometimes wonder whether anything I have said or done has made any difference.

BARUCH: Of course it has! You are a man of prayer, a leader unlike any other I have ever known.

JEREMIAH: And you have been a friend beyond all other friends. Now write, Baruch, while I have strength to talk.

BARUCH: Yes, Master.

JEREMIAH: Write that a remnant of the flock of Israel will return. They shall be fruitful and multiply. The Lord will set shepherds over them, and they shall fear no more. Write that the Lord will raise up for David a righteous branch; that a King shall reign and prosper, and shall execute judgment and justice in the earth. Write that men shall no more say, "The Lord liveth, which brought up the children of Israel out of the land of Egypt"; but, "The Lord liveth, which led the seed of the house of Israel out of the North country, and from all countries whither I had driven them; and they shall dwell in their own land."

BARUCH: Will you not rest now?

JEREMIAH: Is your wrist tired with writing?

BARUCH: No, no. I meant that—

JEREMIAH: Don't worry about me, Baruch. I want you to write, while my heart is full of the Lord's words. But first give me some water.

BARUCH: Yes, Master. Here! (JEREMIAH *drinks it.*) You still feel hope? I was afraid that what happened today would kill you with sorrow.

JEREMIAH: It was a sad day. The fate of all of us who came to Egypt is sad also. We cannot hide from Babylon here. Babylon can eat up Egypt, as easily as locusts eat an orchard. And to see our women, led by the Princesses of our royal house, turn to a silly Babylonian superstition is grievous also. If we looked no farther than Egypt, we could have no hope. But there is hope from the North, Baruch. I once told my Father, "The North will bring destruction." He didn't listen; nor did they in Jerusalem. But now write this: "From the North will come new life for Judah." You remember the letter which you wrote for me, to the first of the exiles in Babylon?

BARUCH: Of course I remember! "Build houses and live in them! Plant gardens and eat of the fruits! Seek the good of the City to which I have sent you as exiles!" I remember how strange it seemed to write those words.

JEREMIAH: And I remember how long I prayed, before I knew that the Lord meant me to write that letter. But it was true! One day salvation will come to Sion from the Jews of Babylon. Write that also, Baruch!

BARUCH: I have written it.

JEREMIAH: We have had too much suffering: too many years when the fathers have eaten sour grapes, and the children's teeth have been set on edge. But write that a new day is coming! The Lord has sworn to me that he will make a new covenant with Israel. It will not be like the old covenant which he made with the people whom he brought from Egypt. These are the words of his promise for the future: "I will put my law in their inward parts, and write my covenant in their hearts; for I will forgive their iniquity and forget their sin."

BARUCH: All that you have said is written, Master.

JEREMIAH: Then my work is done. If it is his will, my words will be remembered. It has been a long road, Baruch, since he called me, and I shrank from his call. A long and hard road. Moses did not see the people return to the land of promise; and I shall not see it. But they will return!

BARUCH: And they will read these words, if it is in my power to make them live. I will make a book, with all the prophecies which you have spoken, since the Lord called you—

JEREMIAH: (*Laughing.*) And this time King Jehoiakim is not here, to cut it in pieces and burn it! Well, Baruch, the book will endure, if it is God's will. Now leave me for a little while. I think that I can sleep.

9. THE EXILE AT BABYLON

The exile lasted about 60 years. After the terrible march from Jerusalem to Babylon, the Jews seem to have been well treated. Following Jeremiah's advice, they settled down and became prosperous. Ezekiel and the "Second Isaiah" were outstanding spiritual leaders at this time. The following brief scenes show the context in which they wrote.

During the unspeakable sufferings of World War II, many Jews must have read these two books with deep feeling.

SCENE ONE: JEREMIAH'S LETTER

Bible reference: Jeremiah 29, 1-14

CHARACTERS: A JEWISH HOUSEHOLDER IN BABYLON
                  *ELASAH
                  *GEMARIAH } *Messengers from Jerusalem*
                  CROWD OF JEWS, *men and women, mostly young*

The setting is a small house in Babylon. The JEW *and the* MESSENGERS *are standing. The rest sit on the floor.*

JEW: My friends, I gathered you together because these two messengers have arrived, with news from Jerusalem. They bring a letter from our great Prophet, Jeremiah. I will ask Elasah, the son of Shaphan, to read you that letter.

ELASAH: Thank you, sir. And greetings to all of you from the remnant of our people! We bring many messages from your families. I and my friend Gemariah will give these to you, and answer your questions as best we can. But first let me read to you the Prophet's letter.

"Fellow Israelites, in the sufferings of our people I send you greetings, and bid you never lose your faith in God. He has caused you to be led away by your captors. Now he says this to you: Build houses, and live in them! Plant gardens, and eat the fruit that grows there! Marry, and raise your families in Babylon, so that your numbers grow in this time of exile, instead of dwindling away! Work for the peace of Babylon! Yes, pray for your masters! In their peace you will enjoy peace.

"Take no notice of false prophets, who talk of doom or resistance! Your exile must last a man's lifetime. But then I will come to you, and lead you back to your own land. For toward you I have thoughts of peace, not thoughts of evil. I will listen to your prayers. Seek for me, and if you seek with your whole heart you will find me. I will gather you back from exile, wherever you are, and restore you to the land of Israel when the time is ripe."

That is his message, my friends.

(*Improvise the rest of the scene. The* MESSENGERS *hand out letters—small rolls of paper—and answer many questions about conditions in Jerusalem. Look up Jeremiah 40-42 and Lamentations 5 for a vivid picture of the sufferings and helplessness of the people left behind in Jerusalem.*)

SCENE TWO: THE VISION OF EZEKIEL

Bible reference: Ezekiel 37, 1-14

CHARACTERS: EZEKIEL THE PROPHET, *a young Jewish Priest*
           VOICE OF GOD

The setting is a hillside, above a deep valley, outside Babylon. EZEKIEL is praying. Make up a prayer which he might use, asking for God's guidance and help for his fellow exiles, and for the families whom they have left behind at home.

VOICE OF GOD: You have come, Ezekiel, in answer to my call.
EZEKIEL: Yes, Lord. You told me to come and look down on the valley where the refuse and garbage of the city is thrown. What do you want me to do?
VOICE OF GOD: You see all the bones that lie scattered here?
EZEKIEL: Yes, Lord. It is a sad and ugly sight to see them rotting here.
VOICE OF GOD: Do you think that they can live again, Ezekiel?
EZEKIEL: Live again? Dead, scattered bones? Only you know the answer, Lord. But how could that be?

VOICE OF GOD: Pray over these bones! Tell them that I will bring them together again. I will put flesh and muscles around them, and cover them with skin, and then put breath in them. Tell them this, Ezekiel!

EZEKIEL: The dry bones of my people! Oh, God, I understand your word! But am I worthy of this vision?

VOICE OF GOD: Do you hear the noise? Do you see them coming together, Ezekiel, bone fitting bone? And now the flesh and the skin?

EZEKIEL: Yes, Lord. But they still have no breath—no life.

VOICE OF GOD: Then cry to them in my name! Cry to the wind, and say: "God commands you to come from North and South and East and West, and to put breath into these dead men, so that they shall live."

EZEKIEL: Wind, hear the voice of God! Come and give life to these men!

VOICE OF GOD: You see, Ezekiel? You see how they live? If these dead bones can live again, tell my people that they must not give way to despair. Israel will be brought together again, and will live also!

SCENE THREE: THE LATER YEARS OF EXILE

Bible reference: Isaiah 40; 42; 44; 53

CHARACTERS: A TEACHER, *the writer of the second part of the Book of Isaiah*
A CLASS OF BOYS AND GIRLS (*The speaking parts may be assigned to more than one of each*)

(*The setting is a small house. The* TEACHER *stands, the* CHILDREN *sit on the floor.*)

TEACHER: That ends today's lesson from the Scriptures. Do you want to ask any questions?

BOY: Do you remember Jerusalem, sir?

TEACHER: No, Ezra. I was born here in Babylon.

GIRL: Do you think you will ever see Jerusalem?

TEACHER: I think so, Sarah. I know that our people will return there. The trials of Jerusalem are nearly over, I believe. Her punishment has been heavy, but God has always promised forgiveness. The glory of the Lord is going to be revealed to all the world.

BOY: But we can't fight the Babylonians, sir, can we?

TEACHER: Not in war. I don't think God has chosen our people to be victors in war, or to rule Empires. Remember that he can measure the ocean in the hollow of his hand, and weigh the mountains on scales. Human boasting and worldly success mean little to him. But I believe that he watches us with tenderness, like a shepherd with his flock of sheep. One day he will send a Messiah to lead us—

BOY: Then we shall win battles, surely?

TEACHER: Perhaps. But I think God's true Messiah will come like a servant, not like a tyrant. He will open the eyes of the blind and free the prisoners. Love will be his means of victory; and if we are to follow him that is the kind of victory that we must seek.

GIRL: Will people follow a leader like that?

TEACHER: I don't know, Sarah. He will be despised and rejected by some; but it will be for us that he will face wounds and punishment and humiliation. Let us hope that there will be some who will understand that this is the true leadership.

GIRL: Some people say that God has given us up, and that is why we are kept here in Babylon. My Aunt Miriam—

TEACHER: Do they think that everlasting God grows faint and tired? I think it is the faint and tired whom he helps and inspires. If we wait for the right time, we shall soar back like eagles, through his strength.

BOY: You make it sound true, sir. But we seem to be so weak; and the Babylonian Army is the best in the world, or so they say. Is God really stronger than the idols in their temples?

TEACHER: Numbers mean nothing to God—nothing. Whole nations are like a drop in a bucket to him. Or it is as though the whole sky were the size of a tent; and we are like grasshoppers in his eyes. You simply can't talk about God in terms of size. As for idols and temples, Ezra, what are they? Wood and stone! They take half a tree, and make it into the statue of a God; and they burn the other half on the fire! Those things don't last, any more than grass or flowers. But God's glory does not wither or fade.

BOY: Grasshoppers! Are we that small?

TEACHER: Grasshoppers, or fleas—the smallest thing you can think of! And that includes the King of Babylon! It's our hearts that matter, not our height or our muscles. We may be flea-sized in comparison with the sun and the stars, but he cares for every one of us. Never forget that! You are not forgotten by God, any of you. (*A bell rings.*) There goes the bell. Learn your lesson well, and we will talk about it tomorrow.

Read Psalm 137 with the class. If you had been carried away by violence, and wrenched from your family; if your home had been burned, your father killed, and your city left in ruins, do you think that you could have avoided feeling the hatred which is expressed in the last verses?

SCENE FOUR: THE END OF THE EXILE

Bible reference: Ezra 1; Psalm 126

CHARACTERS: CYRUS, *King of Persia and conqueror of Baby-lon*
SECRETARY TO CYRUS
TWO JEWISH LEADERS, *an old man and a young Priest*
CROWD OF JEWS

The setting is CYRUS' *headquarters in the newly captured city of Babylon, in 539-8* B.C. *He sits at a table, writing. The* SECRETARY *enters, and bows.*

CYRUS: Well, who comes next?
SECRETARY: Representatives of the Israelites, Your Majesty—or Jews, they are sometimes called.
CYRUS: Oh, yes. I've heard about them. They were forced to come here when Nebuchadnezzar took their city. Is that right?
SECRETARY: That is right, sir. Some have been here for two generations. There are many thousands of them. They keep to themselves, and work very hard. Law-abiding people, I'm told, and very religious, in their own way.
CYRUS: Well, send them in.

(*The* SECRETARY *goes out, and shows in the two Jews. They bow.*)

CYRUS: Greetings, my friends! You are representatives of the Jewish people?

OLD MAN: Of the exiled Jews here in Babylon, Your Majesty. Our people still live in their own land, but they are poor.

CYRUS: Because the Babylonians carried away everything they could lay hands on, including your young men and women? It's a familiar story. I have heard excellent reports about your industry and faith. What is it that you wish to ask me?

PRIEST: My Lord, most of our people have never seen our Holy City, Jerusalem. We have been born in exile, except for a few older men and women, like my friend Simeon. We ask your permission, for those of our people who wish it, to return to our own country.

CYRUS: To a poor country? I understand that many of you are rich men here in Babylon.

OLD MAN: That is true, sir. But what are riches without God's love? We shall not all go. But we beg to be free to choose, and to return to our loved ones if that is our desire.

CYRUS: We have no quarrel with your people, old man. Go, or stay! Only be loyal to Persia and to me.

PRIEST: God be praised! Then you are as they said of you, sir—a just man.

OLD MAN: We will repay you, King Cyrus! Now we must run, and tell our people this great news.

CYRUS: You may do so. I shall sign and seal a decree, and it will be given to you shortly. As for the treasures which the Babylonians took from your city, some reparation will be made. We want our subjects to live good lives, not to starve and cherish hatred.

OLD MAN: May you be blessed forever, Your Majesty!

(*They bow, and hurry out. The scene changes to the street outside the palace. A* CROWD OF JEWS *is waiting for them.*)

OLD MAN: We are free! Men of Israel, come and give thanks!
PRIEST: God bless King Cyrus! We are free!

(*The* CROWD *gathers round them, dancing and shouting. Then the* PRIEST *silences them, and leads them in singing or saying Psalm 126.*)

Ask your class to try to imagine the difference between the forced marches which began the Exile, and the joyful journey home. The

Books of Ezra and Nehemiah, and the prophecies of Haggai and Zechariah, are concerned with the period which followed the return to Jerusalem.

10. JOB

The Book of Job was compiled after the age of the Prophets, perhaps in the fourth century before Christ. Probably the original Book was quite short, and many of the speeches were added later. The Book is a mixture of poetry and prose. But they blend into the greatest of all human works probing the mystery of man's suffering.

Is punishment "an eye for an eye"—God's return for our sins? That conventional answer cannot be right, since it is clear that the innocent suffer, and often the guilty seem to suffer less. Therefore the writer of *Job* takes a just man, and shows us the undeserved pain which God allows Satan to bring upon him. His friends, mouthing pious rebukes and urging him to repentance, give him no comfort.

In his desperation, he hears the voice of God. Not only is this part of the Book unsurpassed in the Bible for its poetic beauty, it is also the most penetrating and powerful of all statements concerning the place of suffering in a world made and loved by God. God tells Job that he cannot understand the majesty and mystery of the created world; and it follows that he cannot know what purpose there may be in the suffering of himself or any other innocent man.

Of course it is not an "answer" to the problem of suffering. The Jewish writer could no more give that answer than could the Greek Tragedians (such as Aeschylus), or modern writers like Thomas Hardy (*Tess of the D'Urbervilles* and other novels) or Dostoyevsky (*Crime and Punishment*). All that a great thinker can do is to lead us to reject superficial answers, and face the deep problems of our lives in honesty and faith.

CHARACTERS: NARRATOR
JOB
JOB'S WIFE
JOB'S SONS AND DAUGHTERS; *in the first scene, at least two boys and two girls, the eldest son being about sixteen. In the last scene, three young daughters.*

ELIPHAZ }
BILDAD   } JOB's *friends*
ZOPHAR   }
VOICE OF GOD
SATAN
SERVANT
MESSENGER
CHORUS, *including more of Job's friends who may come on stage in the family scenes.*

NOTE: The play should be acted in modern dress. Scenery should be very simple, with a plain curtain as background. A front curtain is not needed, and no intervals should be taken between scenes. A table is L.C. downstage all through the play. On it are a punch bowl and cups, and a telephone. Satan needs props to represent an explosive charge (a box of explosive, coil of wire and plunger).

In case you should wish to attempt a musical production of the play, the musical directions have been left in the text. Abbreviations for the stage directions are: C=center; R=right; L=left. If music is used, a piano, downstage R. or below stage, can provide continuity, but there is great scope for a band. Guitar accompaniment is suggested for the NARRATOR. Drums or cymbals are needed for the crashes indicated in the text, and a wind machine or recording of storm and thunder. A selection of the music should be played as an overture.

The setting is the living room of JOB's *house. The stage is brightly lit.* JOB, *his* WIFE, FAMILY *and* FRIENDS *enter as the* NARRATOR *begins to sing, and stand around the table.*

NARRATOR: (*Sings.*) If you saw Job at home
At supper with his wife
You'd say that they were a lucky pair
And had a happy life.

CHORUS: With cattle in the stable
And sheep upon the hills,
Job had the best of everything,
And money to pay the bills.

NARRATOR: Job had a family party;
All his friends were there.
If you saw them all together
You would say their luck was rare.

CHORUS:	The table was well laden With fruit and meat and fish. The servants hurried to and fro With every kind of dish.
NARRATOR:	But all of his good fortune Could never turn his head. His servants thought the world of him, And this is what they said:
CHORUS:	We like Job; he's a very good Master. We like Job; he's a very good Master. We like Job; he's a very good Master.
MEN:	Nobody's afraid of
WOMEN:	Everybody's fond of
CHORUS:	Everybody likes old Job!

JOB: Shall we dance, my friends?

> (*The opening song is played sweetly, in waltz time, and they dance.* SATAN *enters R. and watches. Then he either goes to the piano and whispers to the pianist, or takes over as conductor if there is a band. The tune changes to hot, blaring rhythm, and some of the dancers begin to twist wildly.* SATAN *whirls* JOB'S WIFE *round the stage.* JOB *hurries to the piano and protests, and the music returns to waltz time. Then the dance finishes.*)

JOB: (*Sings.*)	My children, I pray you remember That Jehovah has blessed us indeed; And those whom he blesses with plenty Must give freely to others in need. Thank God for all his blessings! To him be glory and praise! Thank God for all his blessings! Gladly our voices we raise.
JOB AND CHORUS:	For all the things that he gives, for the light upon our way, For all the love and the care that he shows us every day, For the food upon the table, and the roof above our head, God be prais-ed and worship-ped, O! God be prais-ed and worship-ped!

SERVANT: (*Entering L.*) Dinner is served, Mrs. Job.

JOB'S WIFE: Shall we go in, my friends?

(*The family party go off L. Piano plays the opening tune again. SATAN is left alone. He walks to the table. He tastes the punch with an expression of disgust, then picks up an ashtray and empties the cigarette butts into it. Laughing, he stirs the mixture. Meanwhile the NARRATOR is singing.*)

NARRATOR: Satan used to spend his time
　　　　　Waiting, waiting,
　　　　　Finding things that he could spoil,
　　　　　Hating, hating.
　　　　　There was nothing he could make,
　　　　　So he loved to crush and break,
　　　　　Killing for destruction's sake,
　　　　　Waiting, hating.

(*The telephone rings. SATAN answers it.*)

SATAN: Hullo!

VOICE OF GOD: Satan, from whence have you returned?

SATAN: (*Spoken.*) From wandering to and fro in the earth,
　　　　　Thinking of death, and thinking of birth;
　　　　　Seeing men waste their sweat and breath
　　　　　In their twilight life, between birth and death.
　　　　　I saw them mouthing their empty prayers—
　　　　　And grabbing as much as each one dares.
　　　　　If ever things take a turn for the worse,
　　　　　Man's beautiful blessings turn to a curse!

VOICE OF GOD: Did you consider my servant Job?

SATAN: Job? Job?
　　　　　Job is a model of human piety!
　　　　　Job is a pillar of high society!
　　　　　Job behaves with complete propriety!
　　　　　But make him suffer—leave him in the lurch—
　　　　　You'll see if he sticks to his pew in Church!
　　　　　Job leads a privileged existence;
　　　　　His virtue depends on your assistance.
　　　　　Job has no magical resistance!
　　　　　Let me take his cushion away,
　　　　　And you'll hear what Job will have to say!

VOICE OF GOD:	Are you sure that this is true, Satan?
SATAN:	I will prove it, if you give me leave!
VOICE OF GOD:	You may test his faith, but you must not put his life in danger.
SATAN:	Test his faith? He has no faith!
	Faith is a house of cards.
	One push, and over it goes!
	Faith is a myth;
	Faith is a farce;
	As adversity very soon shows.
	Let me plague Job,
	Let me tempt Job!
	Don't protect Job,
	Don't exempt Job!
	And I'll show him to you in a different light,
	Whining and cursing because of his plight.

(*Exit* SATAN *R.*)

NARRATOR: (*Sings.*)	Satan now is all alert,
	Waiting, waiting;
	Thinking how to spoil and hurt,
	Hating, hating.
	Job will soon be forced to learn
	That it is the Devil's turn
	To destroy and kill and burn,
	Hating, hating.

(*There is a crash of cymbals or drums, and the* MESSENGER *runs on R.*)

MESSENGER:	Master! Master!

(JOB *hurries on L. to center downstage, where the* MESSENGER *is kneeling.* JOB *bends over him.*)

JOB:	What is the matter? What is your news?
MESSENGER:	The news is terrible!

(*He mimes the telling of the news, while the* NARRATOR *sings.*)

NARRATOR:	The news is bad for Job;
	The messenger looks grim.
	He says that thieves have seized the flocks,
	And murdered all save him.

JOB: What the Lord gave the Lord hath taken away.
What the Lord wills his people must obey.
May the souls of his servants rest in peace!
And to do his will may I never cease!
What the Lord gave the Lord hath taken away!
Blessed be the name of the Lord!

(Piano introduction, the friends sing, standing downstage L.C.)

FRIENDS: When your heart is feeling like a lump of stone,
It is sad to have to bear the pain alone.
In this situation, luckily for him
Job can call on friends like
Eliphaz, Bildad, and Zophar the Naamathite

(each says his own name)

In this situation, luckily for him,
Job can call on friends like us.

It would be a terrible catastrophe
If you could not call upon a friend like me.
In this situation, what a lucky thing
Job has got some friends like
Bildad, Zophar and Eliphaz the Temanite!
In this situation, what a lucky thing
Job has got some friends like us!

When your sins have left you in a dreadful state,
And you can't do anything but pray and wait,
In this situation, luckily for Job,
He can call on friends like
Zophar, Eliphaz, and Bildad the Shuhite.
In this situation, luckily for Job,

He can call on friends like us.

ZOPHAR:	Goodbye, Job!
ELIPHAZ:	Let me know if I can do anything.
BILDAD:	You know you only have to ask.

(*They hurry off L.* JOB *and his* FAMILY PARTY *follow. Piano plays the opening tune, and then changes to the Satan theme when the stage is empty. The lights are lowered to half-strength.* SATAN *has watched the last scene from the side of the stage R. A* MAID *comes in bringing a fresh tray of food and drinks.* SATAN *comes up behind her and strangles her with a scarf, then drags her body to stage R., miming the actions (there is no need to have the materials in his hands). He then lays a charge of explosive under the table and uncoils wire across stage to R. He stands ready to detonate it with a plunger.* JOB'S SONS *and* DAUGHTERS *enter, laughing and talking, and help themselves to the punch. Suddenly there is a flash and loud sound as* SATAN *detonates the charge. They all scream and fall left of the table, except for the eldest* SON, *who falls C. Blackout and silence. Then a spot lights up the boy's body and* JOB *and his* WIFE *hurry on L.*)

WIFE: O God! O, my son, my son!

(*They kneel by his body under the spot. After a short pause piano gives her a chord for her song.*)

WIFE: My son! My son! How can this pain be
                               borne?
                               How can God bear to do such things to
                               you?
                               O husband Job! How can you now be-
                               lieve?
                               If God so mocks our prayers, how can he
                               care?

JOB: What the Lord gave the Lord hath taken
                               away.
                               What the Lord wills, his people must
                               obey.
                               May the souls of his servants rest in
                               peace!
                               And to do his will may I never cease!
                               What the Lord gave the Lord hath taken
                               away.
                               Blessed be the name of the Lord!

WIFE: Blessed be the name of the Lord? I curse
                       his name,
                       and so should you. It is a lie, a lie, a lie!
JOB: Wife, be calm! Come with me, and pray.
                       Perhaps God calls him to a brighter day.
                       We must have faith, even when things are
                       black.
                       God gives us love, and we must love him
                       back.
WIFE: God gives us love! His love is all a lie.
                       Now all I want is to curse God and die.

(*Black-out. All go off L. while* NARRATOR *plays Satan-tune
on guitar.* SATAN *enters from R. and stands C. under the
spot.*)

VOICE OF GOD: Satan, from whence have you returned?
SATAN: (*Tense and frus-
trated.*)
                       From wandering to and fro in the earth,
                       Thinking of death, and thinking of birth;
                       Seeing men waste their sweat and breath
                       In their twilight life, between birth and
                       death.
VOICE OF GOD: Has my servant Job forsaken me?
SATAN: Skin for skin, yea, all that a man hath
                       will be given for his life. But put forth thine
                       hand now and touch his bone and his
                       flesh, and he will curse thee to thy face.
                       Job has borne nobly the pain and death of
                       others—O yes, nobly! Let us see how he
                       will bear his own pain!

(*Black-out. Roll of drums, and from off stage L.* JOB *cries out
in pain. A few seconds later the Spot comes on C., and* JOB
*staggers on, followed by his wife. He kneels C., and she
stands by him. He is covered with sores.*)

WIFE: Now will you not curse God and die?
JOB: Though I curse the day on which I was
                       born, I will not curse God. Only so can I
                       guard my integrity.
WIFE: Your integrity! How can you speak of
                       that, when we would all be better dead?

(*Sings.*)

Why do we have to be born,
If this is the world we are born in?
Why are we sentenced to live,
If this is the way of our living?
Why give us hearts that can love,
If love must be tortured and riven?
Why give us life, which is better not given?

Why do we bother to pray,
If this is the fruit of our praying?
Why give our service to God,
If this is the God we are serving?
Why should we worship his name,
Amid all our pain and our grieving?
Curse God and die, and have done with
believing!

Job:

I cannot curse him. I cannot live without
integrity.

(*Sings.*)

I will keep my integrity as long as I have
breath,
For without my integrity my life is only
death.
All the pain and the wounds cannot make
a slave of me,
If I can guard my integrity.

I will keep my integrity as long as I survive,
For without my integrity my soul is not
alive.
Though his flesh be destroyed, and his soul
in agony,
Yet man can live with integrity.

Now my faith is my shield in perplexity,
While I strive to remain what the Lord
would have me be.
Though his limbs are in chains, yet a man
is truly free
If he can guard his integrity.

(*He lies, with his wife kneeling by him. Friends come on R.,
whistling "When your heart . . ." They then stand near him*

R.C. *Their lines are spoken, but they sing the refrain line each time it occurs.*)

ELIPHAZ:	When things are turning worse and worse
ALL THREE:	What a man needs is friends.
BILDAD:	When he has grievous wounds to nurse
ALL:	What a man needs is friends.
ZOPHAR:	When Providence's blows have struck
ELIPHAZ:	(Though he may call it "cruel luck")
BILDAD:	And foes are keen to stir the muck
ALL:	What a man needs is friends.
ZOPHAR:	When suffering makes his spirit weak
ALL:	What a man needs is friends.
ELIPHAZ:	When hostile tongues are quick to speak
ALL:	What a man needs is friends.
BILDAD:	When he is left without defense
ZOPHAR:	And difficulties are immense
ALL:	He longs for men with common sense—
	What a man needs is friends.

(*Music as before.*)

When your heart is feeling like a lump of stone,
It is sad to have to bear the pain alone.
In this situation, luckily for him,
Job can call on friends like
Eliphaz, Bildad, and Zophar the Naamathite.

(*each says his own name*)

In this situation, luckily for him,
Job can call on friends like us.

When your sins have left you in a dreadful state,
And you can't do anything but pray and wait,
In this situation, luckily for Job,
He can call on friends like
Zophar, Eliphaz and Bildad the Shuhite.
In this situation, luckily for Job,
He can call on friends like us.

ELIPHAZ: (*The oldest of the friends, a man of distinction and*

*learning. He begins quietly, but soon a note of venom enters in,
all the worse because it is combined with an outward dignity.*)
We have come to talk to you, Job, out of our great regard for
your character and position. This is a moment when no true
friend could withhold advice. You must remember that all this
cannot have happened to you without good reason. Those that
plow iniquity, and sow wickedness, reap the same . . . never forget that! The roaring of the lion, and the voice of the fierce lion,
and the teeth of the young lions are broken. The old lion per-
isheth for lack of prey, and the stout lion's whelps are scattered
abroad. That is the case with you, is it not? You are broken,
and your whelps are scattered and destroyed. Do not try to be
more just than God, but commit your cause to him, who saves
the poor from the sword, and whose hands make whole. Listen
to what we say, and be sure that it is said for your own good.

JOB: Oh, that my grief were thoroughly weighed, and my calamity
laid in the balances together! Does the wild ass bray when he
has grass? Am I complaining without a cause? If God is so
mighty and just, why should man be so miserable? Why should
this happen to me? Look at me now? What is my strength, that
I should hope? Is my flesh made of brass? Leave me alone, till I
swallow down my spittle. I have sinned. . . . I know that I have
sinned; but what does God want me to do? Can he not pardon
me, instead of marking me down for destruction and making my
life a burden too hard to bear?

BILDAD: (*A mixture of blundering kindness and brutality.*) How
long are you going on with this windy talk? Your children are
dead, and it is plain that their sins brought all this upon them
and upon you. As for you, if you were so pure and upright, God
would be giving you happiness. There is no smoke without fire,
you know, and reeds don't grow without mud. God finds out the
sinners and the hypocrites, and makes their hopes like spiders'
webs. You should realize that from the lessons of the past.

JOB: I know it, I know it. But how can a man face God? How can
I answer him, or reason with a God who alone spreads out the
heavens, and treads upon the waves of the sea? He torments the
innocent and the guilty, and there is no respite. Let him take his
rod away from me, and cease to use fear as a weapon against
me! Then I would speak to him; but he gives me no chance. Oh
God! You have poured me out as milk, and curdled me like
cheese. You hunt me down like a lion. Why was I born at all?
Could I not have died in my mother's womb, and been carried

straight to my grave? Let me alone for the little time that I have to live! Soon I shall go to a land of darkness, and never return.

ZOPHAR: (*More hot-tempered than the other two, and at the same time bitingly rational.*) Somebody must answer these lies of yours. I wish that God himself could speak, and show you his wisdom. He is punishing you far less than you deserve, and it is blasphemous for you to try to examine his conduct. Your questionings and complaints are monstrous. Stretch out your hands toward him, and put your wickedness away! Then he will lift up your face, and you will remember your wickedness as waters that pass away. But rest assured that the eyes of the wicked shall fail, and they shall not escape!

JOB: My friends, I am sure that you are very wise—none wiser. But I have some understanding also. I see what is happening around me. The just, upright man is laughed to scorn, and men that provoke God are secure. Have I no right to wish to speak to God, and to reason with him? It is you who are the liars, and who speak wickedly in his name! I will trust in him, though he slay me; but I will maintain my own ways before him. If I hold my tongue now, I shall give up the ghost. Oh, God! Make me to know my transgression and my sin; but do not break a leaf driven to and fro, and haunt all my footsteps! Man that is born of a woman is of few days, and full of trouble. He comes forth like a flower, and is cut down. He flees like a shadow, and does not live. Let him rest until he fulfills his days! When he dies, he wastes away; and in life his flesh has pain and his soul knows mourning. But I will wait until my change comes. You will call, and I will answer you; for in all my sufferings I will put my hope and my trust in you.

ELIPHAZ: You crafty, ignorant windbag! What do you know that we do not know, you, who drink iniquity like water?

BILDAD: So we are vile in your sight? You would like this world changed to suit you, no doubt . . . the rocks moved! But like all the wicked you will have your light put out, blown out like a candle; and your own feet will cast you into a net. You will be chased out of the world in terror, and clean forgotten.

ZOPHAR: Yes, a hypocrite never triumphs for long. He may swallow down riches, but he vomits them up again. He shall not feel quietness in his belly! Heaven will reveal his iniquity, and earth will rise up against him.

JOB: I tell you, you cannot kill hope in me, though you kill pity in yourselves. Oh, that my words were written! Oh, that they were printed in a book! That they were graven with an iron pen and lead in the rock forever! For I know that my redeemer liveth, and that he shall stand at the latter day upon the earth. And though after my skin worms destroy this body, yet in my flesh shall I see God; whom I shall see for myself, and mine eyes shall behold, and not another!

ELIPHAZ: Liar!

BILDAD: Sinner!

ZOPHAR: Hypocrite!

This shorter alternative version of the conversation may be easier to use in some productions.

ELIPHAZ: We have come to talk to you, Job, out of our great regard for your character and position.

BILDAD: This is a moment when no true friend could withhold advice.

ZOPHAR: You must remember that all this cannot have happened to you without good reason.

ELIPHAZ: Listen to what we say! And be sure that it is said for your own good.

JOB: Leave me alone! I have sinned—I know that I have sinned; but what does God want me to do? Can he not pardon me, instead of marking me down for destruction and making my life a burden too hard to bear? O God! You have poured me out as milk, and curdled me like cheese. You hunt me down like a lion. Why was I born at all? Could I not have died in my mother's womb, and been carried straight to my grave? Leave me alone for the little time that I have to live!

ZOPHAR: Somebody must answer these lies of yours! I wish that God could speak, and show you his wisdom.

BILDAD: He is punishing you far less than you deserve, and it is blasphemous for you to try to examine *his* conduct.

ELIPHAZ: Stretch out your hand toward him, and put your wickedness away!

JOB: My friends, I am sure that you are very wise—none wiser. But I have some understanding also. It is you who are the liars, and who speak wickedly in God's name. I will trust in him, though he slay me; but I will maintain my own ways before him. O God! Make me to know my transgression and my sin; but do not break a leaf driven to and fro, and haunt all my footsteps!

ZOPHAR: You crafty, ignorant windbag! What do you know that we do not know, you, who drink iniquity like water?

BILDAD: So we are vile in your sight? You would like the world changed to suit you, no doubt! The rocks moved!

ELIPHAZ: A hypocrite never triumphs for long. He may swallow down riches, but he vomits them up again.

JOB: I tell you, you cannot kill hope in me, though you kill pity in yourselves. For I know that my Redeemer liveth, and that he shall stand at the latter day upon the earth. And though after my skin worms destroy this body, yet in my flesh shall I see God!

ZOPHAR: Liar!

BILDAD: Sinner!

ELIPHAZ: Hypocrite!

JOB: (*Still kneeling under Spot C., sings.*)

> I'll believe in God as long as I can,
> If I have to believe alone.
> I'll believe that this is part of his plan,
> But my heart isn't made of stone.
> I'll believe he shares all our hurts and cares,
> Even when it is hard to feel.
> I'll believe that he watches over me;
> But my heart isn't made of steel.

(*Roll of drums. Friends shrink back into the shadows,* JOB *and his* WIFE *kneel and look up.*)

VOICE OF GOD: Who is this that darkeneth counsel by words without knowledge? Gird up thy loins like a man! For I will demand of thee, and answer thou me!

(*Sings.*)

> Can you draw Leviathan with a hook?
> Can you write the power of God in a book?
> Did you make the Pleiades?
> Did you frame the seven seas?
> Can you draw Leviathan with a hook?

Can you yoke the unicorn to the plough?
Can you make the Behemoth's head to
bow?
Can you cause the buds to spring?
Can you paint the peacock's wing?
Can you yoke the unicorn to the plough?

Have you seen the place where the dead
must go?
Do you know what womb conceived ice
and snow?
Can you make the eagle fly?
Stay the bottles of the sky?
Have you seen the place where the dead
must go?

Where were you when the earth was born?
When the stars sang to greet the dawn?
Did you give the heavens their laws?
Did you shut the sea with doors?
Where were you when the earth was born?

(*This song should form the climax of the play. It ends with
another clap of thunder or roll of drums. During the thunder,
black-out.* JOB *and his* WIFE *go off L.* JOB *quickly changes,
during a short pause when the stage is dark and the piano is
softly re-playing "What the Lord gave the Lord hath taken
away . . ." Then the full lights come up, and as the piano
starts the next chorus* JOB'S FRIENDS *from the opening scene
come on L., followed shortly by* JOB *and his* WIFE. *They stand
round the table exchanging happy greetings.*)

NARRATOR: (*Sings.*)   So the Lord blessed Job,
And he came back home.
The Lord blessed Job
And caused him to rejoice.
Yes, the Lord blessed Job,
And he came back home.
And Job blessed God with a mighty voice.

(*The* FRIENDS *come and kneel in front of* JOB *center.*)

ELIPHAZ: Pardon us, Job.
BILDAD: We have sinned before God.
ZOPHAR: We spoke foolishly. Pardon us.

JOB:
I will pray God to pardon you.
We have all sinned,
but God is good to those who repent.

NARRATOR: (*Sings.*)
So the Lord blessed Job;
And he gave him daughters,
Jemima, Karen-Happuch and Kezia

(*The three small girls enter from the audience.*)

And he lived at home
With his wife and his daughters;
And his wife loved Job, and Job loved her.

CHORUS: (*Including all on stage.*)
And they all thanked God
For his gifts and his blessings;
They all gave God both glory and praise.
Yes, they all thanked God
For his gifts and his blessings;
And Job had joy for the rest of his days.

JOB:
Thank God for all his blessings!
To him be glory and praise!

CHORUS:
Thank God for all his blessings!
Gladly our voices we raise!

For all the things that he gives, for the light upon our way,
For all the love and the care that he shows us every day,
For the food upon the table, and the roof above our head,
God be prais-ed and worshipp-ed
O! God be prais-ed and worshipp-ed!

For all the things that he gives, for the light upon our way,
For all the love and the care that he shows us every day,
For the food upon the table, and the roof above our head,
God be prais-ed and worshipp-ed
O! God be prais-ed and worshipp-ed!

(*Black-out or final curtain.*)

PART II
THE LIFE AND TEACHING
OF JESUS

There are four sections in this Part of *The Bible As Drama.*

1. Ten scenes from the Life of Jesus, and notes on them.
2. A Verse Play: "Good Friday."
3. Eight short parable scenes.
4. Two more Verse Plays: "The Prodigal Son" and "The Wedding Feast."

The object of all the scenes and plays is to introduce the types of people and situations which Jesus encountered during his ministry; the types which he also described in his teaching.

Those who followed him, and those who opposed him, were ordinary people, living lives in many ways like ours. In my experience, the dialogue form used in drama brings this fact out more clearly than purely descriptive writing. To put it simply: if you BECOME Peter, or the Elder Brother of the Prodigal, or the Greedy Guest at the Wedding Feast, you understand what they felt like.

Take Peter as an example. Have you ever thought of his different responsibilities and priorities, after Jesus called him? Of course the top priority was to follow Jesus, and be a fisher of men. But he had a wife (who apparently still travelled with him twenty years later: I Corinthians 9:5); a mother-in-law, and presumably other family members (Mark 1:29-31). He also had business partners in the fishing fleet (Luke 5:1-11).

Turning to the other two examples: the Elder Brother has to decide whether he gets over his natural feelings of resentment against the Prodigal at the final supper—or does he remain as mean and jealous as ever? And the Greedy Guest has the attention of the audience all to himself for a little while, as he displays his total indifference to the meaning of the refreshments which he is guzzling.

There are nearly one hundred characters, big or small, in this book. Even the reading of a small part should make you think hard about a Bible situation. Your one or two lines will be vital, in relationship with the other characters involved with you. For example, a lot turns on the attitude of the hesitant Rabbi (p. 144) and the Priest in the Good Samaritan (p. 192).

The scenes only cover a small part of the Gospel story. This is not intended to be a text book. It will only give you a partial knowledge of the events of Jesus' life. But its object will have been achieved if you find the stories and characters real. Then you will want to go further, applying the same method to other incidents. A few of the New Testament people not mentioned in these scenes are: John the Baptist, Mary and Martha of Bethany, Nicodemus, and Herod Antipas. You could set about writing your own scenes, to include these and many more.

If you combine careful reading, some simple background research, and your own imagination, you will be able to identify yourself with Jesus' friends and enemies, to the enrichment of your understanding. Furthermore, the drama method ensures that you *share* the enjoyment and the discoveries with other people. Give your insights to them, and learn from theirs; and my hope is that the Bible will become a warmer, more meaningful book to you, through your involvement in these scenes and plays.

The three Verse Plays were written as musicals, and some of the original stage directions are retained (in italics) in case you wish to attempt a musical production. For the musical scores (also by the author, price $1.50 each) write to: Religious Drama Productions, 5910 Camino de la Costa, La Jolla, Ca. 92037.

USEFUL BOOKS. The only essential companion to the reading of these plays is a Bible.

Of the many translations now available, the *Jerusalem Bible* has the advantage of useful short introductions and notes. I have made a number of references to these: JB, followed by a number, refers to the pages in the New Testament.

The *King James* (*Authorized*) *Version* remains the most beautiful, but it should be used together with a more modern translation. I have made extensive use of the *New English Bible*, and of J.B. Phillips' translation.

If you need a commentary with more detailed notes than the *Jerusalem Bible* offers, there are many available in libraries. Look through them, to find the level of detail that you need. I have given references to Peake's *Commentary on the Bible* (1962 Revised Edition). This is a very thorough and scholarly book. It has full bibliographies at the end of each Book: e.g., section 714b for Mark, 734g for Luke. Numbers refer to sections, not pages, in Peake.

Jesus in His Time by Daniel-Rops is a good book for background, attractively written. My references to Daniel-Rops give page numbers in this book. I have also made some references to a very good Gospel commentary, Vincent Taylor's *Gospel According To Saint Mark*.

Who's Who In the New Testament, edited by Ronald Brownrigg, contains clear, concise biographies of all people mentioned in the New Testament.

1. TEN SCENES FROM THE LIFE OF JESUS

These scenes have been written with two objects in view. First, they may be used as part of a worship service, to give a continuous picture of the life of Jesus, up to his last journey to Jerusalem. Second, they may be used for reading and study by classes. The *Notes* are intended to point the way toward further reading and discussion.

When a Church performance is planned, the following guidelines should be observed:

The actors should be concealed from the Congregation, except for the Narrator.

Microphones will almost certainly be needed. It is essential that the actors should rehearse carefully with these. This is especially important for the crowd scenes, which need very thorough rehearsal for timing and volume. The Crowd *must* give a convincing impression of urgency and emotional involvement.

A suggested order of service would be:

Opening Hymn, sung by the Congregation.

Prayers by the priest or minister.

A short musical introduction to the scenes: hymn or folk song.

One similar hymn or song, after scene 4, 5, or 6.

One more song at the end of the scenes.

Final prayers.

Final hymn.

This makes up a service of about one hour.

Following the dramatic presentations, beginning on page 155, are background notes for each of them, including Bible references.

SUGGESTED DIVISION OF PARTS
(Numbers refer to scenes)

NARRATOR: Man or Woman

JESUS (*except scene 1*)

JESUS (1); he can also be LEBBAEUS (4), and BOY (6)

MEN

1. PETER (3,6,9)
   FIRST RABBI (1)
   SECOND MAN (4,5C,10)

2. ANDREW (3,6,7,9)
   NATHANAEL (1)
   SERVANT (5E)

3. SATAN (2)
   SIMON (5E)
   JUDAS (9)
   SECOND RABBI (1,4)
   SECOND VOICE (8)

4. JOSEPH (1)
   JAMES (3,6,7,9)
   TAX-COLLECTOR (7)

5. FIRST RABBI (4)
   DOCTOR (5B)
   PHARISEE (7)
   VOICE 4 (8)
   THOMAS (9)

6. JOHN (3,7,9)
   THOMAS (1)
   FIRST MAN (4,5C,10)
   FIRST VOICE (8)

7. ZACCHAEUS (10)
   JOEL (1)
   PHILIP (6,9)
   JAIRUS (5A,5B)
   THIRD VOICE (8)

WOMEN

1. LADY (4)
   MOTHER (5B)
   MIRIAM (10)

2. MARY (1)
   WOMAN (5C)
   WOMAN (5E)
   WOMAN (10)

3. WOMAN (4)
   WOMAN (5A)
   WOMAN (5D)

SCENE ONE: JESUS IN THE TEMPLE

NARRATOR: We bring to you scenes from the life of Jesus of
Nazareth, from the time of his childhood to the day on which he
turned toward Jerusalem, to face his death.
We know very little about Jesus' home and upbringing. Saint
Luke tells just one story of his boyhood. He writes that Jesus'
parents took him on their yearly visit to Jerusalem when he was
twelve years old. A large company went from Galilee; and after
their visit to the Temple they started on the long journey home.

NATHANAEL: Less than a mile to go, Joseph. We've had a message
that the camp site is set up for us this side of the village.
JOSEPH: That's good! I feel ready for supper, and a long night's
sleep.
NATHANAEL: I must begin to get my family together. I haven't
seen some of the children since we started out.
MARY: You must find our son too, Joseph.
JOSEPH: I will. He's probably running around with Joses and
Simon and the girls.
NATHANAEL: It's the biggest Passover caravan I can ever re-
member.
JOSEPH: Yes. It's good to see all the children having such a great
time.
MARY: But they must be tired by now.
NATHANAEL: I'll see you in the village in a few minutes. (*He walks
away, calling his children.*) Ananias! Rachel! Where are you?
(*Fainter*) Ananias! Rachel!
JOSEPH: I'll walk back down the line and find Jesus, Mary.
MARY: He must be further back. We should have seen him if he
had passed us walking up to the front.
JOSEPH: (*Voice fading.*) Jesus! Jesus! (*Pause, then louder again.*)
Jesus! Have you seen that son of mine, Joel?
JOEL: I don't think he's back here, Joseph. Try the front!
JOSEPH: No, I'm sure he must be near the back. Jesus! That's
funny. It's not like him to be hard to find.
JOEL: You're sure he started out with you?
JOSEPH: Well, of course. I mean, where else would he have gone
from the Temple? Mary dear, I can't seem to find him. Oh,
Thomas. You were right at the back when we set out. Did you
see our boy Jesus at all?

THOMAS: No, Joseph. A lot of the kids have been racing around, but I haven't seen him.

MARY: Joses and Judas were here a minute ago. They say they haven't seen him since the Temple.

JOSEPH: The Temple! You don't think—

MARY: Yes, Joseph. That's what must have happened. I believe he was so absorbed in everything that was going on—

JOSEPH: That he never even realized we were leaving! Look, dear, you must stay with the caravan. I'll go back and look for him.

MARY: No, husband. You're not going without me. Let us turn back at once!

JOSEPH: We can't travel through the night. What we must do is eat and rest at the camp, and start before dawn. That boy!

NARRATOR: So Joseph and Mary turned back toward Jerusalem, anxious and puzzled. It was only on the third day that they found Jesus in the Temple.

JESUS: But, Rabbi, what is the true meaning of sacrifice?

FIRST RABBI: Read the Scriptures, my son. Listen to what your teachers say. You are too young to be questioning such things.

JESUS: I know the Scriptures, Sir. Burnt offerings, peace offerings, sin offerings, clean and unclean animals—I have studied all this.

SECOND RABBI: Then you have learned all that a boy should learn. Why

JESUS: Yes, Sir. But in our class at school I asked the teacher to explain why Micah the Prophet wrote: "I desire mercy, and not sacrifice"; and King David said in his Psalm, "Sacrifice and meat-offering thou wouldest not"—

FIRST RABBI: This is indeed a boy who searches the Scriptures! But be careful, child! Remember the Proverb, "Make your ear attentive to wisdom, and incline your heart to understanding—"

JESUS: That's just it, Rabbi! It goes on—don't you remember?— "if you cry out for insight and raise your voice for understanding—" Surely we are meant to think for ourselves, and to try to find God's will for us?

SECOND RABBI: To think for yourself! No, no, my son! Learn from your Masters, and from those who have gone before you. It is dangerous to put yourself forward—

JOSEPH: Jesus! What are you doing here?

MARY: Oh, my boy! You gave us such a fright.

FIRST RABBI: Is this your son?

JOSEPH: Yes, Sir. We have looked for him everywhere, and—

JESUS: Oh, Mother, Father! I'm sorry! I was so excited, coming to Jerusalem. You mean you left without me?

MARY: We thought you were with all the other children in the caravan, Jesus.

JESUS: I didn't mean to give you this trouble.

JOSEPH: I hope he hasn't been making a nuisance of himself, Sir.

SECOND RABBI: Far from it. This is a remarkable boy.

FIRST RABBI: He has great potential, for good or for harm. Watch over him carefully. He has amazed us—the things he has said.

JESUS: I had to do my Father's work. I could think of nothing else.

MARY: Your Father's work? You can't work for him here. He needs you in the carpenter's shop at home.

JESUS: No, Mother, you don't understand. I have to do the work to which my Father in Heaven calls me.

SCENE TWO: THE TEMPTATION BY SATAN

NARRATOR: That is all we know about the youth of Jesus. When the Gospel story begins, he is a mature man, strong in body and mind and spirit. He is ready now for the work to which he is called; and so he goes to the wilderness to prepare himself. There, as he thinks how to use the great gifts of power and love which he has brought to the world, Satan speaks to him.

JESUS: Father, I am ready. Show me your will, and I will go back and find laborers for your vineyard.

SATAN: You have fasted enough, Jesus. Now you are ready to eat, and then to show your power to the world.

JESUS: Is that your voice, Satan? Can you never stop trying to tear down and spoil the love of God?

SATAN: Whatever I do is misinterpreted. I am not trying to tear down, but to build up. First, you must build up your strength. You can do no work for your Father while you are fainting with hunger. Pray that these stones become bread, and eat!

JESUS: Man does not live by bread alone, Satan. I will eat when it is time to eat.

SATAN: Very well. You know best about that. But now you are ready to show God's people your power. They are waiting for you, Jesus! They are longing to know that the Messiah has come. Climb with me to the Temple roof! Descend among the people, and display your power! He has said himself, "He will give his angels charge over you—They will bear you up, lest you strike your foot against a stone."

JESUS: Yes, he said that. And it is also written in his book: "You shall not tempt the Lord your God."

SATAN: Tempt? I am not tempting you, Jesus, I am helping you! You are so hesitant, so weak! Together we could rule the world. Look! Don't you see? All the Kingdoms of the world, waiting for us! Work for me, work with me, and nothing can resist us!

JESUS: Oh, Satan, go! You have no power over me. You have forgotten the only truth that matters. "Worship the Lord your God, and serve him and him alone." Go, and leave me to my prayers!

SATAN: You weak, goody-goody fool! Do you really think mankind is worth what you are doing? Love, service! They will mock you first, then beat you, then murder you! God has gone mad, sending you here in rags—mad, mad!

SCENE THREE: THE CALL OF PETER

NARRATOR: When Jesus began his work of teaching and healing, he needed friends to share the burden. He must have thought hard, and prayed for his Father's guidance, before he chose his twelve Apostles. The Gospels tell us how some of them were called.

ANDREW: Another blank night.

SIMON PETER: That's right, Andrew. Not a fish to be seen.

ANDREW: Well, that's Galilee for you. Shoals of fish, or none.

SIMON PETER: Hey, James! John! Catch anything?

JAMES: Two miserable little fish—we threw them back.

SIMON PETER: Too bad! Well, let's get these nets done, and go home to bed.

(*Crowd voices: "Jesus!" "Jesus of Nazareth!" "Heal my son!" "Master, help me!"*)

JESUS: Be quiet, my friends! Please be quiet!

ANDREW: Good morning, Jesus.

SIMON PETER: Can we help you? Things seem to be a little out of hand.

JESUS: Thank you, Simon Bar-Jonah, and you, Andrew. If I could borrow your boat for a few minutes.

SIMON PETER: Of course.

JESUS: It means putting off that sleep, Peter.

SIMON PETER: How did you know I was talking about that—

JESUS: Just by looking at the rims around your eyes.

ANDREW: I'll launch the boat. There! Get in!

(*Crowd voices: "Don't go, Jesus!" "Don't leave us!" "Heal my son!", etc.*)

JESUS: Friends! Please, please! I am not leaving you. I will pray with every one of those who seek healing. But you must not press forward as you did just now, or more people will be hurt, not healed. That is why I asked these fishermen to lend me their boat. You see them mending their nets? The Kingdom of God is like a net. The fisherman draws it back into his boat, and sorts out the fish—the good ones and those that are tasteless or rotten. He throws these back into the water. So God has sent me to gather into his Kingdom all who are clean and who seek to be near him; but those who reject him, he will reject. Now, please walk back quietly to the village square, and lay the sick there. I will return soon, and pray for them to be healed, if that is God's will.

(*Crowd voices: "Let's go!" "It's all right, Jonathan." "Don't cry!" "Come along!"*)

SIMON PETER: Let me give you a hand. There!

JESUS: Thank you, Simon.

SIMON PETER: That's all right, Master. Any time.

ANDREW: We'll do anything to help you, Jesus.

JESUS: Is that true? Let me put you to the test. How about postponing that sleep a little longer, and catching some fish?

SIMON PETER: Catching some—Look, Jesus, I meant we'd do anything that makes sense. There aren't fish out there. We tried all night. You're a carpenter, not a fisherman.

ANDREW: He means it, Simon.

JESUS: Andrew is right. I promise that, if you launch out into the deep you will catch fish without number. Your life will never be the same again, but you will catch fish.

SIMON PETER: All right! It's crazy, but let's get it over. Hey, James! We're going out!

JAMES: You must be kidding!

SIMON PETER: All right, we're kidding. Come on, let's get ready!

NARRATOR: Simon Peter and Andrew launched their boat. They were not prepared for what happened next.

ANDREW: Here, what's going on?

SIMON PETER: Heavens above, it's a shoal! James! John! Quick!

JOHN: What is it?

JAMES: They're sinking! Come on! Hold on, Simon!

(There are sounds of a struggle.)

JAMES: They nearly pulled us down. What a catch!

SIMON PETER: Master, leave me alone! I'm a sinner. You've shown me that.

JESUS: Don't be afraid, Simon! I wanted to show you that I need you.

SIMON PETER: Need me?

JESUS: Yes, You and Andrew, and the sons of Zebedee. I need you all.

ANDREW: We're just four ordinary fishermen, Jesus.

JESUS: That is what I need. Ordinary men with faith and courage. Fishers of men.

SIMON PETER: If you say so, Master, it must be true. What do you want us to do?

JESUS: First let's go to the village. The people are waiting for me there. Perhaps we can go to your home after that, Simon? I should like to meet your family.

SCENE FOUR: CROWDS AND HEALING

NARRATOR: When Jesus healed the sick in public places, the crowds pushed and jostled to get close to him. Once, they broke open the roof of a house to lower a paralyzed man. Lepers, cripples, epileptics, the blind, deaf, and dumb, and many who were mentally sick swarmed around him to be touched.

(Crowd voices: "Let me get through, please!" "Please, Jesus! Heal me!" "Out of my way!" "I must get near him!")

JESUS: Please, be quiet! *(Voices continue.)* Silence! That's better! You make me sound like a Roman Centurion. Be patient, and I will come and pray with each of you. And you must all pray for each other. Lady, you have waited a long time. Is this your son?

LADY: Yes, Master. He's deaf and dumb. Please, in God's name—

JESUS: You have had faith, to bring him to me. What is his name?

LADY: Lebbaeus, Sir.

JESUS: Come, Lebbaeus! Let me touch your ears and your tongue. Pray, all of you! Let the ears and tongue of Lebbaeus be opened, and his spirit be filled with peace and joy!

FIRST MAN: The old mud and spit cure!

SECOND MAN: A lot of good that will do!

JESUS: Please be quiet. Nothing can be done for this boy unless he is surrounded and supported by faith and prayer. Now, Lebbaeus, open your ears. (*Louder*.) Open your ears! And loose your tongue! Do you hear me, Lebbaeus? You—can—hear.

WOMAN: He nodded his head!

FIRST MAN: It's a trick!

JESUS: Lebbaeus, you hear me? Good! Now say, "I hear you, Master." Speak! (*Loud*.) Speak!

LEBBAEUS: I—hear—you—

LADY: (*Hysterical*.) Oh, no! It can't be true! My boy! My boy!

LEBBAEUS: It is true, Mother. I can hear, and speak. Don't cry, Mother!

> (*Crowd voices: "It's true!" "He really healed him!" "That's no trick." "The boy never spoke before!" "Jesus, heal me next!"*)

FIRST RABBI: Well, Rabbi, what did you think of that?

SECOND RABBI: I don't know what to think. Where did he get this power, this authority over men and spirits?

FIRST RABBI: What power? Don't ask me to believe that the son of Joseph the carpenter has power to heal sickness and forgive sins! He casts out devils through Beelzebub, the chief of the devils.

SECOND RABBI: But you saw—the boy—

FIRST RABBI: Very convincing! We'll see what the High Priest has to say when he hears about it. Come along, Rabbi! We must go and make our report.

SCENE FIVE: WOMEN WHO CAME TO JESUS

EPISODE A

NARRATOR: This was only one of hundreds of healings which Jesus performed. As Mark wrote, "As many as touched him were made whole." We hear more of the men who left their work to follow him, the twelve whom he called Apostles. But there were many women also, who came to him as healer and teacher and gave themselves to his service.

(*Crowd voices: "Make way!" "There's a girl dying." "Let Jesus through!" "Come on!" "Where's he going?" "To Jairus' house, the Synagogue leader." "His daughter's dying." "Make way, please!"*)

JESUS: Stop!

PETER: What is it, Jesus?

JESUS: Who touched me?

PETER: Who *touched* you? Are you—

JESUS: Am I crazy? No, Peter. I know people are jostling us all the time, but this was different. It was you, Lady?

WOMAN: Oh, Sir, I'm sorry. I didn't mean—

JESUS: You didn't mean me to know? You touched the hem of my robe. Did your wonderful faith bring you healing?

WOMAN: Yes, Sir. (*She is sobbing.*) I can feel the flow of blood stopped—after all these years.

JESUS: I knew, as soon as you touched me, that strength had gone from me to heal you. How wonderful that you believed in me!

JAIRUS: Please, Jesus, hurry! My little girl—

JESUS: I'm coming, Jairus. God bless you, my daughter! May you be whole in body and spirit!

EPISODE B

NARRATOR: At Jairus' home Jesus fought for the girl's life. They had run out to tell him that she was dead; but he came and stood at her bedside.

JESUS: She is not dead. She is asleep.

MOTHER: Asleep! Oh God, no! She's dead—dead!

DOCTOR: I happen to be a doctor, Sir. You're talking nonsense, I'd have you know.

JESUS: Please, be quiet! I must wake her. Sarah! Sarah! Wake up!

MOTHER: Leave her alone! Can't she even die in peace?

JAIRUS: Be quiet, my dear. Jesus is a great healer.

JESUS: I understand what you are feeling; but you can help me by praying for her. Sarah! Sit up! You're a big girl, Sarah. I can't lift you if you won't help. Now, sit up! Up! That's right, up!

DOCTOR: God Almighty! It's incredible!

JESUS: Look after the doctor, will you? I think he's going to faint.

MOTHER: Oh, Sarah, my darling!

JESUS: She'll be all right now. Don't make a fuss over her. Just give her something to eat.

EPISODE C

NARRATOR: John tells of the woman who was caught in the act of adultery and the men who were about to kill her by stoning.

FIRST MAN: There she is, Jesus! Caught in the act!

SECOND MAN: We found her in bed! And now she's going to die!

JESUS: Of course! That is what she deserves, isn't it?

FIRST MAN: Let's get on with it!

JESUS: May I make a suggestion? You are going to stone this woman. Let the man who is without sin among you come forward, and throw the first stone. (*Silence.*) Well? (*Pause.*) What is your name, girl?

WOMAN: Susanna, Sir.

JESUS: Susanna, the men who were going to stone you have gone away.

WOMAN: You saved my life!

JESUS: Yes, Susanna. Go, and sin no more. Make your life an act of thanksgiving to Almighty God.

EPISODE D

NARRATOR: And there was a woman who was not a Jew, a woman of Phoenicia, who asked a favor of Jesus.

WOMAN: Sir, heal my little girl!

JESUS: Woman, I am a Jew, sent to minister to my own people.

WOMAN: Sir, I need you. My daughter is so sick. Please help!

JESUS: How can I take the children's food, and throw it to the dogs?

WOMAN: People give the dogs scraps, Sir. Surely you can spare a little from the table.

JESUS: I cannot refuse faith like yours. Go home! You will find your little girl cured—not by me, but by your own shining belief.

EPISODE E

NARRATOR: And, at the house of Simon the Pharisee, another woman who was a sinner knelt at Jesus' feet.

SIMON: Sit down, Jesus. Supper will soon be ready.

JESUS: Thank you, Simon.

SIMON: There are some important questions that I want to ask you—

SERVANT: Excuse me, Sir.

SIMON: Yes? What is it? I don't want to be disturbed.

SERVANT: This woman, Sir. I tried to keep her out, but—

WOMAN: Let me wash your feet, Master. I will not disturb you.

SIMON: Get the woman out of here! She's nothing but a common prostitute. This is a respectable home!

JESUS: Let her alone, Simon. You wanted to question me?

SIMON: How can we talk with that woman here? Don't you know what she is? I thought you were meant to be a prophet!

JESUS: I know what she is, Simon. A sinner, who hates her sin, and is seeking God's love. You gave me no water to wash my feet; she is washing them with her tears, and drying them with her hair. You offered me no oil; she is anointing my feet with perfume. You were cold and correct; she is warm and full of love. God protect me from the chill of righteousness!

SIMON: I'm only trying to tell you what this woman is—

JESUS: And I tell you I know what she is. Have you finished, Mary?

WOMAN: Yes, Sir.

JESUS: Thank you. You are asking forgiveness of your sins?

WOMAN: Oh, yes, Sir! If I could only start afresh—

JESUS: Your faith has earned you a fresh start. Go away now, and sin no more. Now, Simon, your questions—

SCENE SIX: FIVE LOAVES AND TWO FISHES

NARRATOR: All that men had to give, Jesus took and used, and consecrated to God's service. He made men whole in body and mind and spirit, and the wholeness gave them joy. Even if they could only give a little, he could turn it into riches.

PETER: Master, don't you think we should turn back?

JESUS: Perhaps we should, Peter.

ANDREW: There must be five thousand people out there, Master.

JAMES: I'm afraid they're going to get restless. It's been a long day, and everyone's hungry—

JESUS: I agree, James. They need to rest and eat.

PETER: That's the point, Master. We're five miles from the nearest village, let alone a decent market.

JESUS: How about it, Philip? How do you think we can give these people bread?

PHILIP: You know the answer to that, Jesus. We'd need hundreds of dollars to give them a meal.

JESUS: Well, first let us ask them to rest. There's plenty of grass. Ask everyone to sit down. Don't bunch them together too close. Seat them by companies.

PETER: That's all very well, but—

JESUS: Would you do what I say, Peter? Please remember a morning when you didn't want to go fishing.

PETER: Oh, all right, Lord! I'll do it, if you say so. Come on! Let's get them seated!

> (*Voices: "Would you all please sit down?" "Some of you over here?" "What's the idea?" "I'm hungry." "I have to get home." "Please sit down!" "The Master will tell you what to do." "I don't know." "I only know he wants you all to—"*

BOY: Sir.

ANDREW: Yes? What is it, boy?

BOY: Can I speak to you?

ANDREW: That's what you're doing now.

BOY: No, I mean over here, where it's quiet.

ANDREW: All right. Now, what's your name, and what can I do for you?

BOY: I'm Levi, Sir; from Bethsaida.

ANDREW: That's my home town too, Levi.

BOY: Yes, Sir, I know. I've seen your boat by the lake.

ANDREW: Well, Levi?

BOY: I've got this, Sir.

ANDREW: Your lunch? Good! You're luckier than most of us. Oh, I see. You want to share it?

BOY: Well, Sir, I wondered. I mean, if it's any use to the Master —to Jesus—I thought—

ANDREW: Thank you, Levi. That's wonderful of you. Why don't we ask him?

BOY: Oh no, Sir. I'd be frightened to do that. I thought you looked as though you might take it to him. I mean, I didn't think you'd tell me it was a dumb thing to do—bringing it—

ANDREW: It isn't a dumb thing to do, Levi. Now I want you to come and meet Jesus.

JESUS: Who is this, Andrew?

ANDREW: This is Levi, Master, from Bethsaida. He wants to give you something.

JESUS: How do you do, Levi? Is this what your Mother gave you?

BOY: Yes, Sir. She ran after me, and told me to take it. Can you —I mean, is this any use, Sir?

JESUS: Five bread rolls and two lake fish, beautifully grilled? Yes, Levi. Sit down over there, and we will ask God how we may use your gift. Later, I'd like you to walk with me on the way home.

BOY: Yes, Sir. Thank you very much, Sir.

JESUS: Out of the mouths of babes and sucklings! Oh, Andrew, it isn't the rich who give us of their riches, but the simple-hearted who give all that they have. Bless you, Andrew, for the love that showed through in your face, and brought that boy to me! And now, Father, consecrate this precious gift to your glory, and feed all who are hungry!

SCENE SEVEN: DISCIPLES AND CRITICS (1)

NARRATOR: As he went from town to town, preaching and healing, Jesus was preparing his close friends, both men and women, for the day when they would stand alone. Sometimes he taught them by themselves; at other times he spoke to crowds. Sometimes he told them stories, or parables, to make his teaching more vivid. Sometimes he answered the questions which arose from their experience together.

ANDREW: Master, how would you define righteousness? How can we try to be truly righteous in God's eyes?

JESUS: I'm not sure I know how to define righteousness, Andrew. I didn't come to look for righteous men; and, if I had, I'm afraid it would have been a disappointing search.

JAMES: Is nobody righteous then?

JESUS: Put it like this, James. Happy are they who hunger and thirst for righteousness! Those are the people I came to find. They will never rest content, or think themselves good enough.

JOHN: But the Law gives so many rules, Jesus. If you try to keep them all—

JESUS: I don't want to destroy the Law, John. I want to fulfill it; but in the spirit, not only in the letter. The Law is dead without love. Let me tell you a story. Two men went to the Temple to pray. One, who sat in the front row was a Pharisee. You can imagine his prayer.

VOICE OF THE PHARISEE: Lord God, I give thanks that I am not as other men are: not like the tax-collector sitting near the door! Why people like that bother to come and pray, I can't imagine. Adulterers, criminals, extortioners—thank God I am not like them! I keep the Law, Lord. I pay all my dues and pledges, observe all the fasts—

JESUS: So you see? Here was a righteous man; but so far from God, if he only knew it! Listen to the prayer of the tax-collector, at the back of the Temple!

VOICE OF THE TAX-COLLECTOR: Oh, God, God! Have mercy on me! I know that I have sinned. I have done evil, and left good undone. Be merciful to me, O Lord!

JESUS: I tell you, my friends, he went home closer to God than the Pharisee. God loves the humble, but the proud shut him out.

SCENE EIGHT: DISCIPLES AND CRITICS (2)

NARRATOR: Often, on the edge of the crowd, there were men listening, and noting down what Jesus said. They were the Scribes and Pharisees, who resented his popularity, and were shocked by his bold teaching. Their questions were asked to trick him, not to learn from him.

FIRST VOICE: Is it lawful to pay tribute to Caesar, Jesus?

SECOND VOICE: Why do your disciples not keep the fast, Jesus?

THIRD VOICE: Why do you eat with tax-collectors and sinners, Jesus?

FOURTH VOICE: How can you heal on the Sabbath, Jesus? Why don't you keep the Law?

JESUS: Please, gentlemen! One question at a time! You ask about the Sabbath? I love to keep the Sabbath, as much as you do. But the Sabbath was made for man, not man for the Sabbath. You asked me that question, Sir?

FOURTH VOICE: Yes, I did. I want to know why you healed a man on the Sabbath.

JESUS: Surely the important thing is that he was healed.

FOURTH VOICE: That's not the point—

JESUS: I think it is the point. If you are honest, you will admit that you would lift one of your sheep out of a ditch on the Sabbath, not wait and let it die.

FOURTH VOICE: This man would not have died if you had waited—

JESUS: Oh, my dear Sir! Aren't you making rules stand above the love of God? It seems to me God is much more like a shepherd than a Rabbi! God does not love by rule. He will search for one of his lost sheep at any time, day or night, Sabbath or not.

FIRST VOICE: So you are our interpreter of God's will, a Galilean workman!

JESUS: God is your shepherd, and I am the door of the sheep. That is the task he has laid upon me.

SECOND VOICE: Blasphemy!

THIRD VOICE: I have heard enough. Let us go!

SCENE NINE: WHO ARE YOU, LORD?

NARRATOR: As they grew closer to Jesus, the Apostles knew that he was not simply a great teacher. God was calling them to know and follow the Way, the Truth, and the Life. But who was Jesus, and what was his relationship with Jehovah, the Father Almighty?

PETER: Master, we have left our homes, and our jobs, and our families, to follow you. We have no regrets. But isn't it time you told us who and what you are, and what you are calling us to undertake?

JESUS: Yes, Peter. It is time.

ANDREW: Who are you, Lord?

JESUS: Who do men say that I am?

JAMES: Some people say you are Elijah, come back again.

JOHN: Yes, I've heard that. And some say Jeremiah, or one of the other prophets.

ANDREW: Or that John the Baptist didn't really die: he lived on in you.

JESUS: So that is what they say. What do you think yourselves?

PETER: We think that there is only one thing you can be, Master. You are the long-awaited Messiah—and you are the Son of God.

JESUS: Oh, Peter! Blessings be upon you! God the Father has

shown you the truth. You are truly like rock—the kind of rock my Church will need for its foundation.

JOHN: So it is true! God has come down to men!

JESUS: Yes, John. God has loved his world so much that he has given his Son. Those who follow him will inherit eternal life in God's presence.

THOMAS: I don't understand! I'll follow you anywhere, Lord, but this talk bewilders me.

JESUS: I'm sorry, Thomas, I don't mean to deceive you or keep you in the dark. You have learned the way to follow, and I want you all to know where that way is leading me.

THOMAS: But that's just it, Lord! We don't know where you are going, or what your relation is to the Father. How can we find our own way?

JESUS: I am the way, Thomas. You have to come to the Father through me. You have been loyal to me, and so now you are close to the Father.

PHILIP: Can't you show us God the Father, Jesus? Show him to us, and we shall be satisfied!

JESUS: Don't you know me, Philip? After all this time that we have been together? I am one with the Father. If you have seen me, you have seen him.

JUDAS: That means you can show your power, Lord, and establish your Kingdom! That is what we are waiting for!

JESUS: I can show power, Judas. I can establish my Kingdom. But it is not the kind of Kingdom you mean. My Kingdom is not of this world.

SCENE TEN: JERICHO

NARRATOR: At length the time came when Jesus knew that he must turn toward Jerusalem. He had prepared his friends for the road of sacrifice. He had taught them that they must take up the Cross, and be prepared to lose their lives in order to gain them. Now he must show them that the Son of God would give his life for his friends. On this last journey together, they came to the City of Jericho. A great crowd waited along the roadside.

(*Crowd voices: "Here he comes!" "Look, on the donkey!" "It's Jesus all right!" "Make way, there!" "Don't push!" "Jesus! Let me get close!"*)

JESUS: Thank you for your greeting, my friends. Please stand back!

MAN: Do you need a room for the night, Master?

WOMAN: You can come to our house.

FIRST MAN: All the sick will be brought to the marketplace an hour before sunset, Master.

WOMAN: Please come, Sir!

JESUS: Thank you. Thank you all. I see one of you even thought it worthwhile to climb a tree to greet me.

MAN: Don't talk to him! That's Zacchaeus—the swine!

ZACCHAEUS: It's all right, Master. Take no notice of me. I just wanted to watch you; and you see I'm too short.

JESUS: I thank you for the trouble you took, Zacchaeus. Would it be asking too much to invite myself to your home to rest?

MAN: Not with him, Jesus! He's a tax-collector—a swindler!

JESUS: Sometimes I find the swindlers need me more than those whom they swindle. May I come, Zacchaeus?

ZACCHAEUS: Of course, Master, if you wish. But—

JESUS: Don't worry about being unworthy. You climbed a tree, and that was an act of faith. Let us go!

WOMAN: Doesn't he know a crook when he sees one? A shame, I call it! Turning down respectable people!

NARRATOR: Later, at Zacchaeus' home, Jesus talked again of his journey to Jerusalem.

ZACCHAEUS: Can't I come with you, Lord? I'd give up everything to follow you.

JESUS: No, Zacchaeus. Your witness must be here in Jericho. You have promised to pay back all you owe, and to do your work with honesty and compassion.

ZACCHAEUS: I swear I will, Lord. Life can never be the same again—not since you called me down from that tree!

JESUS: And you, Miriam? Will you help your husband to keep his promise?

MIRIAM: Yes, Sir. I'm so happy! I never wanted all this money. It only made everyone hate us.

JESUS: You see, Zacchaeus? If you stay here, and witness to God's love at the Tax Collector's desk, you will be serving me best.

ZACCHAEUS: I know nobody's going to believe it, Lord.

MIRIAM: My husband an honest man! That will be the biggest story in Jericho in my lifetime! (*They are laughing.*)

ZACCHAEUS: The truth is, Lord, this is the happiest day of my life.

I wish you could postpone your visit to Jerusalem, and stay here with us a little while.

JESUS: I wish I could do that, Zacchaeus. Your hospitality and your new-found joy warm my heart. But the Passover is near, and I must do what my Father has told me to do. Let us go now! The sick will be waiting for me in the marketplace.

NARRATOR: And so, from Jericho, Jesus and his disciples started out on the steep, dusty road which led to Jerusalem.

THE LIFE OF JESUS: BACKGROUND

SCENE ONE: JESUS IN THE TEMPLE

This story is told in Luke 2, 41-51.

This is the only story of Jesus' boyhood in any of the Gospels. It anticipates two vital elements of his teaching: the "authority" with which he spoke, to the amazement of his listeners and the indignation of the established leaders; and the order of priorities shown in his own life and in the demands which he made upon his followers.

Mark at once comments on this authority: 1, verses 22-28. Independent thinking was not by any means encouraged in Jewish education; but Jesus showed independence and originality, based on a thorough knowledge of tradition and a deep respect for the Law.

The quotations used in this scene are from: Hosea 6, verse 6 (twice quoted in Matthew: 9, verse 13 and 12, verse 7); Psalm 40 verse 6; and Proverbs 2, verses 2-3.

When Joseph and Mary enter, Jesus makes his statement about the priorities of his life. It is not a rebuke to his parents that he puts his Father's business first. As far as we know, their home remained his home for another twenty years. Discuss Jesus' attitude to tradition, and find examples of his originality. Subjects you might well examine are: Sacrifice and the teaching at the Last Supper; the Sabbath; and the various aspects of the Law covered in Matthew 5, verses 17-48.

For Jesus' home and family, see Mark 6, 2-3; 3, 31-35; John 7, 2-9; Acts 1, 14; and notes in Peake on these passages. Also Daniel-Rops, pages 111-120, and Taylor, page 247.

Find out what you can about Jewish education in Jesus' time. A great deal of it consisted of learning the Scriptures by heart. Also look up Peake 44n, on the city of Tiberias, and see its place on the map in relation to Nazareth. If there was a building boom going on not far from Nazareth, a carpenter's family would be busy.

SCENE TWO: THE TEMPTATION BY SATAN

This story is told briefly in Mark 1, 12-13; and at greater length in Matthew 4, 1-11, and Luke 4, 1-13. Luke puts the "kingdoms of the world" before the "pinnacle of the Temple."

Compare Satan in this episode with the Satan of Job, chapters 1 and 2. There, as in the temptations of Jesus, the devil is pictured as switching from one line of attack to another, probing for a weakness that will give him success. His power is great, but it is negative and destructive. He is the spoiler of good. In the case of Jesus, Satan's only chance was to spoil the power of love by diverting it to wrong ends. Jesus knew that he had the power, and had gone to the wilderness to dedicate himself to its proper use. He refused to cheapen it, as Satan hoped to persuade him to do.

Points for discussion are:

a) How did Jesus use his power? Look up some stories of miracles, and see how he shrank from any open display of power: for example, Mark 1, 40-45; John 2, 1-11, especially verse 4.

b) Jesus all through his life identified himself completely with ordinary people. His home was normal. His work was normal. He was baptized, in spite of John's protest, "Comest thou to me?" (Matthew 3, 13.) And in this incident he was assailed with what one might call normal temptations; for all of us who have any kind of power are tempted to misuse it. The consecration of our power and influence is one of the great tests of the quality of our lives.

c) This story can only have had one source: Jesus himself. None of the Apostles was there to hear what happened. Can you think of any other incident in the Gospels which Jesus' friends only knew about from his description? It is a good habit, when you are reading the Bible, to think about the sources of the stories, insofar as we know them, and to study what Commentaries say about them.

SCENE THREE: THE CALL OF PETER

This story is told in Luke 5, 1-11.

Another version of the calling of Andrew and Peter is given in John 1, 35-42. The two are not inconsistent. We can surely assume that Jesus knew his friends well before he faced them with the ultimate challenge to discipleship.

The Gospels tell us very little about the Apostles, since the writers were not concerned to give any information which did not bear directly upon Jesus' own teaching. Even their names are not all known for certain. Look up the lists in Mark 3, 16-19; Matthew 10, 1-4; Luke 6, 14-16; Acts 1, 13. There is a story of the call of

Philip and Nathanael in John 1, 43-51; and of Matthew's call from his desk as tax collector in Matthew 9, 9.

As the four fishermen were "partners" (Luke 5, 10), they were probably not poor men. Zebedee had hired servants working in his boat. Jesus' followers seem to have come from all walks of life, and from many different backgrounds. There was Joanna, the wife of Herod's steward Chuza (Luke 8, 3); Joseph of Arimathea, described as a rich man and a counsellor; and at the same time many who came from occupations which were despised by society.

A careful study of the little information given about the Apostles leads to the conclusion that they must have had great happiness during Jesus' ministry, as well as accepting hardship and danger. The prevalence of nicknames among them is surely a mark of close friendship and enjoyable shared experiences. Peter was the Rock; James and John the Sons of Thunder; Thomas the Twin; the other Simon perhaps "Eager Beaver" . . . The Zealot; the other James perhaps "Little James."

Discuss their character and backgrounds. What kind of homes and families and jobs do you think they had? Paul's indignant comments in I Corinthians 9, 1-14, give some interesting indications about the life of the Christian preachers of the first generation. Acts 1, 44-66, and 4, 32-37 show the way in which they shared their resources; but it is also clear that Paul tried to pay his way on his journeys by working.

Look up the Bible references in Peake; and also Daniel-Rops, pages 219-224, Taylor, pages 239-244.

SCENE FOUR: CROWDS AND HEALING

One advantage of reading the Gospels in Greek is that the descriptions become more vivid. Especially in Mark there is a roughness and vigor which makes everything come to life, sometimes with a shock. We discover that Jesus' hearers were "thrown off balance" or "knocked sideways" by his originality and authority. We read of him complaining angrily about the disciples' "calloused minds." Those who hunger and thirst after righteousness will be "gorged." The word for the crowds "pressing upon" him, *thlibo*, is a constant companion in the Greek text. With my Greek classes I have coined the word, "to be thlibbed," so as to remind ourselves of what it was really like to be at the center of a volatile,

violent mob, turning so easily from anger to joy, from wild enthusiasm to skepticism, fear or disgust.

It is very well worthwhile to look up carefully Mark's descriptions of crowds, and then to compare them with Shakespeare's
treatment of the mob in *Julius Caesar* and *Coriolanus*. See, for example, Mark 1, 33 (pressure all round Peter's home); 2, 2-4 (the
tearing of a hole in the roof); 3, 9-10 (Jesus has recourse to a boat
to get away); and 5, 7.

Many things combined to increase the strain of Jesus' public life.
Usually there were critics in the crowd, taking note of anything
which they could use against him. Then there was the violence and
noisy reaction of many of those whom he healed. See for example
Matthew 17, 14-22 (the epileptic boy), Mark 1, 26 (where the common New Testament verb, *krazo*, I yell, makes its first appearance),
and 5, 7 (Legion's unclean spirits).

The original words also make clear the great effort, physical and
spiritual, which was needed when Jesus healed the sick. When
Jesus is described as "taking the damsel by the hand" (Mark 5,
41) the Greek word implies effort and the concentration of power.
He felt this kind of power drained from him when the woman with
an issue of blood touched the hem of his garment. That he needed
to get the confidence and prayers of others on his side, and to
build up a concentration of love and support for the sick, is shown
by the startling fact that in the skeptical atmosphere of Nazareth
he "could do no mighty work" (Mark 6, 5).

That is why the crowd is so important in these Scenes. There
should be a note of near-hysteria in their cries, and a feeling that
they are physically close to Jesus all the time, and keeping him
under rigorous pressure.

The name Lebbaeus I made up, and the story of his healing is a
combination of Gospel passages. Read a wide selection of these
passages, and discuss how in each case Jesus made the sick man or
woman "whole" (Mark 6, verse 56). Some needed to be made
whole physically, some mentally, some spiritually.

Jesus made Peter a whole man, and Mary Magdalene a whole
woman, just as much as he made paralytics or cripples whole.

SCENE FIVE: WOMEN WHO CAME TO JESUS

References for these stories are: Mark 5, 24-34; and 35-43; John
8, 1-11; Mark 7, 24-30; Luke 7, 36-50.

Discuss the place of women in Jesus' ministry. Their work was absolutely necessary for the success and support of the men, but it is only seldom mentioned, in passages like Luke 8, 3, and John 12, 1-3. Look up what is known about these women, in *Who's Who in the New Testament*.

Also discuss Jesus' attitude toward Gentiles. When the Syro-Phoenician woman approached him, he seemed to tell her that he regarded his ministry as being confined to Jews. Realistically, this had to be true, for he needed to concentrate on the training of a few unbreakable friends, rather than to spread himself more widely. When he did meet Gentiles, he treated them with courtesy and respect. compare Luke 7, 1-9 (a Centurion), and John 4, 5-30 (a Samaritan woman).

The name Susanna is made up, in section (c). The name Mary in section (d), is given to the woman at Simon's house, because it is often assumed that she was Mary Magdalene.

SCENE SIX: FIVE LOAVES AND TWO FISHES

The feeding of the five thousand is to be found in all four Gospels, which is unusual for a narrative incident. See especially Mark 6, 30-44 and John 6, 5-13. The feeding of the four thousand is described in Mark 8, 1-10.

This very beautiful story opens up many important points for discussion.

a) It is another example of a person being "made whole." (Compare the note on Zacchaeus in Scene 10.) The boy had a small thing to give; but it was freely given, offered in God's service. This made its potential unlimited. Therefore the story contains a parable as well as a miracle. If God could do this with the boy's picnic lunch, what can he do with Paul's brains, Francis' unselfishness, Livingstone's courage, Schweitzer's dedicated talents? And what about you and your gifts?

b) It raises the question, what is a miracle? How did Jesus work miracles? There is no easy answer. Certainly most Christians in our day do not believe that Jesus could without any effort suspend all natural laws and do what he liked. God *could* have come into the world in that way; but the truth of the Incarnation makes the miracles more of a mystery and more of a precious heritage for the followers of Jesus. His miracles were just the opposite of those which Satan urged him to perform (see Scene three). They represented power and love concentrated and dedicated to men's service; and they cost him great effort. Jesus never made an empty display of power.

c) Commentators who were worried about the impossibility of a material miracle of this kind used sometimes to explain it away by saying that Jesus began to offer the boy's lunch to the company of Five Thousand, and then all those who had brought food with them brought it out and shared it, so that there was enough for everyone. This is a beautiful idea; and it may surely have happened, in addition to the miraculous use made by Jesus of the loaves and fishes. But to explain away the miracles is to make out the Gospel writers to have been credulous or dishonest, to a degree which simply cannot square with their general down-to-earth reliability. Get someone in your group to look up, and report on, Luke's record as a historian. You will then see the absurdity of taking out large slices of his writing and labelling them impossible because they have reference to miracles. (Luke: see Peake 715a-716b. For Mark's historical value see Taylor, pages 130-145. See also Alan Richardson, "The Miracle Stories of the Gospels.")

d) Jesus constantly uses bread as a symbol of the sacramental way of life. Read on through John, chapter 6, especially verse 51; and compare Matthew 16, verses 6-12; 13, verses 33-34. Bread was the symbol of man's daily need, as Jesus said in the Lord's Prayer. If simple things like bread can be treated as gifts from God, to be used for service and love, they are transformed. Thus the same sacramental use can be made of other ordinary things in daily life: a cup of coffee becomes a sacrament of friendship; a dollar bill a sacrament of work and service; your car a gift from God to use with consideration and dedication. Discuss this idea, using further examples.

As Jesus often taught his friends in this way, they were ready for the final teaching of the Last Supper and the Eucharist; and in the rest of the New Testament the Breaking of Bread becomes the symbol of the sacramental life: see Luke 24, 30-31; Acts 2, 42; I Corinthians 11, 23-28.

SCENES SEVEN AND EIGHT: DISCIPLES AND CRITICS

This Scene contrasts those who came to Jesus to learn, and to offer their lives in his service, and those who came to collect information for use against him.

Jesus' mistrust of the "good" or "righteous" is deep-seated. The classic statements of this occur in the fourth Beatitude (Matthew 5, 6), and in his comments at dinner in Levi's house (Luke 5, 29-32): "They that are whole need not a physician; but they that are sick. I came not to call the righteous, but sinners to repentance." Notice also Jesus' reply to the rich young man who addressed him as "Good Master." Jesus immediately questioned his use of the word "good"—nobody is good except God. (Look up note in Taylor, pages 426-427, on Mark 10, 18-19.)

Jesus' attitude toward the Law is best seen in Matthew 5, 17-48. He reverenced the Law and the traditions of Judaism; but people came first to him, and laws served people. Hence his frequent clashes with those who challenged him over the literal interpretation of the Law. For these clashes, look up Mark 2, 1, to 3, 6; and also 7, 1-23. The highly dramatized story of the blind man, in John 9, typifies the opposition to Jesus' healing and teaching.

The Gospel writers probably accentuated these clashes. Although the opposition was very real, and resulted in the death of Jesus, we must remember that he could only find a possible context for his ministry among the Jews. We are told that some of the leading Jews came to listen, not merely to criticize: for example Nicodemus (John 3, 1-21) and Joseph of Arimathea. But to the circle of the High Priest Jesus represented a danger politically. They wanted peace and quiet, with themselves in control as far as Roman power allowed. A "Messiah" incident was the last thing that they would welcome with Pilate in Jerusalem, ready to crush any sign of unrest.

Look up Annas and Caiaphas in Commentaries, and in *Who's Who in the New Testament.* Try to put yourself in their place, and discuss their reasons for helping bring about Jesus' death. Also look up the beliefs of the Pharisees, and their attitude toward tradition. It is not hard to see why they were shocked at what Jesus taught. (See Daniel-Rops, pages 209-215.)

SCENE NINE: WHO ARE YOU, LORD?

References used in this scene are: Matthew 16, 13-20; John 6, 66-69; John 3, 16-17; John 14, 1-14; John 18, 36.

One difficulty about reading the Gospels is that they do not give us a clear chronology of Jesus' ministry. The record is very faithful; but the stories and teachings put together by the Gospel editors did not come to them in an orderly form. Brief, vivid word-pictures of incidents in Jesus' life were passed on from person to person in the early Church; and collections of sayings, parables and events were grouped together, not necessarily in their true chronological order. An example of this is the "conflict stories" grouped together in Mark 2 and 3. (For the formation of the Gospels, see Peake 596a—597d and 653a—658c.)

The realism of the Gospel is not in any way reduced by this absence of a clear time scheme. But it leaves us uncertain how Jesus explained his own place in God's plan to his friends. It is usually assumed that he did this gradually; and the incident recorded in Matthew 16 bears this out. Here, at a late point in the ministry, the Apostles are told that Jesus is the Messiah, the Christ. In John's Gospel, his revelation of the truth about himself comes in many forms, and at many different stages in the story. The "I am" sayings (the Bread of Life, the Door, the Light of the World, etc.) are part of this unfolding picture.

Look these passages up, and discuss what the Apostles and other friends of Jesus may have thought about him. The Incarnation must remain a mystery, however much theologians write about it. But the more you read the Gospels, the more it becomes plain that Jesus identified himself with God, yet lived with the real experiences and emotions of a man in his context.

SCENE TEN: JERICHO

This scene comes from Luke 19, 1-10.

Here is another example of a man being made whole. (See again Mark 6, 56) In the case of Zacchaeus, the sickness was materialism. His money, dishonestly acquired, was only leading him to misery. He was hated and despised. His wife and family are not mentioned in the Gospel; but we can imagine what it must have been like to go shopping as the wife of the ostracized tax-collector, or to walk to school as his son or daughter.

There is humor and beauty in the description of Jesus calling Zacchaeus down from the tree. Then comes the familiar reaction of the respectable bystanders: "Fancy Jesus associating with a rat like Zacchaeus!"

Jesus had no set formula in his teaching about money and possessions. Zacchaeus was not told to give everything away. He was to make just restitution, and then to remain in Jericho, doing his job honestly.

To the rich young man (Luke 18, 23) Jesus had said, "Give everything away"; knowing that in his case possessions were the barrier between him and God. To the Apostles, when they went on a preaching mission, he had given clear instructions to take nothing but bare necessities with them. But he presumably did not tell Peter to sell his house and leave his wife to live on charity, when he accepted the call to be an Apostle.

Discuss these and other passages which deal with materialism. Among them are:

Luke 6, 30-34, on generosity and lending.

Luke 8, 3, on those women who made good use of their money to help Jesus in his preaching.

Luke 9, 58 where Jesus comments on his own acceptance of unselfish standards, in a proverbial form.

Luke 10, 21, the significant phrase, "Rich toward God."

Luke 10, 23, on the ravens; and the fuller parallel passage in Matthew 5, 19-34.

Luke 16, 19-31, Dives and Lazarus.

Luke 18, 18-30, the incident of the rich young man, and the Apostles' answer to Jesus' teaching about the "eye of a needle."

Is not the clue to all of Jesus' teaching the need for priorities? The vital thing about our attitude to possessions is to have them in perspective. Where your treasure is, your heart is. This is the lesson of the five loaves and two fishes in different words. Use what you have, as a gift from God. Then it will grow, and you will grow. Give freely of yourself, and you will receive abundance (Luke 6, 38). But bury your talent in the ground, and you condemn yourself to a narrow, unfruitful, selfish existence (Matthew 25, 14-30).

2. GOOD FRIDAY

CHARACTERS: NARRATOR
CENTURION
TWO SOLDIERS
CHORUS, *made up of a crowd of bystanders*
TWO DISCIPLES
TWO BYSTANDERS
THREE YOUNG LADIES

NOTE: This version of the story of Good Friday and Easter can be used in several different ways:

—It can be read as a Verse Play, in conjunction with study of the Passion Story in the four Gospels.

—It can be presented on stage or in a church, rather as a pageant than as a play. Directions are given in the text for a simple form of production.

—It can be presented—with or without the musical score—while a series of slides is shown to the audience. I have used it in this way on many occasions. I have built up gradually a set of about one hundred slides which fit the words. You should consider doing this. Discuss among yourselves what pictures will make the most impact. My set has resulted in a blend of famous pictures (Michelangelo, Grünewald, Rouault, etc.) and sculptures, with modern works, including photographs. This form of presentation can be very effective.

With the stage in darkness, the tune of the opening song is played softly. A trumpet or cello solo would be effective. As it is played, the lights come up. We see, L., the JEWS, DISCIPLES *and* BYSTANDERS, *looking off-stage. Down-stage R., the two* SOLDIERS *are playing dice. All except the* SOLDIERS *are quite still as the opening music plays.*

NARRATOR

At dawn on the day when Jesus was crucified, there were many people watching and waiting. Very different feelings, different hopes and fears, filled the hearts of men and women in Jerusalem, as that Good Friday began.

(A spot now follows the different groups as they are described.)

There were those who hated him, *(pause)* those who loved him, *(pause)* and those who cared little about him either way, but were still affected by what was to happen on Golgotha Hill that day. And there were soldiers, waiting for their orders as the trial of Jesus drew to a close. *(pause)* When Pilate gave in to the pressure of the Jewish leaders, and consented to the Crucifixion of Jesus, there was work for the soldiers to do, *(Enter* CENTURION *L.)* carpenter's work, to nail to the Cross the Son of God, himself brought up as a carpenter.

CENTURION *(sings)*
Take some beams, and make three crosses!
There'll be an execution on Golgotha today.
Take some beams, and make three crosses!
There'll be an execution on Golgotha today.

CHORUS and SOLDIERS
Golgotha! Golgotha! There'll be an execution,
There'll be an execution on Golgotha today.

(As the CENTURION *sings, the* SOLDIERS *fetch the beams and tools from off R., and begin to nail the cross or crosses together.)*

CENTURION
Nail them firm, and join them tightly!
There'll be an execution on Golgotha today.
Nail them firm, and join them tightly!
There'll be an execution on Golgotha today.
Harden your heart, and do your job!
It's not for a soldier to sigh or to sob.
Nail them firm, and join them tightly!
There'll be an execution on Golgotha today.

CHORUS
Golgotha! Golgotha! There'll be an execution,
There'll be an execution on Golgotha today.

CENTURION

Call them out to bear their crosses!
There'll be an execution on Golgotha today
Call them out to bear their crosses!
There'll be an execution on Golgotha today.

CHORUS

Golgotha! Golgotha! There'll be an execution,
There'll be an execution on Golgotha today.

(*While the lights fade to black-out, this tune is played again on a single instrument. Then the sound of mallets and hammers is heard off R. As the lights come up slowly, the shadow of a cross is seen against the back of the stage, R. The* JEWS, DISCIPLES *and* BYSTANDERS *enter L., and the two* SOLDIERS *enter R. at the same time. They hold back the others C. and L.C.*)

FIRST SOLDIER: Keep back, there! Keep back! No crowding round the crosses!
FIRST JEW: I am an official observer. I—
SECOND SOLDIER: Sorry, sir. Governor's orders. You can see all you want from here.
FIRST DISCIPLE: Oh, God! It can't be true. It can't be happening!
FIRST BYSTANDER: Can't we get any closer?
SECOND BYSTANDER: I guess not. We'll have to watch from here.
FIRST BYSTANDER: It always happens to me. I'm always at the back. (*He sings.*)

I'm always on the edge of a crowd,
   Looking over someone's shoulder;
Following any voice that's loud,
   Looking over someone's shoulder.

(*Lines marked with an asterisk (*) may be spoken or shouted.*)

BOTH BYSTANDERS

*   "Hosanna in the highest!"
That was the cry I heard.
"Hosanna in the highest!"
And I echoed every word.

SECOND BYSTANDER

I'm always on the edge of a crowd,
   Looking over someone's shoulder;
Following any voice that's loud,
   Looking over someone's shoulder.

BOTH BYSTANDERS

*   "Hail to the mighty healer!
*   Blessed be Jesus' name!
Hail to the mighty healer!"
They cried, so I cried the same.

FIRST BYSTANDER

I'm always on the edge of a crowd,
    Looking over someone's shoulder;
Following any voice that's loud,
    Looking over someone's shoulder.

BOTH BYSTANDERS

*   "Down, down with the blasphemer!"
The angry voices said.
"Down, down with the blasphemer!"
So I followed where they led.

SECOND BYSTANDER

I'm always on the edge of a crowd,
    Looking over someone's shoulder;
Following any voice that's loud,
    Looking over someone's shoulder.

BOTH BYSTANDERS

*   "Crucify him! Crucify him!"
That is the leaders' cry.
"Crucify him! Crucify him!"
They shout—and so do I.

FIRST BYSTANDER

I'm always on the edge of a crowd,
    Looking over someone's shoulder;

SECOND BYSTANDER

Following any voice that's loud,
    Looking over someone's shoulder.

(*While the* CENTURION *comes in slowly from R., the second half of the tune of the next song is played on a single instrument. He tosses the robe down by the* SOLDIERS, *who sit R.*)

CENTURION (*sings*)

There's a strange, strange man on the cross in the center,
    With his life just ebbing away.
While the nails drove through, still his face was tender,

And I thought I heard him say;
"Father, forgive them!"—that was what he said.
"Father, I pray to you!
Father, forgive them!" I heard him cry,
"For they know not what they do."

FIRST BYSTANDER (*spoken*): Who is his father? He asks him to forgive—
SECOND BYSTANDER: But he does not say to him, "Father, let me live!"
FIRST DISCIPLE: Who is his father?
SECOND DISCIPLE: Tortured now, and torn,
Can he think of dying as waiting to be born?
FIRST JEW: He is a blasphemer, dying for his sins!
SECOND JEW: He is a deceiver, and falsehood never wins!
FIRST JEW: We have tried to save him, but he paid no heed.
SECOND JEW: Every chance we gave him to be spared and freed.

CENTURION (*sings*)
Then the thief next door ceased his raging and crying,
And I heard his halting word:
"O, remember me!" with the voice of the dying,
"When you come to your kingdom, Lord."
"I will remember!"—that was what he said,
Love shining from his eyes.
"I will remember! Today you shall be
With me in Paradise."

(THREE YOUNG LADIES *enter from L., and look over the shoulders of the others.*)

FIRST YOUNG LADY: What's happening?
SECOND YOUNG LADY: Oh, an execution! How horrible!
THIRD YOUNG LADY: Let's get away! It's nothing to do with us.
FIRST YOUNG LADY: Wait a minute! I want to know who that man in the middle is. Excuse me, sir! Can you tell me who it is up there—the middle one?
FIRST JEW: A false Messiah.
SECOND JEW: His death was unavoidable.
SECOND YOUNG LADY: Excuse me! What has the one on the center cross done?
FIRST BYSTANDER: I don't really know. I overheard someone saying it was blasphemy.
SECOND BYSTANDER: We're just passing by, like you.
THIRD YOUNG LADY: Excuse me! (FIRST DISCIPLE *falls to his*

knees, weeping) Oh, is he a friend of yours?

SECOND DISCIPLE: He is our Savior!

FIRST DISCIPLE: I cannot live without him!

FIRST YOUNG LADY: Come on, girls! We can't do anything.

SECOND YOUNG LADY: No. Come along, Betty! After all, it's nothing to do with us.

(*They advance to the front of the stage, C. Other lights go out, and a spot picks them up.*)

FIRST YOUNG LADY: If a man by the roadside has suffered an assault,
 It's nothing to do with me.

SECOND YOUNG LADY: It's risky to help him, and it's probably all his fault.
 It's nothing to do with me.

THIRD YOUNG LADY: Why pick on me to stop and lend a helping hand?

FIRST YOUNG LADY: Why can't an ostrich hide his head in the sand?
 I tell you, it's nothing to do with me.

ALL THREE: It's absolutely nothing to do with me.

SECOND YOUNG LADY: If the man next door gets drunk and beats his wife,
 It's nothing to do with me.

THIRD YOUNG LADY: A girl must be practical in twentieth-century life.
 It's nothing to do with me.

FIRST YOUNG LADY: Am I my brother's keeper when he gets into a jam?

SECOND YOUNG LADY: Can't you see how overworked and put upon I am?
 I tell you, it's nothing to do with me.

ALL THREE: It's absolutely nothing to do with me.

THIRD YOUNG LADY: If three gasping criminals are dying on the cross,
 It's nothing to do with me.

FIRST YOUNG LADY: I don't care for bloodshed; but they probably aren't much loss.
 It's nothing to do with me.

SECOND YOUNG LADY: Isn't it disgraceful that there's such a wave of crime?

THIRD YOUNG LADY: I don't know much about it, for I haven't got the time,

And surely it's nothing to do with me.

ALL THREE: It's absolutely nothing to do with me.

FIRST YOUNG LADY: If some far-off Africans are fighting all the time,
    It's nothing to do with me.

SECOND YOUNG LADY: With things as they are, I have to think of every dime.
    It's nothing to do with me.

THIRD YOUNG LADY: We want to live our lives in peace, and keep them clear of fuss.

ALL THREE: Of course it would be different if disaster threatened us!
    But so far it's nothing to do with me.
    It's absolutely nothing to do with me.

(They go out L. Spot C. off. Lights up slowly, and the other characters are still where they were.)

CENTURION *(sings)*
Then I heard him say to his friend and his mother,
    As they watched him, silent and grim,
That he gave them charge each one of the other;
    And they took fresh strength from him.
"This is your mother!"—that was what he said.
    "Mother, behold your son!
This is your mother!" I heard him cry,
    When his course was almost run.

Then his lips would move in a soundless praying,
    And he whispered many a word;
Till he raised his voice in a tortured saying,
    And I watched him while I heard.
"Father, O Father!"—that was what he said,
    "Have you forsaken me?
Do not forsake me!" I heard him cry,
    As he hung in agony.

FIRST DISCIPLE: *(Spoken)* Is God his father? And has God ceased to care?

SECOND DISCIPLE: How can he forsake him, if his son is dying there?

CENTURION
He had spurned the drug that was there for his easing,

When the pain was at its worst;
But he raised his head, when his strength was ceasing,
    And I heard him say, "I thirst."
"See, he is thirsting!" they cried below.
    "Reach him the draught to drink!
"See, he is thirsting!" I heard them say,
    As his head began to sink.

He's a strange, strange man on the cross in the center,
    Who has drawn his dying breath.
In the midst of pain, still his face was tender,
    And he seemed to conquer death.
"Now it is finished!"—that was what he said.
    "Father, the hour is come!
Into your keeping I give my soul!"
    And then his lips were dumb.

(*At the words, "Now it is finished," the* DISCIPLES *fall on their knees and hide their faces. The* BYSTANDERS, *moved in spite of themselves, are looking toward the cross.*)

BYSTANDERS (*sing*)
    It's sad to see that man die;
    Nobody seems to know why.
They say he was a sinner; but he healed the sick.
    It's sad to see that man die.

    It's sad to see that man killed;
    It's sad to see his blood spilled.
They say he was a traitor; but his ways were pure.
    It's sad to see that man killed.
    It's sad to watch that man now;
    It's sad to see his head bow.
They call him a blasphemer; but his words were of love.
    It's sad to see that man now.

(*When the* JEWS *sing, we know that they are not gloating over Jesus' death. They are grimly satisfied that justice has been done, but moved by what they have seen and heard.*)

JEWS (*sing*)
    Stubborn and unbending, he defied the Law.
    Now you see the ending: he will lie no more!
This is the man who trusted in God, that he would deliver
    him!

This is the man who mocked at our Law, and said we should trust in him!

This is the man who led them astray—the "Christ" from Nazareth!

This is the man whose folly and pride have led him to pain and death!

NARRATOR (*spoken*)

The soldiers threw dice for Jesus' robe, because they did not want to tear it. The one who threw highest took it for his own.

(*We see the* SOLDIERS, *down-stage L., throw the dice as the* NARRATOR *sings.*)

NARRATOR

Now the coat was without seam, woven from the top throughout;

And so was the life of him who died, who was God's own son, no doubt.

And the soldiers played at dice that day for the coat that had no seam;

But they tore the flesh of him who died, as they nailed him to the beam.

CHORUS

O, my Lord! The coat was woven whole.

O, my Lord! You died to save my soul.

NARRATOR

A soldier won the seamless coat, and took it for a prize;

And the seamless Lord, from his burning pain, looked down with loving eyes.

For the soldiers played at dice that day for the coat that had no seam;

But they tore the flesh of him who died, as they nailed him to the beam.

CHORUS

O, my Lord! The coat was woven whole.

O, my Lord! You died to save my soul.

NARRATOR

Now the lives of men are frayed and torn, like a robe all frayed and patched;

But the dying Lord was clean and whole, whose brow the thorns had scratched.

And the soldiers played at dice that day for the coat that had
  no seam;
But they tore the flesh of him who died, as they nailed him to
  the beam.

CHORUS

  O, my Lord! The coat was woven whole.
  O, my Lord! You died to save my soul.

NARRATOR

Now the robe that Jesus wore that day was made in a single
  piece;
And the love of the Lord who wore that robe will live and
  never cease.
And the soldiers played at dice that day for the coat that had
  no seam;
But they tore the flesh of him who died, as they nailed him to
  the beam.

CHORUS

  O, my Lord! The coat was woven whole.
  O, my Lord! You died to save my soul.

(*The* SOLDIERS *go off L. toward the crosses. A sound of ham-
mering is heard. The* DISCIPLES *remain kneeling as they sing.*)

DISCIPLES

I tried to serve him,
    Body and soul,
Because I came to him empty,
    And he made me whole.
I tried to give him
    All that's best of me,
Because I was a prisoner,
    And he set me free.

Is there a gift worth giving
To one who has made you live?
A richer and better living
Is all that I have to give.

I tried to serve him,
    Body and soul,
Because I came to him empty,
    And he made me whole.

        I tried to give him
            All that's best of me,
        Because I was a prisoner,
            And he set me free.

    (*There is a crash of thunder or roll of drums, and a bright
    flash. The shadow of the cross passes from the back curtain.
    The* CENTURION *enters from R., the* SOLDIERS *behind him.*)

CENTURION: (*Sings*) It is finished! His life is done. Carry him to
    the grave!
JEWS: It is finished! The fight is won; but him we could not save.
BYSTANDERS: It is finished! Time to depart. Nothing left to see.
DISCIPLES: It is finished! O, valiant heart! Death has set you free!

    (*The lights slowly fade to a black-out. After a short silence,
    spot L. shows the* THREE YOUNG LADIES *by the TV set down-
    stage extreme R.*)

FIRST YOUND LADY: I'm bored! What can we do?
SECOND YOUNG LADY: Watch TV, I suppose. What's on?
THIRD YOUNG LADY: Let's try to get the news. I'd like to hear
    something about that man we saw on the cross.
FIRST YOUNG LADY: Oh, who cares about that?
SECOND YOUNG LADY: It probably wouldn't mention him anyway.
    Just another crucifixion. (*Reading from TV listings*) Look, let's
    get Channel 4. It's the Scarabs!

    (*She turns on the set. They remain quite still, gazing at the
    screen.*)

                    CHORUS (*sings*)
        Is it nothing to you, all ye that pass by?
        Is it nothing to you, if the people die?
        Can you close your eyes to the grief and pain?
        Can you close your minds to the jailer's chain?
            Is it nothing to you?

        Is it nothing to you, all ye that pass by?
        Is it nothing to you, if the lonely sigh?
        Can you close your ears when the hungry call?
        Can you close your hearts when the wounded fall?
            Is it nothing to you?

        Is it nothing to you, all ye that pass by?
        Is it nothing to you, if the stricken cry?

Can you close your eyes to the victim's need?
Can you close your ears while the helpless bleed?
    Is it nothing to you?

(*Spot L. goes off. The lights slowly come up on stage. It is dawn, and the stage is empty. Just off-stage R. is the tomb of Jesus, from which a light shines. During the next song, the two* DISCIPLES *come on L., and kneel R.C. Then small groups come on and kneel facing the tomb. There are rich and poor, sick and whole, white and colored, in the dress of many different nations. The* CHORUS *singers from the area of the piano may be among those who now come on stage.*)

CHORUS (sings)

Comfort ye! Comfort ye! Comfort ye, my people, saith your
    God!
Speak ye comfortably to Jerusalem!
Cry unto her that her warfare is accomplished!
Cry unto her that her warfare is accomplished!
Her iniquity is pardoned.
Comfort ye! Comfort ye! Comfort ye, my people, saith your
    God!

(*There is a flash of lightning, and a noise of thunder or drums.*)

But the light of the lamp which the Cross has lit
    Will shine till the world shall end;
For the rock-sealed grave could not shut in
    The soul of the sinners' friend.
He broke from the grave-clothes, burst from the tomb,
    And conquered the clouds of night!
For nails and spear and lash and cross
    Could never put out that light!

(*The last four lines are repeated, in a rising spirit of triumph. Kneeling figures now fill the stage, and the light increases. Still facing the tomb, they all repeat the* DISCIPLES' *earlier song.*)

CHORUS

I want to serve him,
    Body and soul,
Because I came to him empty,
    And he made me whole.

I want to give him
  All that's best of me,
Because I was a prisoner,
  And he set me free.

Is there a gift worth giving
To one who has made you live?
A richer and better living
Is all that I have to give.

I want to serve him,
  Body and soul,
Because I came to him empty,
  And he made me whole.
I want to give him
  All that's best of me,
Because I was a prisoner,
  And he set me free.

(*The lights come up full, and all the people on stage turn to the audience.*)

Chorus

All of the people,
In every land,
Must hear of this story
And understand.
Tell all the peoples
Of every land,
Love won the victory
By Jesus' hand.

Tell of his caring
So much that he came!
Tell of his sharing
Sorrow and shame!

All of the peoples,
Over the earth,
Must hear of his coming,
Hear of his birth;
Hear of his living
True to his call,
Hear of his dying,
Savior of all.

Tell of his prizing
Poor men as friends!
Tell of his rising,
To the world's ends!

All of the peoples,
In every land,
Must hear of this story
And understand.
Love won the victory
By Jesus' hand.
Tell all the peoples
Of every land!

(*As the song ends, the lights fade to a black-out.*)

3. SOME PARABLES OF JESUS

In this section some of Jesus' parables are put in dialogue form. A "parable" means literally, in Greek, the "throwing alongside" of two ideas. A story, or word picture, is used by a speaker or writer to illustrate the situation which he is describing.

Such illustrations are used in every language. They may be one-word metaphors: *burning* anger, a *tower* of strength, anxiety *gnawed* at him. Or the illustration may be expanded into a simile: "He was led like a lamb to the slaughter" (Isaiah); "The Assyrian came down like a wolf on the fold" (Byron); "Like quills upon the fretful porcupine" (Shakespeare). These similes, or comparisons, may spread out over several lines.

Another form of illustration is the parable, or story comparison. Aesop's fables were famous examples, and they have been copied in many languages.

When Jesus used parables, his listeners were already familiar with this type of illustration. There are some well-known examples in the Old Testament: Jotham's parable of the Trees seeking a King (Judges 9, 7); Nathan's rebuke to David in the story of the ewe lamb (II Samuel 12); and Isaiah's picture of God and the vineyard of Israel (Isaiah 5).

Jesus used this method of teaching to perfection. He took familiar situations, and told vivid stories, in which not a word was wasted. In the shortest parables there is hardly a story: for example, the Mustard Seed (Matthew 13, 31-32). But the longer parables introduce a large number of characters, each wonderfully described in a very few words. Even a four-verse parable like "The Widow and the Judge" (Scene Two) brings the characters to life with amazing clarity.

The stories are usually timeless. They do not depend upon an ancient setting to be understood. We all lose money. We all know men who are obsessed with possessions. We all see injured people by the roadside. Therefore I have thought it best to use contemporary contexts. You could rewrite the stories in many other ways; and you certainly should look up other parables which Jesus spoke, and make scenes out of them.

SCENE ONE: THE TALENTS

Bible reference: Matthew 25, 14-30

CHARACTERS: THE PRESIDENT, MR. GOLDMAN
      TOM BROWN
      STAN PARSONS
      JOHN TURNER

The setting is the PRESIDENT'S *office of a big corporation. The* PRESIDENT *is at his desk. He picks up a telephone.*

PRESIDENT: Celia? Send Tom Brown in, will you?

 (*He writes for a minute, until* TOM *enters.*)

BROWN: You wanted me, sir?
PRESIDENT: Yes, Tom. Sit down, will you?
BROWN: Thanks.
PRESIDENT: As you know, Tom, I shall be away for nearly six months. We have to expand our foreign markets, and I think I can open up something big. But it will put a lot of responsibility on you.
BROWN: I think I can take it
PRESIDENT: So do I. Now, here's my idea. You will take over full responsibility for production while I'm gone. That means you'll be spending half a million a month. A lot of money, Tom. But you know the opportunities we have, if we're ready to use them.
BROWN: Yes, sir. Don't you worry. I'll be glad to get my teeth into it.
PRESIDENT: Good! And Tom—one more thing. I'm going to put sales in the hands of Stan Parsons. That's another big job. Do you think you two can work together?
BROWN: He's the right man, Mr. Goldman. He'll make a good job of it, and I'm sure we can work things out together.
PRESIDENT: Great, Tom! As you know, that will leave John Turner. He might have been in line for either job, but—well—
BROWN: I think I know what you mean. John's all right while he works under your eye, but— Couldn't he look after our downtown store, sir?
PRESIDENT: That's just what I had in mind, Tom. I'm glad you think it's a good idea. It will give him responsibility, without too big a part in our main operation. Well, thanks, Tom. You've

been a great help. I'll see the other two next. Good luck!

BROWN: And to you too, Mr. Goldman. Have a good trip, but
bust the market open!

(BROWN *goes out.* GOLDMAN *writes for a minute, then asks
his secretary over the telephone to send in* PARSONS. PARSONS
enters.)

PARSONS: You wanted to see me, Mr. Goldman?

PRESIDENT: Yes, Stan. It won't take long, and I hope it's good
news. Sit down!

PARSONS: Thank you, sir.

PRESIDENT: Here it is in a nutshell. While I'm away, I want you
to take over the Sales organization. That means keeping in close
touch with the 18 sales representatives, keeping an eye on pric-
ing, advertising, and a hundred other things. A big job. Will you
do it?

PARSONS: Will I do it? Wow! That's the best tonic I ever had, sir.
I'll do it all right!

PRESIDENT: Good, Stan! I like your spirit. We'll have a more detailed meeting tomorrow. I just wanted to be sure that the main
decisions were out of the way today.

PARSONS: Thanks, Mr. Goldman. You won't regret it, I promise
you!

(PARSONS *goes out. After a pause,* GOLDMAN *picks up the
desk telephone.*)

PRESIDENT: Celia? If John Turner is in his office, ask him to come
in, will you?

(*He sits writing, until there is a knock.*)

PRESIDENT: Come in! Oh, hello, John. Take a seat.

TURNER: Thank you, Mr. Goldman.

PRESIDENT: I've been talking to Tom Brown about our operation,
during the time when I shall be out of the country.

TURNER: Oh yes, sir. We're certainly going to miss you. Things
depend on you so much here.

PRESIDENT: Nobody's indispensable, John. You'll all have some
extra responsibility, that's all.

TURNER: Yes, of course.

PRESIDENT: What I'd like you to do is to take charge of our
downtown store, John. Will you do that?

TURNER: The downtown store? Yes, sir, if that's what you'd like me to do. Things have been a bit slow down there lately, haven't they?

PRESIDENT: All the more challenge to build it up, John. See what you can do.

TURNER: I will, sir, of course. I'll try to keep things from slipping.

PRESIDENT: All right, John. Look over this report, and come in and see me later in the week.

TURNER: I will, sir. I'm sure I'll have a lot of questions.

(*Six months later, all four men are sitting in the* PRESIDENT's *office, drinking coffee.*)

PRESIDENT: Well, that's the picture of what I have been doing, gentlemen. Now let me hear from you. Tom?

BROWN: Here are the figures, sir. We've had a great year. As you can see, production rose by thirty per cent. We were able to—

PRESIDENT: All right, Tom. You've said enough. I'll study it all later. But thirty per cent! That's a fantastic achievement. I certainly chose the right man for the job.

BROWN: Stan gave me first class backing, sir. Wait till you hear what he has to say!

PRESIDENT: Well, Stan?

PARSONS: The full effect of Tom's increased production won't be felt till next year, Mr. Goldman; but we've already put our sales up twenty per cent. Here's a summary of the Sales Representatives' reports, and—

PRESIDENT: I think the best thing for me to do is to go away again! You two have worked miracles, and I know it meant long hours and real loyalty to the firm. Thanks, Stan! Now, John, how did things go downtown?

TURNER: So-so, Mr. Goldman. There were a lot of difficulties to contend with, you know, and—

PRESIDENT: We all have those. I don't want to hear about the difficulties. What were the results?

TURNER: Well, sir, my report isn't quite ready yet; but I think we should be just about in the same position as when you left.

PRESIDENT: With a thirty per cent rise in production, and all our other sales up twenty per cent? That isn't good enough, John, is it?

TURNER: But, sir, you have to make allowances for—

PRESIDENT: That's where you're wrong, John. I'm tired of making allowances for you. You're capable, but you just haven't got what it takes. I'm afraid you'll have to look for something easier to do elsewhere, John. You aren't suited for this business. Tom, make arrangements to take over John's work in addition to your own, will you? You've shown you can do it.

TURNER: But, sir—

(*More dialogue could be improvised. Let the* PRESIDENT *report on his foreign tour, and all of them discuss future plans.*)

POINTS FOR DISCUSSION: Do you use your talents? A large part of our sinfulness consists of wasted opportunities—running away from responsibility.

SCENE TWO: THE WIDOW AND THE JUDGE

Bible reference: Luke 18, 1-8

CHARACTERS: THE JUDGE
HIS GOLFING PARTNER
THE WIDOW

The setting can be a golf course. The JUDGE *is talking to his* PARTNER, *as they walk to the tee. Improvise conversation about the game, the weather, etc. The* JUDGE *gets ready to drive off his ball, as the* WIDOW *enters.*

WIDOW: Judge Walters!

JUDGE: Who is it? What are you doing here?

WIDOW: I have to see you.

JUDGE: Out here? This is my day off. Call my Secretary for an appointment. (*He turns away, and prepares to hit the ball.*)

WIDOW: I have called, many times. You're always too busy to see a woman with no money.

PARTNER: Now, look here, woman, you're being a nuisance. Get away!

WIDOW: A nuisance! Oh, yes! If you'd suffered as I have, you would be a nuisance. I'm going to get the Judge to listen, if I have to follow you both all around the course.

JUDGE: For the last time, will you leave me alone?

WIDOW: For the last time, no! I want justice. You may be the laziest man in the City, but you are the Judge. Now will you listen or will you not?

JUDGE: I will not. And in a minute I shall call the Secretary of the Club and have you thrown out.

(*She quickly picks up his clubs and begins to run away.*)

WIDOW: All right. You asked for it.

JUDGE: (*Running after her*) Stop! What are you doing? Stop her, somebody! Look—come back here, and tell me what you want.

WIDOW: You mean that?

JUDGE: Yes, yes. Anything to get you out of here.

WIDOW: (*Returning*) All right. You've made a promise. If you'll just listen it won't take five minutes.

JUDGE: Sorry, John. It's the only thing to do. Now, sit down on this bench and tell me about it.

(*Ask the girls in the class to make up stories for the* WIDOW *to tell the* JUDGE.)

POINTS FOR DISCUSSION: Verse one: "Men ought always to pray, and not to faint" (that is, give up). If a lazy, bad-tempered Judge listened because he saw no way out, surely a loving God will listen to our prayers. Do you care about praying as much as the Widow cared about getting justice?

SCENE THREE: OUT-OF-TOWN GUESTS

Bible reference: Luke 11, 1-13

CHARACTERS: THE MAN AT THE DOOR
THE MAN IN BED
THE WOMAN IN BED

The setting is a home, at night. The sleeping family can have as many members as you wish, although there are only three speaking parts. The family are sleeping and the room is dark. A clock strikes midnight. A loud knock on the door.

MAN IN BED: What on earth was that?

WOMAN IN BED: Mm?
MAN IN BED: I thought I heard something.
WOMAN IN BED: Mm.
MAN IN BED: (*Angrily*) I suppose I dreamed it.

(*Another knock.*)

MAN IN BED: Who could that be?
MAN AT DOOR: Jim! Sally! Are you there?
MAN IN BED: Who is that? What do you want?
MAN AT DOOR: Jim, we've just had guests arrive from out of town. Could I borrow some bread?
MAN IN BED: At this time of night? Go away, for Heaven's sake!
MAN AT DOOR: Oh, come along, Jim. I really need it. These people—
MAN IN BED: Look, we're all in bed. Can't you leave us alone?
MAN AT DOOR: What sort of neighbor are you? Can't you see this is a crisis?
MAN IN BED: Sally, can't you get rid of the man? Get him his bread, and maybe he'll go away.
WOMAN IN BED: Mm? (*She never wakes up all through the scene.*)
MAN IN BED: Oh, Sally! You're hopeless!
MAN AT DOOR: I wouldn't bother you if there were any stores open, Jim. But—
MAN IN BED: O-o-o-o-h! (*He jumps out of bed and runs to the kitchen and then to the door.*) Take your bread and get out of here, you idiot! I hope it's stale.
MAN AT DOOR: Well, don't make such a song and dance. I only asked for a little bread. Some people just can't—
MAN IN BED: (*Slamming the door and stumbling back to bed*) A-a-a-a-h! Guests from out of town! Now I shall never get back to sleep.
WOMAN IN BED: Mm?

POINTS FOR DISCUSSION: Notice that this humorous story, very similar to the previous parable, is placed by Luke immediately after the Lord's Prayer. Jesus would often be asked, "Does God really care about our prayers?" Yes, he says. Even you would grudgingly get out of bed to give a neighbor bread at night, if he went on asking you. Surely God is much more ready to hear our prayers. The thing that must hurt him is if we are too indifferent to ask.

Act the scene again, this time swapping the roles of the 'Man in Bed' and the 'Woman in Bed.' Let him be the one who sleeps through the incident.

SCENE FOUR: THE CARS ON THE HILL

Bible reference: Luke 18, 9-14, the parable of the Pharisee and the Publican

CHARACTERS: The Cadillac Driver
His Wife
The Jalopy Driver
His Girlfriend

The setting is a steep hill: first, the road near the bottom of the climb; then, near the top; then near the bottom again. A very old jalopy is broken down by the roadside. The girl stands by it. The boy who owns it is stretched out underneath it.

GIRL: Oh, John! Are we ever going to get up this hill?
BOY: Don't worry! We will, one day.
GIRL: Here comes a Cadillac. Maybe they'll help. (*She waves at the Cadillac as it passes, but the people in it take no notice.*) No good! What do they care about people like us?
BOY: If we can just change that wheel, and stop the clutch slipping and then get her to start, we'll make it yet!
GIRL: Oh, John! All those things?

> (*The scene changes to a place near the top of the hill. The Cadillac engine fades out, and it comes to a halt.*)

OWNER: What's wrong with this car?
WIFE: Try starting it again, dear!
OWNER: What do you think I'm doing? These modern engines are hopeless!

> (*Continue this dialogue. He gets more and more angry.*)

> WIFE: I hardly like to mention it, but don't you think we may be out of gas?
> OWNER: Out of gas! You know I never run out of gas.
> WIFE: The gauge did say empty—

OWNER: Then it must be out of order. I *know* I had plenty of gas.

WIFE: Yes, dear. Only—

OWNER: Look, Helen, if you don't have anything more helpful to say, please keep quiet. I tell you, I never ran out of gas in my life.

WIFE: No, dear. Then we'll wait for someone to come by, shall we?

(*The scene returns to the car at the bottom of the hill.*)

GIRL: That sounded more hopeful.

BOY: Yes, I believe she's going to start. (*Continue this dialogue until he jumps in the car with a shout of triumph.*) We did it!

GIRL: Poor John! You do look a sight.

BOY: What does that matter? Let's go. (*They begin to climb slowly. They come opposite the Cadillac.*)

WIFE: Here comes someone. 'Oh, it's that old car that was stuck at the bottom of the hill.

BOY: (*Stopping just in front of them*) Can we help you, sir?

OWNER: Thank you. If you would be so good as to call the Auto Club and ask them to come and tow us in—

BOY: What's the trouble?

OWNER: Just the usual bad workmanship. None of the cars are properly built nowadays.

BOY: Mind if I have a look? I just fixed this old bus up.

OWNER: If you like. (*He climbs out, and the* BOY *gets in and tries to start the car.*)

BOY: Sir, I think I know the trouble.

OWNER: Oh, really? What is it?

BOY: It's very simple. You're out of gas.

OWNER: Don't be ridiculous! Do you really think I don't know how much gas I have? Now please go and let someone tow us in.

BOY: But—all you need is a little gas. As it happens, I have a spare can.

OWNER: Look, boy, I asked you a simple question. Will you, or will you not, go and call the Auto Club? I am not out of gas!

WIFE: Henry, please—

OWNER: Be quiet, Helen! You know nothing about the car.

GIRL: Come on, John. Let's go!

BOY: O.K. If that's the way he wants it. But even a Cadillac won't run without gas.

POINTS FOR DISCUSSION: In the Life of Jesus, Scene Seven, we met these two men as Jesus originally described them: the self-satisfied, smartly dressed man in the front pew, counting his virtues ("I've made my pledge to the Church; I gave to the United Fund; I contribute to my Service Club, and to the Hospital"); and the man from skid-row, desperate and degraded, who has crept into a Church because he longs to find God, but who doesn't think himself good enough to be there at all.

Jesus made it clear that there are no "righteous" people; only those who long to be better, and those who are satisfied with themselves as they are. The former have a chance to reach God, however far away they are—the Prodigal Son started his return journey from a pig-sty. The latter can never move nearer God until they admit their need.

Bunyan's description of the Hill Difficulty, in *Pilgrim's Progress*, would make a good companion story to this scene.

SCENE FIVE: THE RICH FARMER

Bible reference: Luke 12, 15-21

CHARACTERS: TOM DRAKE, the farmer
                  NORA, his wife
                  LEN DAVIS, a builder
                  DOCTOR BENNETT

The setting is the living room of a big farmhouse. TOM *and* LEN *are looking at plans laid on a table.*

LEN: You're sure you want a silo that big, Tom?
TOM: What do you mean? You're a builder, aren't you? Get on with it and build what I ask for.
LEN: Oh, sure. I'll build it. I just don't want you to change your mind in the middle.
TOM: Look, Len. I've worked my heart out on this land, and now I've got my reward. Since I bought out Stevens, and added the

land beyond the Highway, I've trebled my crop. And it's going on up and up. I need that silo, and I need it quickly!

(NORA *enters during this speech.*)

LEN: O.K., I'll have it up for you in three months.

TOM: Make it two, Len!

LEN: What's the mad rush?

TOM: To store my crop, man! I can't let good grain rot. We've got to expand.

NORA: Here's your coffee. Now don't get excited, Tom. You know what Doctor Bennett said.

LEN: That's right, Tom. Take it easy! What's the sense in trying to be twice as rich as you are already?

TOM: Stop bugging me, both of you! (*Shouting*) Do I own this place or do I not? I want that barn pulled down and the new silo built by—

(*He collapses, his hands to his chest.*)

LEN: On the couch, quick. I'll loosen his collar.

NORA: Oh, God! Tom! Tom!

(LEN *runs to the telephone.*)

LEN: Doc Bennett? Len Davis. I'm at Tom's. He's had a heart attack, I think. Yeah. At once. O.K. He'll be here as soon as he can.

TOM: What happened? I—

LEN: Now, Tom. Don't try to talk.

TOM: Build—the silo!

LEN: Yes, yes, Tom. Don't worry!

NORA: Oh, Tom! We don't need more money. I only want you well. I wish I knew what to give him.

LEN: He's unconscious.

(DOCTOR BENNETT *hurries in.*)

NORA: Oh, Doctor. Thank you for being so quick.

DOCTOR: All right, let's have a look at him. (*He examines Tom. A long pause.*) Hm.

NORA: Well, Doctor? How is he?

DOCTOR: Nora, you're a brave woman, and I've known you a long time. It's no use telling you lies. Tom is dying.

NORA: Oh, no! (*She weeps.*) Why couldn't he slow down? Why did he have to drive himself to death?

DOCTOR: That's the way he is, Nora. Tom had to have things bigger and bigger.

LEN: The last thing he said to me was, "Build the silo!"

DOCTOR: Poor old Tom! I'm afraid that new silo was one excitement too many. I'll do what I can, Nora; but I don't want you to have any false hopes. Would Tom like to see the Pastor, do you think? He may regain consciousness.

NORA: Yes. Please call him, and ask him to come. Tom is a good man. If only—

LEN: If he'd just given himself time to live.

NORA: We were going on a trip. He talked about retiring, after the silo was finished.

DOCTOR: With people like Tom there's always one more thing, Nora. Now how about you drinking a cup of that coffee, and I'll call Pastor Bowman?

POINTS FOR DISCUSSION: Compare the Life of Jesus, Scene 10, and the notes on it. Clearly the ordinary Christian has to have money and possessions; a job, a car, insurance, etc. But do not most of us make far too much of security, and in many cases greed? Is our materialism a good way to find and share happiness? Jesus criticized not so much the possession of riches as the reliance upon them; and he hated any kind of meanness in face of other people's needs. Nora says that Tom was a good man, and probably she was right; but Jesus uses the farmer as an example of wrong values and priorities.

SCENE SIX: THE LOST SHEEP

Bible reference: Luke 15, 1-7

CHARACTERS: THE SHEPHERD
      THE LOST SHEEP
      FLOCK OF SHEEP

This setting is suitable for very young children, with the teacher or an older student as the SHEPHERD. *The sheepfold is an enclosure of desks or chairs, with a narrow opening. The* SHEEP *are crawling into the fold. The* SHEPHERD *touches them gently with his crook.*

SHEPHERD: Come on, now! Don't push! Plenty of time, twenty-four, twenty-five— Easy, there! You'll get in much quicker if you don't knock each other over. (*Improvise more like this. The sheep can 'Baa' meanwhile.*) Eighty-six, eighty-seven. Nearly in, now. Time for a rest. Ninety-seven, ninety-eight, ninety-nine— Hey, what's this? One missing! In you go! Now you look after yourselves, while I go and find number one hundred. Don't worry! No wolf can jump that wall.

(*He closes the door of the fold, and walks away, calling. For some time he talks to himself, and calls the lost sheep. After an interval, a feeble 'Baa' is heard.*)

SHEPHARD: Where are you? O.K. I heard you, but do it again.
SHEEP: (*A little louder*) Baa!
SHEPHERD: Over there, are you? You silly animal, I still can't find you.

(*Continue this for some time. The* SHEEP *is hidden behind a desk. At length the "Baa" is loud and close. The* SHEPHERD *sees the* SHEEP.)

SHEPHERD: There! Trust you to fall into the first ditch you come across! Now don't struggle. I'm only trying to help you. (*He lifts the* SHEEP, *and starts back toward the fold.*) Hurt? No, I don't believe you are. Just lost and frightened; and that isn't so good, is it, old funny-face? Never mind! We'll soon have you back.

(*Loud "Baa's" from the fold as they approach, answered by the lost* SHEEP.)

SHEPHERD: See? They hear us coming. "Welcome home!" That's what your friends are saying. (*He drops the* SHEEP *into the fold.*) There you go! Just try to keep out of trouble in the future, will you? To oblige me? I have enough walking to do without going back to look for stragglers. All right, now. Settle down, all of you! I'll sing you David's song, shall I?

If possible, sing Psalm 23 or a setting of it—"Brother James' Air," or the hymn "The King of Love My Shepherd Is." David would have used an instrument like a guitar, so a simple setting is best.

SCENE SEVEN: THE LOST COIN

Bible reference: Luke 15, 8-10

CHARACTERS: MRS. MARTINEZ
      MR. MARTINEZ
      MRS. JACKSON
      MRS. BARTON

MRS. MARTINEZ *sits at a table in her small house. She has a teapot·in her hands.*

MRS. MARTINEZ: There! Soon we shall be able to buy our new home, and there won't be all these dirty corners, and a leaky roof. Let me count it again! (*She pours the big gold coins out on the table. Some of them fall on the floor.*) Here, not so fast! Careful! You don't want to run away from me, do you? Now: 1, 2, 3, 4, 5, 6, 7, 8, 9—oh, no! It can't be— Where is it? Oh, God, where is the tenth coin? (*She looks for it desperately.*) Pablo! Quick! Quick! I've lost a coin. Come quickly!

(PABLO, *her husband, comes through the bedroom door, very sleepy.*)

PABLO: What is it, Maria? What are you doing, up at this hour? It isn't even light yet.

MRS. MARTINEZ: I've lost one of our coins. We have to find it! We have to!

(*Improvise dialogue, as they look for it, and begin to quarrel with each other. Enter* MRS. JACKSON *and* MRS. BARTON *by the front door.*)

MRS. JACKSON: Whatever is the matter with you people?

MRS. BARTON: You're waking up the whole street. What is it?

MRS. MARTINEZ: It's nothing. Please go away and leave us alone!

PABLO: Nothing? You lose a tenth of our whole savings, and call it nothing?

MRS. MARTINEZ: Be quiet, Pablo!

MRS. JACKSON: Savings? You mean you've lost some money?

MRS. MARTINEZ: Yes, but I'll find it. I've got to find it. Pablo, hand me that broom! (*She searches under every piece of furniture. The others get in the way trying to help.*)

MRS. BARTON: Try under the rug!

MRS. MARTINEZ: I've looked there. Oh, I wish you'd leave me alone!

MRS. JACKSON: We're only trying to help you.

MRS. MARTINEZ: (*Retrieving the coin from under a corner cupboard*) There! Oh, thank God, I've found it!

PABLO: That's a blessing, anyway. In the future, don't be so—

MRS. MARTINEZ: Stop scolding me, Pablo, and put the coffee on! We're all going to celebrate.

PABLO: Celebrate what? I don't see—

MRS. MARTINEZ: You wouldn't! You're just a man. Sit down, neighbors!

MRS. BARTON: Thank you, Maria.

MRS. JACKSON: Isn't that wonderful for you?

MRS. MARTINEZ: Oh, yes, it's wonderful! To think of it—I thought my coin was lost, and now I've found it!

POINTS FOR DISCUSSION: "Even so, I tell you, there is joy before the angels of God over one sinner who repents." Like the last parable, this one shows how deeply God loves the outcasts, who are hard to reach. Notice that in our scene Mrs. Martinez found the coin by using her broom. To be a broom, doing God's work and looking for the lost and lonely, is the essence of being a Christian.

SCENE EIGHT: THE GOOD SAMARITAN

Bible reference: Luke 10, 25-37

CHARACTERS: A MERCHANT
HIS TWO SERVANTS
TWO BANDITS
THE GOOD SAMARITAN
HIS TWO SERVANTS
INNKEEPER
A PRIEST
A LEVITE, a highly respected religious leader

The setting is the lonely road from Jerusalem to Jericho, not far from an inn. The MERCHANT *walks on, with his two* SERVANTS *behind him carrying his bags. Improvise conversation while they cross and recross the stage. They talk about the heat and are eager to reach the inn a little way ahead. The* BANDITS *are concealed behind "rocks." They jump out and fire repeatedly at the* MERCHANT, *who staggers and falls. The* SERVANTS *hesitate for a moment, then drop the bags and run off.*

FIRST BANDIT: Let's get out of here with this stuff.
SECOND BANDIT: I'll take his wallet. (*He rolls the* MERCHANT *over.*)
FIRST BANDIT: Is he dead?
SECOND BANDIT: Not yet. Here it is. Let's go.

(*They run off. The* MERCHANT *lies still, groaning. The* PRIEST *walks on, sees the* MERCHANT *and stops, looking around nervously*)

MERCHANT: (*Holding out his hand*) Help! They shot me.
PRIEST: I—I'll send help. (*He hurries off.*)
MERCHANT: Don't leave me! Oh, God, God!

(*After a pause, the* LEVITE *comes on.*)

MERCHANT: Sir, Sir! I've been shot by bandits.
LEVITE: Bandits!
MERCHANT: Please help me! Water!
LEVITE: I—I don't dare wait. It would be suicide. (*He runs off.*)
MERCHANT: Oh, God, have pity on me! I'm going to die!

(*After another pause, the* SAMARITAN *comes on, with his two* SERVANTS. *They should be talking cheerfully as they come.*)

MERCHANT: Sir, Sir!

(*The* SAMARITAN *stops.*)

SAMARITAN: You're wounded! What happened?
MERCHANT: Bandits. They—
SERVANT ONE: Bandits! They're probably still here.
SERVANT TWO: Hadn't we better get out of here quick, sir?
SAMARITAN: As soon as we can move him safely. (*He kneels by the* MERCHANT.) Let's try to stop that bleeding.
MERCHANT: May the Lord reward you!
SAMARITAN: Don't try to talk. You'll be fine when we can get you to the Inn. Here, you two. Help me lift him.

(*Improvise dialogue as they lift the* MERCHANT *and carry him*

carefully away. The scene moves to the inn door. The SAMARI-
TAN *knocks, and the* INNKEEPER *comes out.*)

SAMARITAN: Open up! We have a man out here, badly injured.

INNKEEPER: What's this, then? Trouble?

SAMARITAN: Bandits. He's been shot, but I don't think it's too
bad. Can we have a room for him, and send for a Doctor?

INNKEEPER: Sure. Bring him in. Sarah! (*He calls back through the
door.*) Number 17. Get the bed ready. (*The two* SERVANTS *carry
the* MERCHANT *in.*) Looks like a rich man. From Jerusalem, I
suppose.

SAMARITAN: I don't know. I never saw him before.

(*The* PRIEST *and the* LEVITE *come from inside the inn.*)

INNKEEPER: Never saw him before? You took a risk, didn't you,
stopping to pick him up?

SAMARITAN: Traveling is always risky on this road.

PRIEST: Excuse me. What's the trouble?

LEVITE: We saw a man being carried in.

INNKEEPER: Yes. He's been shot by bandits, and this gentleman
picked him up. Excuse me, sir. Where are you from? You don't
look like a Judaean.

SAMARITAN: No. I am from Samaria.

PRIEST: (*Murmurs*) A Samaritan!

INNKEEPER: Is that so? Well, if I may say so, sir, you're a brave
man. Do you mind if I ask about the gentleman's check, sir?

SAMARITAN: Oh, yes. Well, I expect he has money at home, but of
course they will have stripped him for the present. Let me leave
you this; and if there is any difficulty, I shall return this way
when my business in Jericho is finished.

PRIEST: Perhaps I could help, and my friend here. We—

INNKEEPER: Come to think of it, you came down that road, didn't
you? Funny thing you didn't see him.

(*Members of the class could be asked to say how they think the*
PRIEST *and* LEVITE *would answer. Would they lie, or own up to
having "passed by on the other side," and be ashamed. Of course,
in Jesus' story they are not at the inn.*)

POINTS FOR DISCUSSION: The parable is told in answer to
the Lawyer's question, "Who is my neighbor?" Jesus deliberately
took a member of an unpopular group to be the person who

showed courage and compassion. It is a story which challenges "good" and respectable people to look at their lives, and to ask themselves whether their goodness is a facade which covers over their selfishness. How much do we go out and look for the people who need our help? How much courage do we show in giving help when it could easily be dangerous? Do we retreat into the easy way of giving pocketbook help, but little or none of the effort which costs sacrifice of ourselves?

Ask the class to make up instances of "Good Samaritan" situations in our own time, or to quote real cases. As we know too well, a Samaritan who stops to give help can end up in bad trouble. You could rewrite the play, making the "Merchant" a plant, in league with the bandits, so that when the Samaritan stops to help him he is surrounded and held up himself.

The parable is one of the simplest which Jesus told, and it raises the central question of a Christian's life: How do we put into action the commandment to love our neighbors?

4. THE PRODIGAL SON

Bible reference: Luke 15, 11-31

CHARACTERS: NARRATOR
FATHER (JOE)
MOTHER (MARY)
ELDER Brother (PETE)
PRODIGAL SON (JOHN)
STEWARD
DEVIL
GIRL IN THE TAVERN
BOY IN THE TAVERN
BARMAID-WAITRESS
THREE TEMPTRESSES
CHORUS of guests and servants

NOTE: This play is designed for reading or for presentation in modern dress, with or without the musical score.

SCENE ONE   Main room of the Father's house
SCENE TWO   The Prodigal's bedroom
SCENE THREE   A roadside
SCENE FOUR   A tavern
SCENE FIVE   A pigsty
SCENE SIX   Outside the Father's house
SCENE SEVEN   Main room of the Father's house

Only the simplest props are needed to suggest these scenes, as in-dicated in the stage directions.

SCENE ONE: MAIN ROOM OF THE
FATHER'S HOUSE

The stage is empty, except for a dining table, set for four people, C. General lighting, no spots. The FATHER *enters R., reading the evening paper. Then the* MOTHER *enters L., carrying food.*

FATHER: Need any help, Mary?
MOTHER: No, thanks, Joe. It's all in. How was your day?
FATHER: Fine! We're heading for a good harvest.
MOTHER: Were the boys with you?
FATHER: Pete was there, helping Manuel. John never showed up.
MOTHER: It always seems to be that way.
FATHER: I know. The men on the ranch all like John, but—
MOTHER: And the girls! He only needs to turn on that charm—
FATHER: But Pete is the one who does the work.
MOTHER: I'll call them for supper.
FATHER: No. I'll do that. (*He goes R.*) Pete! John!
ELDER BROTHER: (*Hurrying in*) I'm ready for it. That was some
   day!
FATHER: Have you seen John?
ELDER BROTHER: I've heard him—or his stereo, full blast. He gets
   back from the beach when he thinks dinner's ready.
MOTHER: Then why isn't he here?
ELDER BROTHER: Because he's taking a shower—what else? And I
   need to hurry. I've got to get back to the barn before dark, and
   check with Manuel—
PRODIGAL: (*Hurrying in*) What's for dinner?
MOTHER: Oh, John! We've been waiting for you.
ELDER BROTHER: Some of us have work to do.
FATHER: All right. Let's sit down and say a blessing.

   (*They sit,* MOTHER *with her back to the audience,* ELDER
   BROTHER *on her right, the* PRODIGAL *on her left. They all
   hold hands, except the* PRODIGAL.)

PRODIGAL: Do we have to hold hands, like kids?
FATHER: If you want to eat dinner with us, John, you give thanks
   with the rest of us.

   (*He speaks or sings the first line, then the others join in.*)

   Thank God for all his blessings!
   To him be glory and praise!
   Thank God for all his blessings!
   Gladly our voices we raise!
For all the things that he gives, for the light upon our way,
For all the love and the care that he shows us every day!
For the food upon the table, and the roof above our head,

God be praised and worshipped, Oh! God be prais-ed and worshipp-ed.

(*They eat in silence. Lights narrow to spot on* NARRATOR, *off-
stage R., and spot on the dining table.*)

NARRATOR: (*sings*) A certain man had two sons.
      A certain man had two sons.
      One stayed at home, and was solid and slow;
      The other said, Oh let me go!
      The other said, Oh let me go!

(*The* CHORUS *consists of servants and guests, who will come
on stage for the final supper scene. They may be of all ages.
They stand with the* NARRATOR, *offstage R., or below stage.*)

CHORUS (*sings*)

He wasn't a boy, and he wasn't a man,
He was half way between, when the story began.
He was young, he was restless,' he didn't know why,
But he knew there were things he was longing to try.
He was hungry for life, and he wasn't content
To remain in the place where his youth had been spent.
He was headstrong and bold, and he hadn't a care;
He was burning to go, but he didn't know where.

(*At the words, "He was hungry for life," spot on* FIRST
TEMPTRESS, *R. takes spot off* NARRATOR. FIRST TEMPTRESS *is
dressed for the beach, and holds a surfboard, offering it to the*
PRODIGAL. *He gets up and goes toward her, but the spot
blacks out as he approaches her. A spot then shows the* SEC-
OND TEMPTRESS, *L., holding out a motorcycle helmet. The*
PRODIGAL *goes toward her, but the spot blacks out before he
can reach her. Spot R. then shows the* THIRD TEMPTRESS. *She
is obviously drugged, and holds out a hypodermic. The* PRODI-
GAL *goes toward her, stops suddenly, and slowly backs to the
table, and sits. The spot goes off her. The other three have
continued to eat, taking no notice of the* PRODIGAL's *"dream".
A dance sequence for the* PRODIGAL *and the* TEMPTRESSES
would be appropriate. Music of the CHORUS *is played through
a second time during the* TEMPTRESSES' *appearances.*)

(*General lights come on again, as the* PRODIGAL *returns to his
seat. The four are eating.*)

NARRATOR

A certain man had two sons.
A certain man had two sons.
One stayed at home, and was solid and slow.
The other said, Oh let me go!
The other said, Oh let me go!

(*The* PRODIGAL *jumps up from his chair, and moves about the stage as he sings.*)

PRODIGAL

Give me the portion of mine inheritance,
Give me the money that's mine to spend!
Give me the portion of mine inheritance;
I want to live till it comes to an end!
Give me everything I'm entitled to,
It's unfair of you to refuse.
Give me the money in cash immediately;
I'm old enough to spend what I choose!

(*The* FATHER *produces a leather purse from his pocket.*)

I want to go, I want to live,
I want to take what life can give,
I want to have all of the things
That a purse full of money always brings.
Give me the portion of mine inheritance;
I want to live before I must die. (*Snatches the purse.*)
Give me the money that I'm entitled to—
I'm in a hurry to say "Good-bye"!

CHORUS: He's in a hurry to say "Good-bye"!
PRODIGAL: I'm in a hurry to say "Good-bye"!

(*He hurries off right. Black-out. Lights up on front of stage. The* PRODIGAL *comes on from R., with a pack on his back, whistling happily and walking quickly. The* CHORUS *sings the first verse of the next song, "He went into a far country." Going off L., the* PRODIGAL *quickly takes half of the things out of his pack, and opens a map. Then he walks back across the stage to R., slowly and thoughtfully, looking at the map. He sits down, and the front lights go out.*)

CHORUS (*sings*)

He went into a far country;

Watch him make his way.
He went into a far country,
Seeking a place to stay.
Will he find in a far country
Friends to take him in?
Will there be in a far country
Ways that lead to sin?

SCENE TWO: THE PRODIGAL'S BEDROOM

As the front lights go off, a spot comes on L., where the PRODI-
GAL's *bed has been placed. On it there is an untidy mixture of
bedding, clothes and books. The* MOTHER *comes in, stands by the
bed, and sings.*

MOTHER
An empty room, and a rumpled bed,
The clothes he wore, and the books he read,
All of them meaningless, all of them dead.
Whatever happened to love? Oh, whatever happened to love?
What happened to our love,
The thing that mattered most?
What stole away our happiness,
Until our dream was lost?
What happened to our trust,
Our laughter and our joy?
What happened to the tenderness
That tied us to our boy?

At the back of the closet the treasures are piled,
From the days when he chattered and laughed and smiled.
Whatever happened to my little child?
Whatever happened to love? Oh, whatever happened to love?
What happened to the days
When he came running in,
With tousled hair, and dirty face,
All eager to begin
To pour out all the tales
Of things that he had done—
Of joys and triumphs, plans and dreams—
What happened to my son?
What happened to our love? What happened to our love?

SCENE THREE: A ROADSIDE

As the MOTHER's *song ends, the spot goes out, and another spot shows the* PRODIGAL, *sitting R., looking at the map.*

PRODIGAL (*sings*)

There seem to be several people
Locked up inside of me,
Fighting a constant battle
For my identity.
Sometimes they keep me prisoner,
Sometimes they set me free.
Is one of them my true being?
Is one of them really me?
Who am I? Just a dreamer of dreams.
Who am I? Just a failure, it seems.
No—a hero, the idol of the crowd—
Timid, or arrogant; humble, or proud.
Who am I?

There seem to be several voices
Crying inside my heart.
Sometimes they sound in discords,
Each with a different part.
They're crying for recognition,
And sometimes I stop my ears;
For sometimes they bring me gladness,
And sometimes they bring me tears.
Who am I? I'm all ready to go!
Who am I? Why, the star of the show!
Included, respected—neglected, ignored;
Assured, or bewildered—ecstatic, or bored.
Who am I?

There seem to be several people,
Sewn up inside my skin,
Struggling to take possession.
Is one of them going to win?
For I want to know my meaning,
And I want to find my way.
Yes, I want to know why my heart beats so fast
While tomorrow follows today.
Who am I? Just a dreamer of dreams.

Who am I? Just a failure, it seems.
No—a hero, the idol of the crowd—
Timid, or arrogant, humble, or proud—
Accepted, rejected; aggressive, withdrawn;
Never consistent—uplifted, and torn—
A soul, or a robot; a mask, or a face—
Animal, or spirit—I must know my place.
Who am I?

SCENE FOUR: A TAVERN

While the CHORUS *sings the next verse, the bed is removed, and also the dining table. Two small tables are placed C. and R.C., with two chairs at each. The* BOY *and* GIRL, *both young and pleasant-looking, come and sit R.C. The* PRODIGAL *gets up, and slowly walks across stage, and off L. He quickly takes off his pack, smears blood on his face, and tears his shirt. Then he comes on again L., limping. Full lights come on slowly, and reveal the* DEVIL *R. He is smartly dressed in dark clothes, with a cane and bowler hat. The* BARMAID *also comes on R., and exchanges a joke with the* DEVIL. *Then she goes C., to take the order of the* BOY *and* GIRL *from behind their table.*

CHORUS

See him now in a far country,
Money in his purse.
Soon he finds, in a far country,
Things grow worse and worse.
Men may smile, in a far country,
While he pays in gold.
Poor men find, in a far country,
Friends grow hard and cold.

(*During this verse, the* PRODIGAL *has walked slowly C. The* DEVIL *bows to him, and mimes an invitation to enter the tavern and sit down. They sit at the table C., and the* DEVIL *summons the* BARMAID *and orders drinks. Music of the "Far Country" tune continues through this scene. The* DEVIL *takes out dice from his pocket, and rolls them. The* PRODIGAL, *half dazed with the drinks which the* BARMAID *keeps supplying, wins the first time, then steadily loses. After a while, the* DEVIL *points over his shoulder at the* GIRL, *and laughs. The*

PRODIGAL *rises unsteadily, and goes toward the* GIRL. *The*
BOY *rises, and pushes him away. The* PRODIGAL *falls heavily
into his chair. The* DEVIL *whispers to the* BARMAID, *who puts
a drug in the* PRODIGAL's *glass. She steals the purse from his
pocket, and the* DEVIL *snatches it from her. While the* PRODI-
GAL *is drinking, the* GIRL *sings.*)

GIRL

You can buy everything,
Money cannot fail;
But you can't buy happiness,
And love is not for sale.
You can buy flattery,
Comfort, and advice;
But you can't buy happiness,
And love has got no price.

Food and friendship, clothes and drink,
Luxury, and sex;
Music, murder, scent or mink—
You can pay by checks.

You can buy everything,
Money has its way;
But you can't buy happiness,
There is no price for happiness,
And love won't let you pay.

(*The* DEVIL *does not like this song. He hurries over to the
piano, and either plays himself, or causes the pianist to play, a
jazzed-up version of the music. The* THREE TEMPTRESSES
march on, and go through a dance sequence. They pull the
PRODIGAL *up, and each dances with him, though he can hardly
stand. They push him from one to the other, and finally he
falls C., as the music ends. The "Far Country" theme is
played again. The tables are moved, and the* DEVIL *and* BAR-
MAID *drag the* PRODIGAL *off R. A small piece of scenery, rep-
resenting a pigsty, is placed C., and a stool R.C. A little
puffed wheat or other cereal is sprinkled in the sty.*)

SCENE FIVE: A PIGSTY

As the music ends, the PRODIGAL *crawls quickly C., scrambling for
the food in the sty and eating greedily. Spot on the pigsty, other*

lights out. The DEVIL *comes on R., laughing, and sits on the stool.*

DEVIL (*sings*)

Now I've caught him.
Here's another victim, and I've caught him.
   He will not escape me,
For his money is vanished, and he finds he is banished
    And alone
       With me!

In the pigsty,
Literally and morally the pigsty,
   I will keep him prisoner;
He will find life is hollow while he still has to wallow
    With the pigs
       And me!

I must screen him
From the kind of love that could redeem him.
Never in the future do I mean him
To escape my clutches and be free.

I'm his master,
Leading him to ruin and disaster.
   He's an easy victim;
With his wine and his ladies, he will soon come to Hades
    And be friends
       With me!

(*The* PRODIGAL, *still grovelling on the ground, begins to sing. The* DEVIL'*s interjections are spoken.*)

PRODIGAL: (*Sings*) I'm in Hell!
DEVIL: You certainly are well on the way!
PRODIGAL: I'm in Hell!
DEVIL: It's up to me to see that you stay!
PRODIGAL: I'm hungry, I'm dirty, I haven't any friends.
DEVIL: That's usually the way this kind of thing ends.
PRODIGAL: I'm lonely, I'm desperate, my clothes are in tatters.
DEVIL: And you've no way out; that's the thing that really matters.
PRODIGAL: I'm in Hell!
DEVIL: Ah, well, my boy, you've no one else to blame.
PRODIGAL: Living Hell!

DEVIL: Alive or dead, it's very much the same.
PRODIGAL: I feed on scraps that are left in the gutter.
DEVIL: Sad, sad words for a lad like you to utter.
PRODIGAL: I sleep on straw that is foul and musty.
DEVIL: You do look a little bedraggled and dusty.

(*The* PRODIGAL *rises slowly to his knees.*)

PRODIGAL: Oh, God, I'm sorry!
DEVIL: That's quite enough of that; no praying!
PRODIGAL: Please, please, forgive me!
DEVIL: Whatever is the young fool saying?

(*The* DEVIL's *voice in the following lines passes from anger and alarm to a furious scream at the end.*)

PRODIGAL: Perhaps my father will give me pardon.
DEVIL: He won't, I tell you. His heart will harden.
PRODIGAL: Oh, merciful God! Am I damned for ever?
DEVIL: You can't go back, I tell you! Never! Never!

(*There is a clash of cymbals at the end of the song. The* PRODIGAL *sinks down, sobbing. Then, from far away, the* GIRL's *voice is heard. She sings the last verse of her song, unaccompanied.*)

GIRL (*off; singing*)
You can buy everything;
Money has its way.
But you can't buy happiness,
There is no price for happiness,
And love won't let you pay.

(*As the* GIRL *sings, the* PRODIGAL *slowly rises to his knees, to the anguish of the* DEVIL. *While the* PRODIGAL *sings the next song, he rises unsteadily to his feet.*)

PRODIGAL (*sings*)
I will rise and go to my Father,
    And tell him of all my sin.
I will knock at the door and entreat him
    To open and let me in.

I have been the cause of his sorrow,
    And brought disgrace on his name.
I have sinned so much against Heaven
    That I must return in shame.

I will say that I am not worthy
　　For his love to cherish and save.
I will beg for food and for shelter,
　　And work as a humble slave.

For the meanest place in his castle
　　Seems sweeter than life to me;
The home that I have forsaken,
　　The home where I long to be.

(*The* PRODIGAL *goes off R. to begin his journey home. The pigsty and stool are removed. The* DEVIL *goes L. angry and upset.*)

SCENE SIX: OUTSIDE THE FATHER'S HOUSE

The ELDER BROTHER *enters R. The* DEVIL *comes from L. and accosts him.*

DEVIL: Excuse me a moment, sir.
ELDER BROTHER: Who are you? What do you want?

(*The following words are spoken with a background accompaniment of chords on the piano.*)

DEVIL: I have come to give you news about your brother.
ELDER BROTHER: What? My brother?

DEVIL

There's a message he was very keen to send.
　　So I'm glad to have the chance
　　To prepare you in advance.
Understand that I am speaking as a friend.

I have come to let you know that he's returning.

ELDER BROTHER: What? Returning?

DEVIL

You will want to make him welcome, I am sure.
　　For, whatever he has done,
　　He is still your father's son,
And has had a lot of suffering to endure.

　What he needs is understanding and forgiveness;

ELDER BROTHER: What? Forgiveness!

DEVIL

To be treated as if nothing were amiss.
   Now that all his cash is spent
   He is ready to repent.
Greet him gladly, with a brother's loving kiss.

It will not, I think, affect your own position.

ELDER BROTHER: My position?

DEVIL

There is plenty left for him and you to share.
   He has forfeited his claim,
   But you could not bear the shame
Of denying him your tenderness and care.

So be ready any minute to receive him.

ELDER BROTHER: Me? Receive him?

DEVIL

Degradation has not robbed him of his charms.
   You will shortly have the joy
   Of welcoming the boy,
When he throws himself into his father's arms.

(*The* DEVIL *goes out R., laughing. The* ELDER BROTHER *goes off L. The* FATHER *enters, and stands C., looking over the audience for his son. From far away, at the back of the hall, the* PRODIGAL *is heard singing, unaccompanied, in a broken voice. He drags himself slowly toward the stage.*)

PRODIGAL (*sings*)

I will rise and go to my Father,
   And tell him of all my sin.
I will knock at the door, and entreat him
   To open and let me in.

(*The* FATHER *moves down C. As the* PRODIGAL *nears the stage, the* DEVIL *enters and kneels in front of him, making one last plea to him to turn back, but the* PRODIGAL, *now that his face is turned toward home, does not even see him. The* PRODIGAL *falls in front of his* FATHER.)

FATHER (*sings*)
Come home! Come home! Come home to me!
Come home! Come home! Come home to me!
My son was lost, and he is found again;
From far away I hear his voice.
He left his home, and is returned again;
I bid him welcome and rejoice.

FATHER and MOTHER
Come home! Come home! Come home to me!
Come home! Come home! Come home to me!

FATHER
Fling wide the gates, and bid him come again!
Let trumpets call and bells resound!
My son was lost, and he is home again,
My son was lost and he is found!

FATHER and MOTHER
Come home! Come home! Come home to me!
Come home! Come home! Come home to me!

SCENE SEVEN: MAIN ROOM OF THE FATHER'S HOUSE

While they sing, the FATHER *helps the* PRODIGAL *onto the stage. Manuel, the* STEWARD, *runs on from R., and embraces the* PRODIGAL. *He can also, if the director wishes, go to the* CHORUS *and be welcomed by them. After the song, the* FATHER *and* MOTHER *lead the* PRODIGAL *off L. The* STEWARD *summons other* SERVANTS, *including the* TEMPTRESSES, *who are now dressed as maids. They bring in a table, place on it a cloth, silver candlesticks and food and set four chairs behind it. This could be a dance routine, while the* STEWARD *sings.*

STEWARD
Put the best wine out on the table,
See that nothing shall lack!
Bring the fatted calf from the stable,
And welcome the Prodigal back!
Call the men who are out at the reaping,
Bid them hasten and come!

Wake up those who are resting or sleeping;
   Welcome the Prodigal home!
Call them here for the feast and the singing;
   Let the messengers run!
All the bells of the castle are ringing
   To welcome the Prodigal Son!

SERVANTS and CHORUS

Put the best wine out on the table,
   See that nothing shall lack!
Bring the fatted calf from the stable,
   And welcome the Prodigal back!
Call the men who are out at the reaping,
   Bid them hasten and come!
Wake up those who are resting or sleeping;
   Welcome the Prodigal home!
Call them here for the feast and the singing;
   Let the messengers run!
All the bells in the castle are ringing
   To welcome the Prodigal Son!

(*As the song ends, the* ELDER BROTHER *enters L. The* STEW-
ARD *and* SERVANTS *see him, and freeze where they are standing.*)

ELDER BROTHER (*spoken*)
   Why all this fuss?
What has he done to deserve it?
   Why all this fuss?
It makes me sick to observe it!
I'm told that he has spent his time with harlots and with
   thieves,
And eaten up the refuse that a pig or chicken leaves;
And when he comes back crawling, what a welcome he re-
   ceives!
   Why all this fuss?

   Why all this fuss?
Isn't it all rather hearty?
   Who thinks of us?
Why haven't I had a party?
It does me no good slaving here, as far as I can see.
I'm just a humble stay-at-home—no need to think of me!

Far better be a Prodigal, and get your pardon free!
    Why all this fuss?

    Why all this fuss?
What an absurd way to treat him!
    Why all this fuss?
This is a strange way to greet him!
He's cut his father's heritage effectively in half.
His conduct is disgraceful—and it really makes me laugh:
As soon as he comes whining home you kill the fatted calf!
    Damn all this fuss, I say—damn all this fuss!

(*As he finishes, the* FATHER *and* MOTHER *come on L., with
the* PRODIGAL. *He is dressed in clean clothes, and has bandages on some cuts. He limps slightly. While the music of
"Thank God For All His Blessings" is played softly, the* FA-
THER *and* MOTHER *lead the sons to their chairs behind the
table. The* FATHER *stands, with the* PRODIGAL *and the*
MOTHER *sitting to his left, and the* ELDER BROTHER *to his
right. The* SERVANTS *and* CHORUS *move up, and stand behind
the table in a semi-circle, during the third verse of the* FA-
THER's *song.*)

FATHER
There was a good shepherd,
    Who had a hundred sheep;
It was his work, and his delight
    His precious flock to keep.
And in the heat of Summer,
    And in the Winter cold,
He fed them on the mountains,
    And led them to their fold.

This shepherd would number
    His flock from day to day;
And he would leave them in the fold
    If one had gone astray.
He left them there together,
    The ninety and the nine,
And said, "I must seek for
    This one lost sheep of mine."

Now I am your shepherd,
    And master of you all;

And you, my son, have stayed with me
    And lived within my Hall.
But those who dwell in shelter
    Must not grow proud and cold,
But welcome home the lost ones
    Who come back to the fold.

        FATHER and CHORUS
Yes, whose who dwell in shelter
    Must not grow proud and cold,
But welcome home the lost ones
    Who come back to the fold.
So welcome him with feasting,
    And do not count the cost,
For this (my) son is found again
       (his)
(My) son whom (I) had lost.
(His)   (he)

5. THE WEDDING FEAST

Bible reference: Matthew 22, 1-14; Luke 14, 7-10

CHARACTERS: KING
SIMON
BARZILLAI
ELIAS
THREE MESSENGERS
GREEDY GUEST
HUMBLE GUEST
KING'S STEWARD
KING'S PAGE
PRINCE
PRINCE'S BRIDE
PHOTOGRAPHER
CAPTAIN
TWO PHARISEES
TWO FOOTMEN
CHORUS, who also act as wedding guests

NOTE: Dress should be modern and simple. Instead of "wedding garments," use corsages and boutonnieres. Otherwise, dress and props are at the discretion of the director.

SCENE ONE   The King's Palace
SCENE TWO   The Delivery of the Invitations
SCENE THREE The King's Palace

SCENE ONE: THE KING'S PALACE

During the opening chorus verses, the KING *is busily writing letters. He also calls the* STEWARD, *and hands him a check; and, during the third verse, calls the* THREE MESSENGERS *and gives them each a letter.)*

CHORUS (*sings*)
A King made a marriage for his son,
And sent men to summon everyone.
      He wrote the invitations
      To friends and to relations,
And all the noblemen in the land,
To come to the wedding he had planned.

He told all his servants to prepare
A feast for the wedding with due care.
      He gave them all they needed,
      Until they had succeeded
In doing all the things he had planned.
It was the finest wedding in the land.

He sent out his messengers to say
The time of the wedding and the day,
      Then gladly he awaited
      What he anticipated
Would be a joyful day for the land,
The day of the wedding he had planned.

SCENE TWO: THE DELIVERY OF THE INVITATIONS

The curtain closes, and the THREE MESSENGERS *appear in front of
it. During the opening lines of the* CHORUS, *the* MESSENGERS *mime
knocking at three doors, at the middle and sides of the curtain. If
possible, work out an appropriate dance movement for them during
the verses.*)

CHORUS (*sings*)
Opportunity's coming,
Watch his hurrying feet.
What kind of a reception
Is he going to meet?

Don't be deaf when he's knocking!
Don't look at him askance!
Opportunity's coming.
This is your golden chance!

Hello, Mr. Opportunity! Why are you at my door?
Come in, Mr. Opportunity! What are you waiting for?
    You will see my door unlock,
    Soon as I hear you start to knock.
Step up, Mr. Opportunity! Show me something more!

Thank you, Mr. Opportunity! Glad you came my way.
Welcome, Mr. Opportunity! It's my lucky day.
    What are you holding in your hand?
    Let me try to understand!
Surely, Mr. Opportunity, you have come to stay.

(SIMON, BARZILLAI *and* ELIAS *come out center, right and left,
and take the letters. Each writes a few words on the invitation, and returns it to the* MESSENGER *as he speaks his verse.*)

SIMON (*sings*)
Simon the Pharisee thanks the King
For the invitation to his son's wedding;
But business reasons, he is sorry to say,
Will keep him from being free that day.

BARZILLAI
Lord Barzillai is deeply grieved
To refuse the invitation which he has received.
He has taken a wife himself, and so
Regrets that he will be unable to go.

ELIAS
Doctor Elias is most upset
That he has to express his deep regret.
His farming interests keep him tied,
And his time is completely occupied.

(MESSENGERS *go out. The three come to the center in a line.*)

SIMON, BARZILLAI and ELIAS
We find it sad to refuse the King,
Whom we like to obey in everything.
Our regrets, of course, are quite profuse,
But we all with one accord would like to make excuse.

(*They go off. The curtain opens.*)

SCENE THREE: THE KING'S PALACE

The KING *is still writing. The* STEWARD *stands by him.*

KING

Steward, we must reckon
What we shall need,
With a hundred thirsty throats
And a hundred mouths to feed.
Wine?

STEWARD: Eighty flagons. (*He takes notes on a pad.*)

FOOTMAN: (*Entering*) A letter for you, sire.

KING: Put it on the table. Logs for the fire?

STEWARD: Logs from the forest.

KING: What does he say? (*He opens the letter.*)

STEWARD: Lamb and beef and mutton.

KING: Josiah will be away.

STEWARD: Boar's head and venison.

FOOTMAN: Sire, I bring another.

STEWARD: A whole ox for roasting.

KING: What? And his brother? (*Growing more angry with each letter*)

STEWARD: Then the fruits and honey—

KING: This villain shall be hung!

STEWARD: Oil and grain and cheeses—

KING: Steward, hold your tongue!

(*A chain of* SERVANTS *now passes letters across the stage to the* KING.)

FIRST FOOTMAN: Letter after letter,

SECOND FOOTMAN: And the King in a rage!

FIRST FOOTMAN: Look, there's another!

SECOND FOOTMAN: Give it to the Page!

PAGE: Sire, let me give you—

KING: Here! Let me see!

STEWARD: The messengers are back, sire.

KING: Bring them here to me!

(*The* MESSENGERS *enter, and hand the letters to the* KING)

FIRST MESSENGER

Simon the Pharisee thanks the King
For the invitation to his son's wedding;

But business reasons, he is sorry to say,
Will keep him from being free that day.

SECOND MESSENGER

Lord Barzillai is deeply grieved
To refuse the invitation which he has received.
He has taken a wife himself, and so
Regrets that he will be unable to go.

THIRD MESSENGER

Doctor Elias is most upset
That he has to express his deep regret.
His farming interests keep him tied,
And his time is completely occupied.

ALL THREE

They find it sad to refuse the King,
Whom they like to obey in everything.
Their regrets, of course, are quite profuse,
But they all with one accord would like to make excuse.

(*The* KING's *anger increases. During the last verse he beckons to a* CAPTAIN *and gives him orders. Then he jumps up from his chair.*)

KING (*sings*)

Go into the highways!
Go into the byways!
That the wedding be furnished with guests.
Go through the streets and call them here!
Call them from far, and call them from near!
Go into the highways!
Go into the byways!
That the wedding be furnished with guests.
Go to the city, and there proclaim
That I will welcome the halt and the lame.
Go into the highways!
Go into the byways!
That the wedding be furnished with guests.

Go out and call the deaf and the blind!
Call all the poor men that you can find!
Go into the highways!
Go into the byways!
That the wedding be furnished with guests.

(*While the verses are repeated by the* CHORUS, *the* SERVANTS *go out among the audience, and bring back the* GUESTS. *Other* SERVANTS *prepare the feast on stage. As the* GUESTS *come up, they are offered the "wedding garment": A boutonniere for men and a posy for women.*)

CHORUS (*sings*)
They went into the highways,
They went into the byways,
And the wedding was furnished with guests.

They went through the streets and called them there.
They called them from far, and called them from near.
They went into the highways,
They went into the byways,
And the wedding was furnished with guests.

They went to the city, that they might proclaim
That the King would welcome the halt and the lame.
They went into the highways,
They went into the byways,
And the wedding was furnished with guests.

They went out and called the deaf and the blind,
And all the poor men that they could find
They went into the highways,
They went into the byways,
And the wedding was furnished with guests.

(*The* GUESTS *are coming onto the stage, and the* SERVANTS *continue to hand out flowers and prepare the feast.*)

CHORUS (*sings*)
And when the bells began to call,
The people gathered in the Hall;
And man and woman, girl and boy,
Were glad with laughter and with joy.

(*A row of* BLIND *and* HALT *and* LAME *men and women have come to the front of the stage. The* STEWARD *examines them with dissatisfaction.*)

STEWARD: Is this the best that you could find?
HALT: Yes, the halt,
LAME: And the lame,
BLIND: And of course the blind.

STEWARD: Just look at their clothes! Though it's not their fault.
LAME: Yes, the lame,
BLIND: And the blind,
HALT: And of course the halt.
STEWARD: We asked Lords and Ladies—and look who came!
BLIND: Yes, the blind,
HALT: And the halt,
LAME: And of course the lame.
STEWARD: We must make the best of it, and be kind—
HALT: To the halt,
LAME: And the lame,
BLIND: And of course the blind.
STEWARD: It's the savor that matters, and not the salt—
LAME: For the lame,
BLIND: And the blind,
HALT: And of course the halt.
STEWARD: We must carry on, though it's not the same—
BLIND: With the blind,
HALT: And the halt,
LAME: And of course the lame.

CHORUS
The King had taken pains to make that feast
A time of joy for greatest and for least.
By his command, whoever entered there,
A wedding robe was given him to wear.

FIRST SERVANT: Boutonnieres!
SECOND SERVANT: Corsages!
PAGE: Wedding garments! The King would like each of you to
wear one.

(*The two* PHARISEES *walk to the stage through the audience.*)

FIRST PHARISEE: What a collection!
SECOND PHARISEE: I hope the King is taking steps to separate the
real guests from—these!
FIRST PHARISEE: Let us go up higher, to the upper seats!

(*They pass through the* HALT *and* LAME *and* BLIND *with con-
temptuous looks.*)

HALT MAN: Well! He fancies himself, doesn't he?
LAME MAN: Upper seats, indeed! I'm grateful to be here at all.

(Litany of the HALT *and the* LAME *and the* BLIND: *Spoken together by all of them.)*

From the grudging heart and the graceless word,
    O deliver me, good Lord!
From the sneering tone and the lifting brow,
    O deliver me, good Lord!
From the damning voice, and the eyes gone cold,
From the grim face set in a cruel mold,
From the hint half dropped, and the truth half told,
    O deliver me, good Lord!

(Various HALT *and* LAME *and* BLIND *people say these lines.)*

GUEST: I've never been anywhere like this.
ALL: Isn't it wonderful?
GUEST: Me in a Palace! It's simply bliss!
ALL: Isn't it wonderful?
GUEST: Me in a hall with chandeliers!
GUEST: Wearing the flowers that a Princess wears!
GUEST: I shall remember it all my years!
ALL: Isn't it wonderful?

(They all say the next verse together.)

God make me grateful for friendship and care!
God make me grateful for all that is fair!
God bless the King and the Prince and his Bride!
God give them happiness side by side!

STEWARD: Ladies and Gentlemen! Make way for the Royal party!

(The KING *and the* PRINCE *and his* BRIDE *enter.)*

CHORUS *(sings)*
The Prince came with his Bride all dressed in white;
And in that Hall it was a gracious sight
To see the people gathered in a ring,
Rejoicing to be guests before their King.

(The PHOTOGRAPHER *enters, and poses everybody for a group picture, except for the* GREEDY GUEST. *He sits at the front, unnoticed by the others.)*

GREEDY GUEST *(Examining the tables)*
Cheese? Ham? Shrimps? Beef?

Turkey? Chicken? Asparagus? Egg?
Strawberry? Peaches? Pineapple? Punch?
This should make a substantial lunch!
     Get something for nothing!
     That's the motto to keep.
     Get something for nothing!
     Live life on the cheap.
Caviar, sausages, cake, champagne;
Nothing to lose, and plenty to gain—
Better than sitting out there in the rain!
     Get something for nothing!
   That's the motto to keep!

     Get something for nothing!
     That's the way to be smart.
     Get something for nothing.
     That is the wise man's part.
Wine and women and dance and song,
(Give me a drink, and make it strong!)
Everything pleasant that comes along—
     Get something for nothing!
     That's the way to be smart!

(*The photograph is completed. The* CHORUS *begins again, but
breaks off abruptly, with a clash of cymbals, as the* KING *sees
the* GREEDY GUEST.)

CHORUS (*sings*)
The whole Assembly broke into a cheer;
A sound which warmed that good King's heart to hear—

(*spoken*)
But he suddenly saw, at the back of the Hall,
A man who was taking no notice at all.
He had elbowed his way to the drink and the food;
He was noisy and careless and dirty and rude;
He was munching and swilling, and paying no heed,
For his only desire was to drink and to feed.
And the King was so angry, his eyes started out,
And the guests in the Hall heard him suddenly shout:

KING (*sings*)
     How can you stand there
     Without a wedding garment?
     Don't you even care

What the party's about?
If it's only greed
Brought you here to my table,
Get you gone with speed,
Or be driven right out!

How did you get by
Without a wedding garment?
Can't you even try
To behave as a guest?
Do you feel no shame
Without a wedding garment?
Go the way you came,
If you know what's best!

(*The* GREEDY GUEST *is driven out, while the* CHORUS *repeats the* KING's *verses. The* KING *notices the* HUMBLE GUEST, *keeping out of the way at the side of the stage. He leads him to the main table in the center.*)

KING (*sings*)
Friend, go up higher!
Sit at my right hand!
Friend, go up higher,
With the highest in the land!

You, who were humble,
Be my honored guest!
Come to my table!
Eat and drink the best!

You, who were shrinking
From a place of pride,
Eating and drinking
By a poor man's side,

Come by the fire!
Share my wedding cup!
Friend, come up higher!
Come with me and sup!

(*The* KING *stands in the center, with the* GUESTS *gathered round him.*)

KING: Shall we say a blessing, my friends?

KING and CHORUS (*sing*)

Thank God for all his blessings!
To him be glory and praise!
Thank God for all his blessings!
Gladly our voices we raise!

For all the things that he gives, for the light upon our way;
For all the love and the care that he shows us every day;
For the food upon the table, and the roof above our head;
God be praiséd and worshippéd, O God be praiséd and wor-
shippéd!

(*They begin to eat and drink, while the* CHORUS *continues.*)

CHORUS (*sings*)

This is the tale of an earthly King,
Who did a just but a cruel thing;
And of a guest who was rough and rude,
And paid the price of ingratitude.

This is a lesson which Jesus gave
To all the friends he had come to save.
So let the lesson be here renewed,
To keep us all from ingratitude.

Here was a man whose thoughtless greed
Drove the King to a headstrong deed;
For he would not share the wedding food
With a guest who showed ingratitude.

(*The* KING *and his party have gone round the* GUESTS, *greeting them, during these verses. Now they come to the center.*)

ALL (*spoken*)

So serve your God with a thankful heart!
Play your proud or your humble part!
And wear for him, who is just and good,
The clean white robe of gratitude!

God make me grateful for friendship and care!
God make me grateful for all that is fair!
God bless the King and the Prince and his Bride!
God give them happiness, side by side!

For all the things that he gives, for the light upon our way;
For all the love and the care that he shows us every day;
For the food upon the table, and the roof above our head;
God be praiséd and worshippéd! O God be praiséd and wor-
shippéd!

PART III
THE YOUNG CHURCH

The Scenes in this last part of *The Bible as Drama* have as their purpose to give participants a feel for the events of the early Church. While they follow the order of events in Acts, these scenes are not meant to teach a history of this period but rather to introduce ordinary people who sensed that something extraordinary was happening in their lives.

From the choosing of a successor to Judas Iscariot through the post-Pentecost euphoria and then the persecution and growth of the early church, these scenes present a picture of people convinced that they were doing the Lord's work. Enacting these scenes will give a feel for these early very human Christians who spread the good news of redemption at great risk.

While all of these scenes are particularly appropriate for liturgical use during the seasons of Easter and Pentecost, some of them may also be used on saints' feast days. These are, scene one: The feast of Saint Matthias, February 24; scenes seven and eight: The feast of Conversion of St. Paul, January 25; scene nine: The feast of St. Peter, June 29.

SCENE ONE: THE UPPER ROOM

Bible reference: Acts 1, 10-26

Liturgical use: The Sunday nearest to St. Matthias' day (Feb. 24); or the second Sunday after Easter.

CHARACTERS: THE ELEVEN APOSTLES
JAMES ⎫
JOSEPH ⎪ *Jesus' four cousins*
JUDAS ⎪
SIMON ⎭
JOSEPH JUSTUS
MATTHIAS
CLEOPHAS
MARY, *Mother of Jesus*
MARY MAGDALENE

223

MARY, *wife of Cleophas*
SUSANNA
JOANNA
OTHER DISCIPLES, men and women

NOTE: Begin by thinking out the situation. Jesus' followers have been told to wait for the promise of the Father (verse 4), a promise that they would be given power when the Holy Spirit came to them.

Was it easy to wait? Imagine different reactions among the company assembled in the Upper Room. Peter, Simon the Zealot (this might be a nickname signifying his impetuous character), James and John (whom Jesus once called "Sons of Thunder") might have had a problem trying to be patient. Perhaps the women steadied the men. Improvise dialogue along these lines.

The Upper Room may have been in the family home of Mark, where many of the disciples were gathered after Peter's return from prison (see Acts 12, 12). If so, Mark, his Mother (yet another Mary) and the servant Rhoda would be there.

Begin with verse 14: They "devoted themselves to prayer." Led by Peter, act out a spontaneous worship service. Include the Lord's Prayer, prayers for guidance from different people, and a mime of the Breaking of Bread. Then the scene starts. The whole company are lying on rugs or sitting.

PETER: One thing we must do. Judas Iscariot has gone to his death. Someone must be chosen to take his place.
JAMES, SON OF ZEBEDEE: Yes. One of those who have been with us from the start.
PETER: We have prayed that God will guide us in this and all things. Are you ready to offer names?
ANDREW: I propose Joseph Justus Barsabas.
PHILIP: I was going to name him also. He was with us from the beginning.
PETER: Joseph Justus. Matthew, please keep a note of the names. Are there others whom you would put forward?
THOMAS: I propose Matthias.
JOHN: I agree. He was one of the Seventy, and has always been faithful.
PETER: Add the name of Matthias. Are there others?
SIMON THE ZEALOT: Let us choose at once!

PETER: Be patient, Simon! Let us all think carefully. Are there other names?

JOHN: (*After a pause*) I believe those are the clear choices, Peter.

PETER: Is it agreed?

(*All reply with words such as these: "Yes." "We agree." "Agreed."*)

PETER: Joseph and Matthias, are you willing to have this choice made between you, and to abide by the lot which God will reveal to us?

JOSEPH: I am willing.

MATTHIAS: And I.

PETER: Then place the lots in a bowl. Matthew—

MATTHEW: They are ready, Peter. I have marked the pebbles.

PETER: Good! Now let us pray again together in Jesus' name.

ALL: Thou, Lord, who knowest the hearts of all men, show us which of these two thou hast chosen to accept that Apostle's ministry which Judas forfeited to go where he belonged.

MATTHEW: (*After a pause*) The lot has fallen to Matthias.

PETER: Glory be to God! My brother, you are now by his choice one of us. May he bless and strengthen you, and every one of his followers! And you, Joseph Justus, remain faithful and serve the Lord, wherever you may be called.

SCENE TWO: THE DAY OF PENTECOST

Bible reference: Acts 2, 1-41.

FIRST EPISODE

CHARACTERS: The same as in Scene One

NOTE: This is hardly a "scene." Formal dialogue would be impossible to write in this situation; but the scene is far too important to omit.

Imagine a crowded room, in which the mixed company of disciples are praying. It is fifty days after Easter, ten days after the Ascension. The strain and excitement have been almost overwhelming. Acting out this episode will only be effective if the participants understand and enter into this mounting excitement. You can find many examples of similar experiences, especially in the early days of new religious movements. John Wesley's *Diary*, and many accounts of religion on the early American frontier, provide vivid instances of "pentecostal" reactions.

Each member of the group must think his way into the situation. Then individuals begin to repeat, with growing intensity, phrases like this:

"Come, Lord Jesus!"

"The Spirit of the Lord God is upon me!"

"Show us your power, Lord!"

"He has come down! The Spirit of the Lord has come down!"

"Fill my heart, Lord!"

"It is filled with fire!"

"I feel the wind of the Spirit!"

Then PETER cries out:

"Yes! It is the Spirit of the Lord—the wind of God! His fire and power are filling our hearts!

They then all begin to shout:

"Out into the streets! To the Temple!" etc.

As they go, they begin to speak in other tongues. This can be partly conveyed by phrases such as:

"Domine Christe . . . Spiritus Sanctus . . . Kyrie Christe . . . Eloi! Eloi!"

SECOND EPISODE: IN THE STREET

Liturgical use: Whitsunday

CHARACTERS: All of those in the scene above, with the addition of men and women passing by in the streets of Jerusalem.

This scene follows immediately on the last. The DISCIPLES *run out of a door into the street, shouting as before. A number of passersby are jostled by them.*

FIRST MAN: Who are they? Here, look where you're going!

WOMAN: That man in front sounded like a Galilean.

SECOND MAN: That's right. Like those men who came with Jesus—the one who was crucified.

FIRST MAN: Galilean or no, he was shouting what sounded like Latin to me.

WOMAN: If you ask me, I'd say they're drunk!

SECOND MAN: Mind where you're going! Let me pass!

FIRST MAN: Disgraceful! Drunk at this hour of the morning!

ANDREW: No, no! You don't understand! Peter, these people think we're drunk.

PETER: (*Laughing*) Drunk? At nine in the morning? No, my friends, that is not what fills us with such power and joy.

FIRST MAN: Then what is going on? Talking in all these foreign-sounding languages, and pushing us around in the streets—

PETER: Let me try to explain it to you. (*He shouts loudly*) Listen, friends! All of you, please listen! (*They grow quiet.*) I can understand why you are puzzled. But have you never read the prophet Joel? "I will pour forth my Spirit upon all flesh," he says. "Your sons and your daughters shall prophesy, and your young men shall see visions." I tell you, that is what has happened to us. This is it— the day of the coming of God's Spirit! You know about Jesus, who was crucified. I tell you, friends, we know that he is risen from the dead. We were there, and he spoke to us many times. This Jesus, whom King David foretold, and whose works of power and love proved that he came from God—turn to him, men of Israel! Turn your hearts to him!

(*This is followed by a confusion of calls from the crowd. Some cry: "What must we do?" "Tell us what to do?" Others: "Don't listen to him!" "It's blasphemy!"*)

PETER: Change your hearts! Repent, and have faith in him! Any of you who truly accept him can be baptized with water and the Spirit, today! You will be made rich with the same gift which we have.

VOICES: "I repent!"

"Let me be baptized!"

"I believe in him!"

"Save me, Jesus!"

PETER: Oh, God be thanked for this day! Truly his promise has been fulfilled. Come, friends! Let us baptize the new brothers and sisters whom the Lord has called!

SCENE THREE: A PUBLIC MIRACLE
AT THE TEMPLE

Bible reference: Acts 3, 4, 4.

Liturgical use: Soon after Whitsunday.

CHARACTERS: *ELIAS, a cripple
Two MEN who carry him in
PETER
JOHN
MEN and WOMEN passing by
Two JEWISH TEMPLE POLICEMEN

Two men carry ELIAS *in, and set him down by the Temple gate.*

FIRST MAN: There you are, Elias.
SECOND MAN: Comfortable? Here, let me shift this pillow.
ELIAS: Thank you, friends.
FIRST Man: Got all you need? Well, we'll be back for you at five.
SECOND MAN: Have a good day, Elias! Send a message if you need anything.
ELIAS: Blessings on you both! Goodbye!

> (*They go out. Several people walk past. Each time,* ELIAS *says: "Can you help a cripple, Sir?" Some give him a coin, some go by without stopping.* PETER *and* JOHN *enter.*)

ELIAS: Can you help a cripple, Sir?
PETER: Help a cripple?
ELIAS: Just something small, Sir, if you can spare it.
JOHN: No, friend. We cannot give you something small.
PETER: We have no silver or gold.
ELIAS: All right, Sir, no offense, I'm sure. Why are you looking at me like that?
PETER: If you have faith, we will make you whole in the name of Jesus of Nazareth.
ELIAS: Jesus? The one who healed a blind man? The one they—
JOHN: Yes, the one they crucified. But he is not dead, and he still makes men whole in body and spirit.
PETER: It is he that has sent us here today.
ELIAS: It isn't any use. I've tried everything.
PETER: You have not put your faith in him. Many who were dumb

and deaf and paralyzed came to him when they had "tried everything," and had no hope. Many with sick hearts and minds also.

JOHN: Can you have faith in him, and rise up and walk?

ELIAS: You mean it, don't you? You're not lying to me!

PETER: I swear by Almighty God that we are telling the truth. What is your name? And what injury keeps you from walking?

ELIAS: I am Elias Bar-Joseph. It's my ankles, and my feet. I haven't walked in fifteen years.

PETER: Hold my hand, Elias. No, tightly! Now, trust in the power of Jesus! (*Louder*) Get up! Up! (*With great effort,* PETER *pulls* ELIAS *to his feet.*) That's right! Stand and walk!

(PETER*'s loud voice has caused a crowd to gather round them. Voices:* "What's happening?" "What's he doing?" "Elias, what's going on?")

PETER: That's it, Elias! You can walk! Only believe it, and you can!

ELIAS: It's true! God, I can walk! I can walk! God Almighty, I'm healed!

(*Voices:* "It's a trick." "Who is this man, anyway?" "No, that's Elias all right." "Come on, let's get out of here!" "If that's Elias, it's a miracle!")

PETER: Why stare at us, all of you? Is this so astonishing? It is not something that *we* have done, but the power of God, working in the world through Jesus. We are only his instruments.

MAN: Jesus? Jesus of Nazareth? He's dead!

JOHN: No! He rose from the dead. He—

WOMAN: Don't give me that! I saw him crucified.

MAN: You don't rise from the dead when the Romans are finished with you.

JOHN: I tell you, the tomb could not hold him.

ELIAS: Can't you see that I'm walking? If Jesus did that to me, he isn't dead!

PETER: It is true. Jesus has healed this brother of ours through faith. Jesus, who was put to death for us, has been raised in glory, and will give all of you healing and strength, if—

MAN: Look out! Police! (*The crowd begins to disperse hurriedly.*)

POLICE CAPTAIN: What's this disturbance?

PETER: No disturbance, Officer.

ELIAS: They healed me! You know me—Elias—I'm here every day.

POLICEMAN: You aren't Elias. He's a cripple.

CAPTAIN: Just a minute! There's something funny here. That *is* Elias!

ELIAS: They healed me in Jesus' name!

POLICEMAN: Oh, they did, did they? We'll see what the High Priest has to say about that. Now see here, Elias, you'd better go on home, and keep quiet about this. As for you two—what do you think, Sir? Had we better take them in?

ELIAS: What? For healing me? Are you crazy?

CAPTAIN: Watch what you say, Elias! You two, come with us!

PETER: We will come. Elias, give thanks to God, and be a witness to Jesus' power—

POLICEMAN: That's enough from you! Make way, there! Make way!

SCENE FOUR: PETER AND JOHN
BEFORE THE COUNCIL

Bible reference: Acts 4, 5-22

Liturgical use: Soon after Whitsunday

CHARACTERS: CAIAPHAS, *the High Priest*
ANNAS, *his father-in-law*
JOHN, ALEXANDER, *and other members of his family*
POLICE CAPTAIN, *the same as in the last scene*
PETER
JOHN
*ELIAS *the cripple*
MEMBERS OF THE SANHEDRIN, OR JEWISH COUNCIL

NOTE: Bible references to Caiaphas and Annas include: Matthew 26, 3-5; Mark 14, 53-65; John 11, 47-53; and Acts, chapters 4 to 9. There are fuller accounts of these men and their activities in the historian Josephus. All of these references tend to be hostile, and it is important that we should see both sides of the case. If we depended on hostile sources for our knowledge of Christianity now, it would be impossible to arrive at a fair judgment of it.

Briefly, the case of the High Priestly caste was this. Somebody had to represent the Jews under Roman rule. One rich family, of which Annas was the most powerful representative, provided no less than eight High Priests in the first century A.D. They steered a difficult course as religious and political leaders. Their money came largely from the Temple sacrifices. The "tables of the money-changers," which Jesus overthrew, were known as Booths of Annas.

For these men, any new religious movement was a threat. They believed in acceptance of Roman rule, but they could exert strong pressure on Roman officials, like Pilate, to do what suited them. If Jesus had gone on to greater success in his preaching, the position of the High Priest's family would have been threatened. Hence their determination to be rid of him, and to suppress his followers. To put this in perspective, you should try to think of instances in the history of Christianity in which leaders have taken similar decisions to suppress opposition.

Caiaphas was a crafty, unattractive character, according to our sources. Annas was the power behind the throne. I have made Alexander a violent, unthinking opponent of Christianity, as a contrast; but this is imaginary.

The Jewish Council is in session. CAIAPHAS *presides.*

CAIAPHAS: Call the prisoners in! And the so-called cripple, too. And ask Captain Nathanael to come in.
ATTENDANT: Yes, Sir. (*He goes out.*)
CAIAPHAS: This is a delicate matter. I ask you all to listen carefully, and to avoid making hasty judgments.
ALEXANDER: Surely it's obvious that the whole thing is a fraud—
ANNAS: Here they are. We shall be able to judge for ourselves.

(PETER *and* JOHN *are led in, with the* POLICE CAPTAIN.)

CAIAPHAS: Stand here in front of me, prisoners. And you, Captain, step forward, please.
ANNAS: I understand, Captain Nathanael, that you arrested these two men after a disturbance near the Temple yesterday.
CAPTAIN: Yes, Sir.
ANNAS: What are your names, and where do you come from?

PETER: I am Simon Bar-Jonah, of Bethsaida in Galilee. This is my friend, John Bar-Zebedee.

CAIAPHAS: Galileans! I suspected as much.

ANNAS: You are accused of having caused a public disturbance and claiming to work a miraculous cure in order to attract notoriety.

JOHN: It is not a claim, Sir, but a fact. Our friend stands here healed.

ANNAS: Your friend stands here, and you and he claim that he is healed. There is not a jot of proof that you are speaking the truth. You admit that you are responsible for what happened?

PETER: We healed him. If that caused a disturbance, as you call it, then of course we were responsible.

ALEXANDER: And just how did you perform this remarkable cure, Galilean?

PETER: Councillors, I find it strange that we are here in bonds, accused of healing a man. But, since you ask by what power we healed him, I can answer simply; we did it through Jesus of Nazareth. (*Reactions of surprise and anger.* CAIAPHAS *nods: He had expected this answer.*) He was crucified; but he rose again, and told us to heal and preach in his name, by which alone men can be brought to salvation.

ANNAS: These men are peasants. What right have they to talk such nonsense?

JOHN: Sir, the man stands here healed.

ALEXANDER: Be silent, prisoner! How dare you answer back?

CAIAPHAS: It would be wise, I think, to send these men out while we reach a decision.

ANNAS: I should like to hear what Captain Nathanael has to say.

CAIAPHAS: Take them outside! (*They are led out.*) Well, Captain? How do you view the situation in the streets?

CAPTAIN: To be frank, Sir, it is not good. Since this cripple, Elias, was healed—

ANNAS: Come now, Captain! Surely you haven't fallen for that story.

CAPTAIN: Well, Sir, you asked me to speak. I've known Elias for years. He begs every day by the Beautiful Gate—never any trouble before. He's over forty, and in my opinion—

CAIAPHAS: Suppose we do without your opinion, Captain, and you tell us what the state of other people's opinions is. What do the people believe about this healing?

CAPTAIN: The majority are skeptical; but they weren't there. A lot of witnesses can swear to what happened; and it has certainly stirred up interest in this Jesus they talk about.

ANNAS: All right, Captain, you may go. (*He goes out.*)

CAIAPHAS: As I said—a delicate matter.

ALEXANDER: Why not make an example of this so-called cripple? Give him a beating that will cripple him properly?

ANNAS: That would be most unwise. We want to avoid publicity. Besides—

CAIAPHAS: The healing may be genuine. Was that what you were going to say?

ANNAS: God may have healed him. We cannot be sure. The point is that to deny it outright might be inadvisable.

ALEXANDER: Then punish these Galileans.

CAIAPHAS: Alexander, punishment is an excellent thing, if it is effective. But punishment for its own sake has no value. This excitement over Jesus will die down. It would be folly to fan it by the publicity of persecution.

ANNAS: Then what do you suggest?

CAIAPHAS: In the first instance, a stiff warning. If that does not work, I agree with Alexander that harsher measures will be necessary.

ANNAS: Is that the opinion of all of you?

ALL: Yes. Agreed.

CAIAPHAS: Call the two prisoners back. (*They are led in.*) Simon and John, your case has been considered. We have decided to be lenient with you. You will not on this occasion be punished. But it is our duty to warn you bluntly that any further claims made in the name of Jesus will lead you into serious trouble.

PETER: Sir, we have no wish to speak with disrespect before this Council; but you are asking us to put your commands above those of God.

ALEXANDER: How do men like you think that you know what God commands?

PETER: We know what we see and hear, Sir.

ALEXANDER: Ignorant, obstinate fools!

CAIAPHAS: Let us give these men a chance to think it over. You have been warned what will happen to you if you oppose the authority of this Council. It is for us to interpret the will of God, not for individuals with no training. I suggest that we let them go now.

ANNAS: You may go. I trust that we shall have no further trouble with you.

SCENE FIVE: REPRESSION AND GROWTH

Bible reference: Acts 5, 27 - 6, 6

Liturgical use: Soon after Whitsunday

CHARACTERS: The same company of Christians who were in the Upper Room in Scene One. I have given parts in this scene to Mary, mother of John Mark the Evangelist, and to Mark and their servant Rhoda.

NOTE: This scene is imaginary, but based closely on the text. Instead of another scene before the Council, we see Peter and John returning to their friends after the beating described in Acts 5, 40. In Acts 12 Peter returned to Mark's home after he left prison; so that this may have been the regular meeting-place for the Church.

New Testament names cause confusion unless they are carefully distinguished. There are five or six Mary's in the Gospels:

Jesus' mother

Mary Magdalene

Mary, wife of Cleophas (John's Gospel); perhaps the same as

Mary, mother of James and Joses (Matthew's Gospel)

Mary, sister of Martha and Lazarus, of Bethany

Mary, mother of John Mark, who appears in this scene.

The repetitions of James and John and Judas cause similar problems. It is for this reason that I have not given spoken parts to the less known James and Judas among the apostles, or to John the High Priest's relative.

MARY, *mother of Mark, and* RHODA, *with several of the* APOSTLES, *are in the upper room.* MARK *and* ANDREW *are heard climbing the outside steps, and run in.*

MARK: Mother! Peter and John are coming. They are both hurt.

MARY: I know, my son. Thaddaeus saw you coming along the road.

RHODA: We have beds ready for them.

MARY: How badly are they hurt, Andrew?

ANDREW: Not seriously, I hope. Beaten, as we expected.

(*Sounds on the steps.* PETER *and* JOHN *are helped in by* MATTHEW, JAMES *and* THOMAS.)

MARY: Over here, Thomas.

THOMAS: Good! You have everything ready. Easy, Peter!

JOHN: I'm all right. Don't—

MATTHEW: Sit down, John. Take it easy! I'll get you some water.

PETER: That's better! All I need is a little rest.

RHODA: Turn round, so that I can bathe your back.

PETER: Ouch! That Police Captain had a strong arm!

JOHN: They treated you far worse than me, Peter.

PETER: (*Trying to laugh*) Perhaps because I did more talking.

ANDREW: Can you tell us about it? Don't, if you're not up to it.

JOHN: You rest, Peter. I'll tell them.

> (JOHN *sits against the wall.* PETER *lies down. The others gather round.*)

MARY: Drink this first, John.

JOHN: Thank you, Mary. Where would we be without your home and all you do for us? Oh, that tastes good!

MARY: Mark, go and fill the pitcher, please.

MARK: Yes, Mother.

JOHN: There's really not much to tell. We were arrested by the Temple Gate, just like last time. After about two hours of waiting we were taken to the Council Room. All the same people were there; but this time Gamaliel the Pharisee was with them—luckily for us.

PHILIP: I've heard of him. The greatest teacher in Jerusalem, they call him.

JOHN: Well, they repeated what they said last time. The High Priest asked why we had gone on teaching about Jesus; and of course Peter said again, "We can't obey you rather than God." I tell you, at that moment I thought the end might come. That brute Alexander was howling for us to be lynched, and Caiaphas seemed to be on his side—

ANDREW: Surely they couldn't do that!

PETER: I wouldn't be so sure. The way they looked—

JOHN: Rest, Peter! I'll do the talking. Anyway, this Gamaliel really saved us. He asked the High Priest's permission to speak, and he has a way with him that makes everyone listen. He told them to take a hard look at what they were doing. He said that if God wanted us to fail, we'd fail; but if we were speaking God's word, nothing could stop us. I tell you, they didn't like it; though I think at that point Caiaphas, the old fox, swung over to Gamaliel's point of view, and was glad to have Alexander and the rest calmed down.

THOMAS: So what happened then?

JOHN: They chose the obvious way out: beat us, and avoid trouble with Pilate. I kept quiet, and got off lightly; but when the Captain was ready to beat Peter, Alexander said to him, "This will muzzle you, Mister Fisherman!" And Peter said—

PETER: It was waste of breath. I should have held my tongue.

ANDREW: What did you say?

JOHN: He said, "You can't muzzle the word of God"—and of course the Captain laid into him all the harder.

PETER: (*Sitting up*) I feel better. Tell me what happened at your prayer meeting today.

ANDREW: Later, brother. There's no hurry.

PETER: No, no. Jesus' business cannot wait for a few bruises. What decisions did you make?

MATTHEW: None, Peter. We heard the representatives of the Greek-speaking brothers.

PETER: What was their complaint?

THOMAS: That some of their widows are not being fairly treated in the food distributions.

ANDREW: We told them a decision must wait till you came back for a full meeting of the Twelve.

PETER: The Twelve! We are too few to know all their needs. With thousands joining us and turning to Jesus, how can we preach the good news and distribute the bread and keep the money? It isn't like the old days in Galilee.

JAMES: I have a plan, Peter. Rather than try to do all these things ourselves, let us appoint some helpers to do those jobs—look after the money, I mean, and the food.

JOHN: That's right! It was the word that Jesus entrusted to us— the good news. I agree with James. If we are to have our time free for witness and healing, we must appoint others for other tasks.

PETER: Yes. That is what we must do. And we ought to be thankful that the growth of the Church makes it necessary. Andrew and Philip, you know best about the Greeks among our number.* Choose with prayer those whom you think to be best suited for that kind of work.

MARY: Now, no more business for today. Rhoda has supper ready, and you two need rest.

PETER: You are right, Mary. Let us break bread and eat! I rejoice that God has thought me worthy to suffer a little with Jesus. Now we all need new strength, to go out again in his name.

*The names of these two Apostles were Greek, not Jewish.

SCENE SIX: THE STONING OF STEPHEN

Bible reference: Acts 7, 57—8, 1

CHARACTERS: SAUL
STEPHEN
A NUMBER OF JEWISH MEN

NOTE: In Acts 6—7 the story of Stephen is told. This brilliant young man was chosen as one of the seven "Deacons" to help the Apostles with practical work. He soon became an outstanding preacher. When Saul was chosen by the High Priest to suppress the Christian heresy, we can guess that he was both horrified and fascinated by the power of Stephen's witness.

And then, suddenly, came the lynching of Stephen. The importance of this event lies partly in the effect it must surely have had upon Saul. He helped to carry out a brutal, messy killing, and heard Stephen forgive him as he was dying. Saul never forgot it; and it is not fanciful to think that later he almost welcomed suffering, in order to pay for what he had done to Stephen and other Christians.

There can be no set text for this scene. Its effectiveness depends upon the capacity of the participants to make themselves feel the fury of the Jews at what Stephen had said before the Council. He was a traitor to his country and his faith, in their eyes.

They drag him forward, with Saul following. They should be shouting appropriate phrases, such as: "This is far enough." "Here, against this wall." "Let's get it over!" "Keep our coats, Saul!"

They take off their coats, and begin to throw stones at short range. Mime this, and imagine the hate which must have been involved, to give these sincere Jews the endurance to go through with such a horrible process. To kill a man with stones would take minutes rather than seconds.

When you think enough time has elapsed, Stephen should say the words at the end of chapter 7: "Jesus, Lord, receive my spirit!" and "Lord, forgive them for this sin."

Saul has to go forward and verify that Stephen is dead. Improvise dialogue for this. The men then pick up their coats and go away, saying things like: "Let's get out of here." "Do we have to take him away?" "No, leave him." "The sooner we get away the better." Saul should stay a minute after the rest have gone. Ask him to say what his thoughts are.

SCENE SEVEN: THE CONVERSION OF SAUL

Bible reference: Acts 9, 1-9; also chapters 22 and 26

CHARACTERS: SAUL (PAUL)
　　　　　　　　HIS JEWISH COMPANIONS
　　　　　　　　CROWD OF MEN AND WOMEN PASSERSBY
　　　　　　　　VOICE OF GOD

NOTE: When the Bible describes a vision sent from God, we expect to find that the person receiving it has prepared himself for it. Visions come to meet a need, and in answer to a search. This applies to Peter in Acts 10; Paul himself in the dream at Troas (Acts 16); Ezekiel at the Valley of Dry Bones (Chapter 37); Jacob dreaming of the Ladder (Genesis 28).

It is therefore legitimate to think of Saul, on the slow journey from Jerusalem to Damascus, thinking of what lay ahead of him. He must beat, bully and imprison the Christian heretics. All his training has led him to believe that a heresy like this must be stamped out. But he has seen Stephen die, and knows what he died for. I picture him going through a prolonged torment of doubt. Finally, the sight of the city, in which he must carry out his duty, is too much for him. He is ready for the vision which is to change his life.

Again, there is no set dialogue. Saul and his companions are walking along the road; though probably they would have been riding. Improvise conversation: "There it is, Saul!" "Damascus!" "We'll be there in a few minutes now."

Saul is very quiet, hardly answering. Suddenly he cries out, covers his eyes, and falls. What happened after that was naturally confusing, and Luke's three versions do not give identical details.

Act out verses 4 to 6.

"Saul, Saul, why are you persecuting me? It is not easy for you to kick against your own conscience."

"Who are you, Lord?"

"I am Jesus, whom you are persecuting. But now stand up and go into the city and there you will be told what you must do."

The other men listen in astonishment, and their reactions should be improvised. They come forward and begin to lift Saul up. A crowd gathers round. Saul is moaning, and murmuring to himself, only half conscious, and temporarily blind. The crowd members keep asking who he is, and commenting on his Jewish dress. His companions are terrified, and want to get away from him as soon as they can. They say: "Let us take him inside the city. Somebody will look after him. I don't like it." And another could say: "Did you hear that voice?" "I heard something. I was too confused to listen. There was a flash of light."

As with the earlier "situations," with no set text, the impact of this scene will depend upon the imagination and involvement of the actors.

SCENE EIGHT: IN THE HOUSE OF JUDAS

Bible reference: Acts 9, 22. Compare Galatians 1, 13-17 and II Corinthians 11, 32-33

Liturgical use: The Sunday nearest to the Conversion of St. Paul (January 25)

CHARACTERS: SAUL (PAUL)
               JUDAS
               *SUSANNA, *wife of Judas*
               ANANIAS

NOTE: Susanna is an imaginary character, needed to create a natural scene in Judas' home. The names "Judas" and "Ananias" are two more that can cause confusion in the New Testament. Two of the Apostles were called Judas, as well as one of Jesus' brothers or cousins (Mark 6, 3). Look for two other men named Ananias, in Acts 5 and 23. Because it was a common name, Judas and Susanna did not understand why Paul kept repeating it. How could he know the name of an obscure Christian in Damascus, whom he had never met?

> *In a simple room in* JUDAS' *home on Straight Street,* SAUL *lies on a bed.* JUDAS *and* SUSANNA *are with him.*

SAUL: (*Unconscious, muttering*) Who are you, Lord? Ananias, help me! (*He repeats this several times, groaning and tossing restlessly.*)
SUSANNA: It's all right, Saul. It's all right. We are your friends. Three whole days unconscious! He must be so weak!

JUDAS: Saul? Can you hear me? Saul? Rest! You'll be all right.

SAUL: (*Loudly*) Ananias, help me!

JUDAS: Who can this Ananias be?

SUSANNA: He doesn't know what he's saying.

JUDAS: Wait a minute! I think he's opening his eyes.

SAUL: Where am I? Who—

SUSANNA: He's conscious!

SAUL: (*Slowly, with effort*) Please help me! How did I come here?

JUDAS: We don't really know, Saul. You are Saul of Tarsus, aren't you.

SAUL: Yes. Yes, I am Saul.

JUDAS: That's what they said when I found you. It was near the South Gate. You were stumbling along by the wall, and a lot of frightened people were watching. Nobody seemed to want to do anything.

SAUL: I remember. Someone spoke to me. Was it you?

JUDAS: Yes. I don't mind telling you, I was frightened too. I mean, after what we had heard—

SAUL: Why were you frightened? (*A pause.*) You don't mean that you—

SUSANNA: Yes, Saul. We are Christians.

SAUL: But you still helped me?

JUDAS: We had to, Saul. I'm no hero, but the Spirit of Jesus seemed to push me forward. So I brought you here. My name is Judas, and this is Susanna, my wife.

SUSANNA: How do you feel, Saul? Are your eyes—

SAUL: I can see nothing. My right arm is numb. But I feel my strength coming back.

SUSANNA: You're shivering. I will fetch another blanket. (*A knock at the door.*) Oh, God! Who can that be? Not the Police!

JUDAS: I will see. Don't worry! (*He opens the door.*) Ananias!

ANANIAS: Greetings, Judas, and Susanna! I—oh, it's true!

JUDAS: This is Saul of Tarsus.

ANANIAS: I know.

SAUL: Ananias! I knew that you would come!

JUDAS: You knew? I don't understand.

ANANIAS: The Lord told me in a vision that I must come here and find you, Saul. I had just got back from work, and I don't know whether I was awake or asleep. All of a sudden there was this voice. I could hardly believe it—

SUSANNA: So that is why you kept talking about Ananias, Saul.

SAUL: Did I? My mind is still confused. I know that the voice which spoke to me on the road has kept telling me that a man would come to heal my sight—Ananias—

ANANIAS: That's right! The Lord sent the vision to both of us.

SAUL: How could you believe it? You knew who I was, and why—

ANANIAS: I didn't want to believe it, I can tell you. I can remember arguing—that's good, isn't it? Me arguing with the Lord! But I knew I had to come.

SAUL: So it is true that Jesus is Messiah! I should have known! I saw Stephen die. Oh, God! God! God!

SUSANNA: Rest now, Saul! Don't think about that!

JUDAS: If it is God's will that you are to be one of us, look forward! Think of what lies ahead!

SAUL: Yes. (*A pause.*) Though I don't know what else can lie ahead for me but death, when they know at Jerusalem—

ANANIAS: Saul, the Lord has told us one thing clearly. I am to pray with you that your sight may return. Lie back now. I want you to surrender yourself to faith in Jesus. He will make you whole.

JUDAS: We will all pray, Saul. (ANANIAS *puts his hands on* SAUL's *eyes.*)

ANANIAS: Lord Jesus, you have sent me here to our brother Saul, to give him back his sight, and to pray for him to be filled with your Holy Spirit. Let my hands be your hands, Lord! Come with healing power! Come! Heal! (*There is a long silence.*)

SAUL: (*Sitting up quietly*) I can see. My head feels strange, but I can see. (*He tries to get up.*)

SUSANNA: No, Saul, lie down. Before you do anything else, you must eat. You have had nothing for three days.

SAUL: But first, my beloved friends—my wonderful, brave new friends in the fellowship of Jesus, I witness to you solemnly that I give my life to him.

ANANIAS: Let us baptize you at once! Susanna, fetch water, please! You are head of this household, Judas. Give our brother baptism!

SAUL: Wait! Am I worthy to accept this baptism? After I have done what I have done?

JUDAS: We all came to him as sinners, Saul. If you repent, and believe in your heart that "Jesus is Lord," you should be baptized.

SAUL: I do believe. He came to me in my need. Jesus is Lord!

JUDAS: Saul—

SAUL: Don't use that name! It is stained with all that I have done.

Call me Paul—my name among the Romans.

JUDAS: Paul, I baptize you in the name of the Father, and of the Son, and of the Holy Spirit! Now join with us, and say the prayer which Jesus taught us. (*They say The Lord's Prayer,* PAUL *repeating each phrase after the others.*)

SUSANNA: Here, Paul! Wrap this around you.

SAUL: Thank you, Susanna. I shall never forget your kindness. (SUSANNA *goes out.*) Now you must tell me what I can do to serve you.

ANANIAS: Get back your strength first.

SAUL: But I know that if I stay with you you will be in danger.

ANANIAS: If you are to follow Jesus, Paul, you will learn to face danger. We all know that. "Take up the Cross, and follow me!" That was what he said. So far, we have not been interfered with here in Damascus. But we always knew persecution would come one day. After what has happened to you, I suppose it will be worse.

JUDAS: We all share it—that is what matters. It makes danger lighter.

SAUL: I only ask one thing. As I have stood in public places in Jerusalem and denounced Jesus, let me soon go out into the streets of Damascus and witness to him. After that, I will wait for his guidance, and for your advice.

SUSANNA: Here is food, Paul.

> (*Improvise further discussion.* SAUL *can tell them about Jerusalem: Gamaliel's views, and the High Priest's, and what he knows of the church there. They tell him more about Jesus' teaching. What questions would he ask? They discuss the situation in Damascus. Look up Aretas, the ruler, and find out all you can about the city.*)

SCENE NINE: PETER AND THE
BAPTISM OF CORNELIUS

Bible reference: Acts 11, 1-18

Liturgical use: The Sunday nearest to St. Peter's day, June 29

CHARACTERS: PETER
                JAMES, *cousin of Jesus*
                BARTHOLOMEW
                THADDAEUS

NOTE: The scene is imaginary, but based on the text. We do not know who belonged to "the circumcision party" in the Christian Church (verse 2), but their influence frequently appears in Acts and Paul's Letters. They were honestly opposed to the unchecked spread of Jesus' message to the Gentiles.

At this point in Acts, James, one of Jesus' four cousins, becomes prominent. (The death of James, son of Zebedee, is reported in Acts 12.) For a discussion of Jesus' brothers and sisters (or cousins) see JB, 21; Peake 702a. I have chosen Bartholomew and Thaddaeus for this scene as representatives of the more conservative Apostles, because they have Jewish names (unlike Andrew and Philip), and names not easily confused with others. To introduce another Judas or Simon from among the Twelve would be unnecessarily complicated.

The four men enter a room like the Upper Room, and sit down.

JAMES: We wanted to talk to you, Peter, before this evening's meeting.
BARTHOLOMEW: I'm sure you realize that the rumors about what happened at Caesarea have made many people uneasy.
PETER: I certainly do, Bartholomew. And I agree that you should know all the facts, before it becomes a matter of general discussion. I keep telling myself that for all of you, in Jerusalem, it must be quite impossible to understand news like this at second hand.
JAMES: Tell us exactly what happened, Peter, please.
PETER: I was staying at Joppa, with a wonderful Jewish family: Simon the Tanner, his wife and children. They have all accepted Jesus and been baptized. Up there, and in Caesarea, there are

many more Gentiles studying our faith than here in Jerusalem. Quite a few Romans in the Army read the Law and the Prophets, and nobody can help admiring their enthusiasm. I met several of them, and I was really puzzled.

THADDAEUS: I can understand that. It's a new situation. We met so few Gentiles when we were with Jesus.

BARTHOLOMEW: But he always listened to them, and treated them with love and respect. However, that's a very different thing from—

PETER: Wait, please! Don't make up your minds until you hear it all!

JAMES: Go on, Peter.

PETER: I was puzzled, as I say; because with Jesus we were a band of Jews, all united in worship and sacrifice and the Law—and here were these people, trained to read the Scriptures, but not circumcised.

THADDAEUS: That is the point, surely! Jesus never said—

PETER: Wait, Thaddaeus, wait! One day I came in tired to Simon's place, and sat down to rest before dinner. I suppose I was thinking about food, and I was all confused in my mind about these Gentile families. Anyway, I must have fallen asleep, because suddenly, there in front of me, was the most vivid sign from the Lord that I have seen since the Mount of Transfiguration! There was a kind of tablecloth, lowered from above me; and on it there were all the kinds of flesh that you and I are forbidden to eat—every unclean animal you can think of, all piled up in front of me. I felt myself recoil; and then Jesus' voice came—you won't believe this at first, but it's true. He spoke in that same half-humorous voice that he would use when he was getting us to see something, and we were being obstinate —you remember!

BARTHOLOMEW: (*Laughing*) Yes—like when he called James and John "Sons of Thunder," and none of us could stop laughing— and they were so embarrassed!

JAMES: What did he say, Peter?

PETER: "Get up, Peter, kill and eat!"

THADDAEUS: *What?*

PETER: It was just as clear as when you speak to me now. "Kill and eat!" Of course I said, "You can't mean that, Lord—not this pork and all these unclean things!" But all he kept saying was, "Kill and eat!" It happened three separate times. And when I protested, he said, "You must not call what God has cleansed

common." Well, just imagine what happened then! I felt someone shaking me, and saying, "Wake up, Peter! Someone wants
you." So I got up, still dazed and confused, and went to the
door. That was when I knew that Jesus meant me to baptize my
first Gentile converts.

JAMES: Why?

PETER: Because at the door were two Jews, men I knew slightly,
from Caesarea. They had been sent by a Roman Centurion sta-
tioned there, Cornelius. And they told me that he had seen a vision, just like me. The Lord had told him to send for me.
Would any of you have refused to go, in face of that?

BARTHOLOMEW: You couldn't refuse.

PETER: That was the turning point. I found Cornelius to be a fine
man, well known for his generosity, and a student of the Scriptures. He was as sure as I was that God's messenger had stood
by him, and told him to send for me. So I said to him, in front
of a whole company of our Jewish Christian friends, "Cornelius,
this goes against all that I was brought up to believe; but I can
see that Jesus is driving us forward to new understanding. I have
heard his voice in a vision also, and he has shown me that the
old rules of "clean" and "unclean" are not binding any more.
Do you believe that Jesus is Lord?" He said, "Yes, I believe."
And that was it I baptized him, and his lovely wife, and two of
their children, and a God-fearing slave.

JAMES: (*After a short silence*) When you tell that story to the
meeting, Peter, I don't think anyone will deny that you did
God's will.

THADDAEUS: I hope you are right, James. It will still be hard for
some of the company to accept this. They are so afraid that we
are moving out too far and too fast—losing the basis of our belief. But I know that *my* doubts have vanished.

BARTHOLOMEW: Mine also! I thank God for such a clear sign to
lead us!

JAMES: We shall be able to back you up now, Peter. Thank you
for spending this time with us. Let us be on our way!

SCENE TEN: BARNABAS AND PAUL
START ON THEIR JOURNEY

Bible reference: Acts 13, verses 1-4

CHARACTERS: SIMEON NIGER
                 MANAEN
                 LUCIUS OF CYRENE
                 PAUL
                 BARNABAS

NOTE: At least fourteen years separate this Scene from Scene Eight. We know very little about Paul's life in these years. He had no desire to push himself forward as a leader; but he evidently earned the respect and trust of his fellow Christians. And so, when new leadership in the mission field was needed, Barnabas went to Tarsus to persuade Paul to take on fresh responsibilities (Acts 11, 22-26).

The five men begin with a period of silent prayer. Then there is an improvised discussion. Simeon asks them to share the results of their prayers. Barnabas, who came from Cyprus (Acts 4, verse 36), says that he has been thinking of the need to found Churches there. Why only there? The others discuss a wider mission, the theme being that the time is ripe for it.

Paul keeps very quiet. Simeon says that the Spirit has kept on showing him a picture of Barnabas and Paul going together by ship. Manaen says that he too is sure that God means Paul to go on such a journey. Lucius talks about the need for the Church to send missionaries to his native Cyrene. There may have been a Church there already, for it was a man of Cyrene, Simon, who carried Jesus' Cross; but let Lucius try to imagine the situation there, and talk about plans and opportunities.

After a few minutes, Simeon sums up. The Spirit is guiding them to send Barnabas and Paul, with Cyprus as their first objective. Paul is hesitant and diffident at first; but at length he consents to go, if his friend Barnabas will be the leader. So they agree that this will be the plan. They discuss Cyprus, and also the neighboring Roman Province of Cilicia, in modern Turkey. They talk about the opposition they may meet: from Roman officials, priests of the pagan Gods, anti-Christian Jews.

Finally, the other three lay their hands on the heads of Barnabas and Paul, and pray for them to receive the Spirit's blessing and power.

SCENE ELEVEN: JEWS AND GENTILES AT LYSTRA

Bible reference: Acts 14, 8-23

Liturgical use: Epiphany season

CHARACTERS: PAUL
BARNABAS
*PHRIXUS, *a cripple*
*HIERON, *a Jew of Pisidian Antioch*
*FUSCUS, *a Jew of Iconium*
LOIS, EUNICE and TIMOTHY, *Christians of Lystra*
A CROWD OF GENTILES
JEWS, *companions of* HIERON *and* FUSCUS

NOTE: Phrixus, Hieron and Fuscus are imaginary names for the people mentioned in the text. Timothy and his family (mentioned in II Timothy, 1, 5) may not have been Christians as early as this; but it seems legitimate to introduce them among the Christians at Lystra, as Timothy left that city to accompany Paul in Acts 16, verse 4.

You should read the whole account of Paul's first journey, in Acts 13 and 14, to put this scene into its full context.

The scene is a street in Lystra. PAUL *and* BARNABAS *are standing on steps above the crowd of people of mixed races.* PAUL *is in the middle of a sermon. It would be a good challenge for the actor to expand this opening speech, giving other instances in which Jesus accepted and befriended Gentiles.*

PAUL: And so, my friends, though Jesus was a Jew, as I am, and lived among Jews, he was the Savior of all nations. Some of my closest friends in our Christian brotherhood are Greeks; and in our Church at Caesarea we have a Roman Centurion and all his family. God sent his Son to us, to heal the sick and the lame, and to save every tribe and race of men. So now we come to you in Lystra—

(PHRIXUS *has been trying to get to his feet on his crutches.*)

MAN: Here, Paul! There's a sick man trying to come to you.
BARNABAS: Bring him forward!

MAN: Come on, Phrixus! I'll help you.

PHRIXUS: Sir, is it true? That this Jesus can heal a lame man?

BARNABAS: Set him down here!

MAN: He's a hopeless case. He has never walked.

PHRIXUS: You said he could heal me!

PAUL: Yes, friend. What is your name?

PHRIXUS: Phrixus, Sir.

PAUL: Phrixus, God, who gave you life, can now give you healing, if it is his will, and if you have faith.

> (*The crowd presses close. Remarks like: "What's happening?" "Isn't that Phrixus?" "What did he say?"*)

BARNABAS: Please keep back! Keep away from the steps, or someone will get hurt! If you will all be quiet, we will pray together for our brother Phrixus to be healed. (*The crowd is quiet.*)

PAUL: People of Lystra, I have told you about Jesus. His power can heal, even through the hands of a sinner like me, if he wills it. But you must all pray, and have faith. Pray to Jesus! And you, Phrixus, give me your hands! Now look at me, and say this after me: "Lord Jesus, (PHRIXUS *repeats each phrase.*) I know that you can heal me, if that is your will for me. I am going to stand and walk." Now! Stand straight up on your feet! Go on, Phrixus! Stand! (*Both* PAUL *and* PHRIXUS *show signs of great physical effort, as* PHRIXUS *stands.*) You, throw away those crutches! Take them away and burn them if you like!

MAN: Great Jupiter! Phrixus is standing up!

PHRIXUS: I can walk! Great God, I can stand up and walk!

> (*Shouts and excitement among the crowd.*)

PAUL: Silence, please! Friends, do not be amazed at what God has done. Let Phrixus go home quietly. He needs to rest, and be with his family. Is it far to your home, Phrixus?

PHRIXUS: Just round that corner. They never carry me far. God! What am I saying? I don't have to be carried any more!

PAUL: Take it easy, Phrixus! Somebody run ahead to his home, to prepare them. And you, Sir, will you go with him?

BARNABAS: Have something to eat, Phrixus, and don't try to do too much. We will come later and visit you.

> (PHRIXUS *goes out, with one or two of the crowd.*)

MAN: (*Climbing on the steps*) People of Lystra, a wonderful thing has happened in our city. Can you doubt it any longer? The

Gods have come down to us in human form! (*Yells from the crowd.*) I know nothing about Jesus; but this man must surely be Mercury, for he speaks as the messenger of God. And here is mighty Jupiter himself! (*He points at* BARNABAS.)

BARNABAS: Don't say that! It is blasphemy!

MAN: I say we should make a sacrifice to them! (*Voices from the crowd "That's right!" "Call the Priests!"*)

MAN: Lead them to the Temple and sacrifice oxen! (*Voices: "To the Temple!" "They are Gods!"*)

PAUL: Stop! Stop! Stop! (*Silence.*) Oh, men and women of Lystra, why are you doing this? We are not Gods, but ordinary human beings, like all of you! We have come to lead you away from empty superstitions, and turn you to the living God—

> (*Crowd voices: "Take them to the Temple!" "Fetch the Priests!" "The Gods have come among us!" Meanwhile* HIERON, FUSCUS *and other* JEWS *enter.*)

PAUL: For the last time, silence! Listen to me! I want you to understand that this healing was God's work; but I and my friend are not Gods. We are men—

HIERON: Yes, men! Troublemakers, liars!

FUSCUS: Devils, not Gods! (*They push forward to the steps.*)

> (*Crowd voices: "Who are you?" "What do you mean?" "Who are these men?"*)

PAUL: Hieron of Antioch! May God forgive you for this!

HIERON: Traitor! I want to tell you all about these two so-called preachers. I am Hieron, a Jew of Antioch in Pisidia.

FUSCUS: And I am Fuscus of Iconium. We came here with our friends, to warn you about these money-grubbing, cheating hypocrites!

PAUL: Don't listen to them! They are enemies of the light!

HIERON: I'm not here to talk theology. I could prove to you that these men are liars, perverters of our Jewish faith; but all I need say is that wherever they go, trouble follows. They were chased out of Antioch by all the decent citizens—

FUSCUS: Then they tried the same game in Iconium. They stirred up a riot, and we threw them out—

PAUL: That is true! Wherever we bring light, the powers of darkness fight against us!

HIERON: And now I hear they are pretending to be your gods.

BARNABAS: That is a lie, Hieron! We—

FUSCUS: Drive them out of your city!

MAN: He's right. These men are not Gods! They cheated us!

> (*While the crowd shouts: "Drive them out!" "Stone them!"* HIERON *and* FUSCUS *slip away. Stones are thrown, and* BAR- NABAS *is driven away.* PAUL *falls. The crowd disperses. After a long pause,* PAUL *sits up.* BARNABAS *enters with a group of Christians.*)

BARNABAS: Paul! Paul! Thank God you're alive!

PAUL: I shall be all right.

LOIS: We must get your head washed and bandaged.

TIMOTHY: We have to hurry, and take you out of the city.

PAUL: Not so fast, all of you! I don't intend to be driven away by men like Hieron and Fuscus. I'm grateful to you, Lois, and I will come back and rest at your home. It's courageous of you and Eunice to offer it. Meanwhile, Barnabas, you ought to go and see Phrixus. Then we can all meet for the Lord's supper.

EUNICE: I will go ahead and prepare for you, Paul.

PAUL: We have to have faith that this crowd will cool off, and then those whom the Lord calls will surely join us.

SCENE TWELVE: THE COUNCIL AT JERUSALEM

Bible reference: Acts 15, 1-21

CHARACTERS: ALL THE LEADERS OF THE CHURCH
THE APOSTLES, *except for James, Son of Zebe- dee, who had been killed by Herod (Acts 12)*
JAMES, *who presided at the Council (verse 13)*
JUDAS BARSABBAS *and* SILAS, *chosen as envoys (verse 22)*
"ELDERS" *and* "THE PHARISAIC PARTY" *(verse 4)*

NOTE: This meeting was very important for the Church. The Apostles, who had worked with Jesus in a Jewish context within Judaea, now faced honest disagreements within the growing Church. Could it be true that membership of the Christian body was open to Gentiles who did not first accept Jewish traditions?

Parables of seed and growth, like the "Mustard Seed," pointed toward a universal Church; and the last of Jesus' sayings recorded by Matthew was: "Go forth therefore and make all nations my disciples." But it was still hard for some of the traditionalist disciples to accept what was happening in places unfamiliar to them. There are difficulties in reconciling Luke's account of the Council with Paul's letters. These are discussed in commentaries (Peake, 791a-f). From Paul we learn that the decision of the Council did not put an end to the disagreements. For further study of this question, see Romans 14, I Corinthians 10, and Galatians, 1-2.

The whole of this scene is to be improvised. Imagine a crowded room, like the Upper Room of earlier scenes, simply furnished. Choose for James, brother of Jesus, someone who will express a moderate Conservative view. Get him to study the character carefully. Choose several people to take the two opposite sides: the strict Jewish-Christian party, and the Hellenist, pro-Gentile party. Choose others to portray Peter, Paul and Barnabas.

When they have studied their roles, improvise the meeting. James should lead them in prayer, and then open the business. He explains what has brought them together.

Then Peter speaks (see verses 7-11). Questions are asked by several of the others. James then asks Paul to speak, followed by Barnabas. They describe the events of chapters 13-14, including especially the scene at Lystra. Questions follow their speeches. Encourage the two "parties" to put their points strongly, even angrily. James holds the balance, and intervenes when necessary.

At length James says that all the points at issue have been fully discussed, and it is time for a decision to be made. He can either read verses 13-21, or make his own summary of it. When he has finished, they all pray for the future of the Church, and for unity.

Finally, Judas Barsabbas and Silas are appointed to carry the decision to the Church of Antioch.

SCENE THIRTEEN: THE GUIDANCE OF THE SPIRIT

Bible reference: Acts 16, 6-10

NOTE: In Scene Two the Apostles were portrayed when they received the gift of the Holy Spirit, collectively and very dramatical-

ly. This short passage is important, because it shows another side
of the Spirit's work in the Church: guidance given to individuals.
The scene is divided into three episodes.

FIRST EPISODE

CHARACTERS: Paul
                    Silas
                    Timothy

*The three men are in a house, in one of the cities of what is now
South West Turkey. It is not possible to tell from the text exactly
where they were. They are praying together, and trying to make
the right plan for the next step in their journey. Improvise the first
part of the scene. Paul asks for the guidance of the "Spirit of
Jesus." Each of the three prays aloud, using phrases like: "Guide
us, Lord!" "Send your Spirit into our hearts!" "Let us have ears
to hear!" Then there is a period of silence.*

Silas: I had a clear vision of a straight road, leading to the
    North. There were other roads to the right and left, but I knew
    that we should not take them.
Paul: It's strange that you should say that. I was thinking of
    Ephesus, and how I long to go and preach there, in front of
    Diana's temple. But I felt the Lord saying, "Not yet, Paul!" Ti-
    mothy, did God speak through your prayers?
Timothy: I felt confused. I could only thank God for counting me
    worthy to be here with you.
Paul: It is clear to me that the Spirit is directing us toward the
    North. Let us go on toward Mysia tomorrow, and then seek
    guidance again.

SECOND EPISODE

CHARACTERS: Paul
                    Silas
                    Timothy
                    A Family (*imaginary*)

*The whole of this episode can be improvised. The three men have
moved North into Mysia (find it on a map). Imagine them to be*

staying with a Christian family. Make up names, and assign parts to several actors. They are all at supper, discussing plans. Their host talks about Bithynia, the Roman Province along the North coast of Turkey. There are big cities there, like Sinope. It seems a good way to go next.

Then a letter is brought in by a Christian from Troas. It is from Carpus, who is later mentioned in 2 Timothy 4, as a friend of Paul at Troas. PAUL reads the letter aloud. Carpus has heard about Paul's journey, and sends an invitation for him and his companions to come to Troas, and use his house as a base for preaching. He mentions that a Doctor named Luke is staying there also.

They discuss this offer, and agree that it must be a sign from the Spirit that they should turn away from Bithynia and go to Troas.

THIRD EPISODE

CHARACTERS: CARPUS
LUKE
TIMOTHY
SILAS
PAUL

This improvised scene takes place in Carpus' home at Troas. It is breakfast time, and the four men are eating—PAUL having not yet got up. Imagine what they would discuss. As PAUL later left some parchments at Carpus' house, one subject could be the need for writing down the Gospel, and for keeping in touch with the Churches in different cities by letter. They also talk about PAUL, and how soundly he is sleeping. They are unwilling to wake him.

Suddenly PAUL bursts in, and says, "The Lord has spoken to me! I know now where the Spirit is leading us."

They question him eagerly, and he tells them about the dream, described in verse 9. There is much excited discussion about Macedonia; the different cities like Philippi, Neapolis, Thessalonica and Beroea; the types of people they may meet there; and the prospects of finding a passage in a ship.

They send Luke off to the harbor, to try to book passages for all of them except CARPUS, on any ship leaving for a Macedonian port.

SCENE FOURTEEN: THE PRISON AT PHILIPPI

Bible reference: Acts 16, 19-40

Liturgical use: Epiphany season

CHARACTERS: PAUL
                 SILAS
                 *PHLEGON, the Jailer
                 *LUCIA, his wife
                 THEIR SON and DAUGHTER
                 VOICES OF PRISONERS

NOTE: First read Acts 16, 11-18. Improvise scenes at the riverside place of prayer and the confrontation with the owners of the slave girl.

Philippi was an important city, where a colony of Roman veterans had been settled. Apparently there was no synagogue, as Paul went to the open air place of prayer to preach first. The hymn used in this scene can be found in the Episcopal Hymnal (number 336). Use another familiar hymn about the Cross if you prefer. The children may be omitted; but you could also write bigger parts for them.

In the prison, PAUL *and* SILAS *are sitting, with their feet in stocks and chains on their hands. The other prisoners are in a neighboring room, and can be heard through the door.* PAUL *and* SILAS *are singing. I have chosen a familiar modern hymn, whose words fit in well with* PAUL's *later Letter to the Philippians.*

PAUL AND SILAS: In the cross of Christ I glory,
                              Towering o'er the wrecks of time;
                     All the light of sacred story
                              Gathers round its head sublime.
PHLEGON: (*Entering.*) What is this cross you were singing about?
SILAS: The Son of God was nailed to a cross in Judaea, Jailer, to save you and all mankind.
VOICES OF PRISONERS: Sing some more! Don't stop!
PHLEGON: Son of God?
PAUL: Yes. Jesus of Nazareth, your friend and savior. What is your name, Jailer?

PHLEGON: Phlegon, Sir. Here! What am I doing calling a prisoner
"Sir"?

VOICES: Sing! You in there, sing!

SILAS: They want us to tell them Jesus' story, Phlegon.

PAUL AND SILAS: When the woes of life o'ertake me,
        Hopes deceive, and fears annoy,
    Never shall the cross forsake me;
        Lo, it glows with peace and joy.

PHLEGON: I like that song. Tell me—

(*The earthquake shakes the prison. The lights go out: shouting
and confusion.*)

PAUL: Don't panic, any of you! You won't be hurt!

PHLEGON: Oh, God! The doors are open! I shall be beheaded for
this.

(*He draws his sword.* PAUL *can hear this.*)

PAUL: Don't do yourself harm, Phlegon! We shan't run away.

SILAS: Are you all right, Paul?

PAUL: Just shaken. It did me no harm. And you?

SILAS: The same. We seem to be free of our bonds.

PHLEGON: Lucia! Lights! Lights! (LUCIA *comes in with a lamp, the*
CHILDREN *with her.*) Oh, Thank God! Are you all right? And
you, children?

CHILDREN: "We weren't hurt, Daddy." "Didn't it make a terrible
noise?"

LUCIA: The quake seemed to shake the prison, without harming
our house.

PAUL: Thank you for bringing the lights. Everyone keep calm!
You'd better count the prisoners, Phlegon. I don't expect there
are any missing. (PHLEGON *goes into the other room.*)

SILAS: I think they're all too scared out there to run far.

LUCIA: Who are you, Sir? You're not like any other prisoner my
husband ever had in here before.

PAUL: I am Paul of Tarsus, and this is my friend Silas. We were
brought in here because we are followers of Jesus, Son of God.

LUCIA: And you were beaten and put in prison for that?

PAUL: Only partly for that. Some of the good people of Philippi
thought that our teaching was hurting their pockets.

SILAS: So naturally they wanted us out of the way.

PHLEGON: (*Returning.*) I can't believe it. Everyone is here, and no one hurt. There's more going on tonight than I can understand.

SILAS: The hand of God is upon us, Phlegon. He wants to show you his power, and to bring you to salvation.

PHLEGON: What must I do to have salvation, Sir?

LUCIA: Before you worry about that, Phlegon, let me bathe their bruises. Fancy putting gentlemen like this in prison!

PAUL: Our bruises can wait. The important thing is our souls, and yours. Phlegon, this Jesus whom we worship is God himself, but for love of us men he humbled himself, and came to live among us in the form of a man—not a King or a General, but an ordinary carpenter in Judaea. I know that he sent us here tonight to tell you about him. He showed a sign through this earthquake; but his real power lies in acts of love and service. Do you understand this, and believe it?

PHLEGON: I don't know what to believe, Sir. I trust you to speak the truth—I know that.

LUCIA: Please, Sir, come through to our home, and drink some wine. I'll get some breakfast ready, and bathe your wounds. Come and help me, children!

PAUL: Thank you, Lucia. We will come. We shall tell you more about Jesus, and if you believe what we say you shall all be baptized.

SILAS: Will you give us some food and wine to take to the other prisoners, Lucia? We can bear witness to them also, and perhaps they will turn to God.

PHLEGON: That's very irregular, but—oh, it's all too much for me! I'll do anything you say. I expect the Magistrates will send someone to set you free in the morning, anyway.

PAUL: Oh, no, Phlegon! I have decided to give our friends at City Hall a slight lesson. They have beaten and imprisoned two Roman citizens without trial, and they can—

PHLEGON: Roman citizens! You mean you let them beat you, and never said anything about it?

PAUL: We had a good reason, Phlegon. Jesus allowed himself to be scourged and crucified. We will tell you more about his death later, and how he rose from the dead to assure us of everlasting life.

SILAS: And there is another reason. If the Magistrates are uneasy about having broken the law in imprisoning us, they will be less likely to make trouble for Jesus' followers here after we have left.

PAUL: If you are to be one of us, Phlegon, we must introduce you to these wonderful people who form our Church here: Lydia, the dye merchant, and Epaphras, and Euodias and Syntyche.

LUCIA: (*Coming back.*) Aren't you coming?

PAUL: Yes, Lucia. We are coming. My back does feel sore, and I shall be grateful to have it bathed.

SILAS: Let us sing as we go, Paul.

PAUL AND SILAS: When the sun of bliss is beaming
                     Light and Love upon my way,
                     From the cross the radiance streaming
                     Adds new luster to the day.

SCENE FIFTEEN: FRUSTRATION AT ATHENS

Bible reference: Acts 17, 16-34

Liturgical use: Epiphany season

CHARACTERS: *CHRYSIPPUS, *a Stoic philosopher*
            *ATHENAGORAS, *an Epicurean philosopher*
            DIONYSIUS, *a member of the Areopagus Council*
            DAMARIS, *a Christian convert*
            PAUL

NOTE: Chrysippus and Athenagoras are imaginary characters. Their types are implied in the text. The Areopagus was a very old religious and cultural body. After having become almost obsolete, it had revived its prestige in Roman Athens. Luke's account of Paul's appearance before this Council is halfway between a Court hearing and a philosophical discussion, in which a foreign teacher's credentials are being checked.

At Athens Paul met with something which he seems to have hated more than persecution: he was patronized. The jail at Philippi and the docks of Corinth gave him hard opposition to cope with; but in Athens he met polish and intellectual curiosity, without any true vitality behind it. I have tried to bring this out in the characters of the philosophers. If students are interested in a follow-up, it would be worthwhile to read more about the Stoic and Epicurean philosophies, and to improvise more discussion.

For Damaris and Dionysius, see verse 34. It appears that both were Gentiles. I have imagined Damaris to be a business-woman, like Priscilla in Acts 18, verse 3.

CHRYSIPPUS, ATHENAGORAS *and* DIONYSIUS *are walking in a portico, or "stoa," in the agora at Athens, the main business and social center.*

CHRYSIPPUS: Well, what did you think of him?

ATHENAGORAS: Paul? Impressive, I thought. Quite a forceful speech; but with a lot of Eastern absurdity mixed up in it.

CHRYSIPPUS: You didn't like what he said about the resurrection of this Jesus, I suppose! You Epicureans don't give an inch on immortality, do you?

ATHENAGORAS: I must say, we prefer our myths in books of fiction, not dressed up as history. For an educated man with a good mind, Paul believes some remarkable things!

CHRYSIPPUS: You're very quiet, Dionysius. What did you think?

DIONYSIUS: You really want to know? What I heard today was the first real message of hope that ever got through to me. I don't know what to believe about Paul yet, or about Jesus. I only know I have to find out more.' If it is even half true, it's the most important thing that ever happened in the history of mankind.

CHRYSIPPUS: Come now, Dionysius! Don't get carried away!

DIONYSIUS: Why not get carried away? In God's name, Chrysippus! You and I have hung around Athens, discussing every dead philosophical idea, for so many years that it sickens me. Here comes a man who is real, and tells us from his own experience that God cares—God is love—

ATHENAGORAS: But is the experience real? I'm sure Paul believes it; but you know what these Easterners are like.

CHRYSIPPUS: There he is, talking to that woman. Who is she?

DIONYSIUS: That is Damaris. She has a flax-importing business. Paul is a tentmaker, and he has been lodging at her home.

CHRYSIPPUS: A tradesman philosopher! Unusual!

ATHENAGORAS: (*As* PAUL *and* DAMARIS *enter.*) Paul! Excuse me for interrupting, Madam, but we were just talking about your friend. My name is Athenagoras, and this is Chrysippus. I think you know Dionysius. That was a remarkably able talk that you gave to the Council, Paul.

PAUL: Thank you. Talk is like seed. The important thing is where it falls, and what fruit it bears.

ATHENAGORAS: You certainly scattered some unusual seed today! Your argument flitted around like a sparrow, scavenging a little from every religion.

PAUL: Then it should be very suitable for an Athenian audience,

Sir. There are more dead religions here than in any other city throughout the Empire.

CHRYSIPPUS: That is an offensive thing to say, Jew! Don't forget that you are enjoying the hospitality of Athens. What right have you—

PAUL: I mean no offense. I say what God commands me, in Jesus' name and through the power of his Spirit. I bear you no ill will; but today I have spoken to men who seem to be all intellect and no heart, no lifeblood. If you patronize my Lord and Savior, it is a waste of time to talk to you.

DIONYSIUS: Paul, may I—

PAUL: Come with me, Dionysius! I watched you at the Council. I know that you need Jesus, and are called to follow him.

DAMARIS: You are welcome to come with us to my home, Dionysius. There is a small group gathered there, and Paul will tell us more.

CHRYSIPPUS: Well! Another new sect! I didn't know you went in for Eastern fads, Dionysius.

PAUL: Chrysippus, I pray from the bottom of my heart that you will one day find out how blind you are. May Jesus come to you both in his love, and enter your hearts! Will you come, Dionysius?

DIONYSIUS: Yes, I will come. Goodbye, my friends!

CHRYSIPPUS: Goodbye! Be careful what lies you swallow! This man would outtalk Socrates. (PAUL, DAMARIS *and* DIONYSIUS *go out.*)

ATHENAGORAS: Extraordinary! I'm all in favor of new approaches, but really—

CHRYSIPPUS: I see what Dionysius means. The man is sincere. If it were not for the fantastic exaggerations, Jesus' teaching would be a very original contribution to religious thought.

ATHENAGORAS: Let us walk down to the Gymnasium. It will be interesting to see how it struck some of the others.

SCENE SIXTEEN: CORINTH

Bible reference: Acts 18, 1-20. See also I Corinthians 8; 11, 1-24; and 13

Liturgical use: Epiphany season

NOTE: Corinth was a cosmopolitan port, full of every variety of human being. The Church there was bound to contain a mixture of people, from all kinds of religious and social backgrounds, and very difficult to keep in harmony. Paul's two Letters to the Corinthians reflect many problems; but he obviously cared very deeply for this Church. In the two episodes, I have combined Luke's account in Acts with some passages from Paul's First Letter. All the characters are mentioned in the Bible in connection with Corinth.

Gallio came from a famous Roman family, which included the philosopher Seneca and the poet Lucan. He probably became Governor, or Proconsul, of Achaea in 51 A.D. (Peake 795k). He appears in this scene as a polished Roman of the aristocratic governing class; a little cynical, but just and intelligent.

FIRST EPISODE

CHARACTERS: GALLIO, Governor of Achaea (Greece)
                      ROMAN OFFICIALS
                      SOSTHENES, *Leader of the Synagogue*
                      JEWISH LEADERS
                      PAUL
                      CHRISTIANS OF CORINTH

The JEWS *and* CHRISTIANS *are seated in a courtroom. They all stand as a* ROMAN OFFICIAL *ushers* GALLIO *in.*)

USHER: Silence in Court! All rise for His Excellency the Governor!

GALLIO: You may be seated. (*He consults a paper in his hand.*) This is an informal hearing of a complaint by the Jewish community against Saul, also called Paul, and his associates, of the sect called Christians. I wish to establish whether there is a case which can be tried under Roman Law. Who represents the Jews?

SOSTHENES: I do, Your Excellency. My name is Sosthenes, leader of the Synagogue.

GALLIO: Which of you is Paul?

PAUL: I am Paul, Your Excellency.

GALLIO: Sosthenes, state briefly your reasons for this accusation.

SOSTHENES: They are simple, Sir. For a long time we Jews have been loyal and law-abiding citizens of Corinth. I think our record speaks for itself; and Roman Law recognizes our rights and offers us safeguards and protection. But in the last eighteen months our Synagogue has been torn by disloyalty and dissension—ever since the arrival of this Paul.

GALLIO: Just a minute. Paul, I understand that you are a Roman citizen.

PAUL: I am, Sir.

GALLIO: But you are a Jew?

PAUL: Yes, Sir, by birth and training—

SOSTHENES: But a traitor and a renegade, Your Excellency!

GALLIO: Be silent! This Court will be conducted in an orderly manner, or else dismissed at once! Answer when I direct a question to you. Is that clear?

SOSTHENES: I apologize, Your Excellency.

PAUL: I am a Jew, Sir; but I am a follower of Jesus, the Christ, the Son of God. He too lived as a Jew, but he taught us that love and faith have no limits of race.

GALLIO: That hardly seems like a dangerous belief, Sosthenes. What is your objection to Paul's teaching?

SOSTHENES: I have no wish to involve you in details about our beliefs, Sir; but I call your attention to the results of this man's attempts to break up our Synagogue. We keep to ourselves, and observe our own Law, which is very precious to us. But this man, having ingratiated himself with our members when he first came to Corinth, began to recruit some of them for his sect. We regard this Jesus as an impostor, and Paul's teaching as a debased, false, cheap corruption of the Jewish faith. I hope that you

GALLIO: You said "results," Sosthenes. I am not interested in your theology.

SOSTHENES: Yes, Sir. Well, first he split our membership by persuading our leader, Crispus, to turn Christian. Then he invited half the riff-raff of Corinth, dock slaves, loose women, and criminals, to join his wonderful Church!

GALLIO: That is no concern of mine.

SOSTHENES: It is your concern, Sir, if it causes disloyalty and upheaval, and imperils the peaceful status of the Jewish community. Ask him whether his Christians—

PAUL: May I speak, Sir?

GALLIO: Yes, Paul. In a very few words, what is your answer to these charges?

PAUL: We are not disloyal, Sir. We have caused no upheaval. To us a Phrygian dock-slave is equal in God's eyes to a Jewish Rabbi or a Roman General. We preach love and joy and peace to all, because God does not distinguish between rich or poor, Jew or Gentile.

GALLIO: Thank you. I have heard enough to be quite clear in my mind that there is no case for a Roman Court to try. This is a matter of religious disagreement, which is as old as the human race, I suppose. I am inclined to believe, Sosthenes, that the upheaval of which you speak has come from the Jews, not from the Christians. But I pass no judgment about that. As Governor, I warn you all, Jews and Christians, that violence will be suppressed, and rioters punished. I urge you to solve your differences; or, if you cannot do that, to keep clear of each other.

SOSTHENES: Your Excellency, I protest! We—

GALLIO: Sosthenes, I did not invite you to speak again.

SOSTHENES: No, Sir, but—

GALLIO: You are all dismissed.

USHER: The Court is adjourned. (*There is a buzz of comment as they leave.*)

GALLIO: Paul, I should like a word with you.

PAUL: Certainly, Sir.

GALLIO: Sit down. (*They are now alone.*) I confess I am puzzled to find a man of your background and education mixed up in what seems to be a revivalist movement. I would have placed you as a university teacher.

PAUL: You would probably have been right, Sir, if my life had not been changed by Jesus.

GALLIO: You knew this man?

PAUL: Not in his lifetime on earth, Sir. He appeared to me—

(*An* OFFICIAL *hurries in. There is shouting outside.*)

OFFICIAL: Excuse me, Sir. There's some trouble outside.

GALLIO: What kind of trouble?

OFFICIAL: It's that Sosthenes, Sir—the Jew. There was quite a crowd outside, waiting. He's not too popular with a lot of the Greeks; and he got into a fight.

GALLIO: Is it out of hand? Are our men involved?

OFFICIAL: No, Sir. Nothing serious yet. But I thought you ought to know.

GALLIO: Quite right, Metellus. Keep an eye on the situation, but don't interfere unless you have to. It's really no concern of ours.

OFFICIAL: Yes, Sir. (*He goes out.*)

GALLIO: Is this part of your love and peace, Paul?

PAUL: It cannot be my friends who attacked him, Sir. They are sworn to avoid violence. Jesus taught us to love our enemies.

GALLIO: That's sometimes difficult, Paul. If the Romans made that their policy, I think you and everyone else would be in trouble.

OFFICIAL: (*Returning.*) Sir, the crowd has broken up. I think Sosthenes is badly hurt. He's lying in the road.

PAUL: Will you let me go and help him, Sir?

OFFICIAL: I think some of your people are picking him up—the men who were here in Court with you.

GALLIO: Loving the enemy, Paul? All right, go and help. You seem to me to be a sincere man. I hope we may have a further chance to talk. But keep your people out of trouble! I understand that your Jesus finished up on a cross.

PAUL: His work is not finished, Sir. It has just begun. And we do not seek trouble. We have to face it if it comes. I will go now, if I may, and see if I can make my peace with Sosthenes. Goodbye, Sir, and thank you for your impartiality.

SECOND EPISODE

CHARACTERS: PAUL
                AQUILA
                PRISCILLA, *his wife*
                CRISPUS, *former leader of the Synagogue*
                GAIUS (*see I Corinthians 1, 14*)
                STEPHANAS *and his family (See I Corinthians 1, 16)*
                SILAS
                TIMOTHY
                PHOEBE (*see Romans 16, 1*)
                EPAINETUS (*see Romans 16, 6, Phillips' translation*)

NOTE: This scene is imaginary. It is possible that the Sosthenes of the First Episode is the same as "our colleague Sosthenes" of I Corinthians 1, 2, but we cannot be sure. I have imagined a scene at the house of Stephanas, which could have been the church center at Corinth, as Paul baptized all of the household (I Corinthians 1, 16). We could just as well place this scene in the house of Titius Justus (see Acts 18, 7). The advantage of placing the scene in a Christian home is that the characters can have a general discussion, and introduce some of the problems dealt with by Paul in his letters to Corinth.

The setting is the living room at STEPHANAS' *home.* PAUL *and a group of his friends are sitting.* PHOEBE *enters from an inner room.*

AQUILA: How is Sosthenes, Phoebe?

PHOEBE: Much better. He seems to have relaxed since Silas prayed with him. We made him drink some milk, and I think he will sleep soon.

STEPHANAS: Come and join us, Phoebe, unless you are needed in there.

PHOEBE: Your wife and daughter will look after him, Stephanas.

PAUL: We have to think hard about what happened today, and how it will affect our work. Now that we have shared in the Eucharist, do any of you have a message of guidance for us?

EPAINETUS: May I speak? You know I was the first to be baptized in Corinth, five years ago. I've seen this trouble coming ever since; and I don't think we can run away from it. Jesus told us to baptize all nations; and in Corinth that means *all*. So, let's face it, we shall clash with the Orthodox Jews.

STEPHANAS: And we have to stand up for the truth.

TIMOTHY: Truth tempered with love. When Phoebe and Priscilla bandaged Sosthenes' head today, they achieved more than a month of sermons.

AQUILA: What worries me is the Jewish tactics—getting us in trouble with the Romans. Priscilla and I have already had to leave Rome itself. We don't want to be driven from city to city.

SILAS: There's a kind of common sense about most Roman officials. Paul and I know they can be rough in their methods; but I must say I was encouraged by Gallio today.

PHOEBE: We have had no trouble with the authorities in Cenchreae. I suppose we are better off than you in Corinth, because we have very few Jews living there. We have our problems —but not the kind of thing I've seen here today.

STEPHANAS: You're very quiet, Paul.

PAUL: I wanted to listen before telling you what I think. I feel deeply thankful for what the Lord did today. Not for the shedding of blood; but for the chance to witness, even a little, before a man like Gallio; and for the fact that Sosthenes is here in Stephanas' home. Corinth seems made for trouble; but it is made for opportunity also. Where there is vitality, you will have hatred—not a dead wall of politeness such as I met in Athens. As for what Timothy said about tying up Sosthenes' head, I agree. It is faith which brings us to Jesus, but it is love that shows him to other people: not eloquence, or prophecy, or almsgiving, or even martyrdom, unless love shines through them. Here in Corinth, with Venus' temple breeding vice on one side,

and the dock slums on the other, we need to show a patient
love, constructive and self-effacing; not out to make an impression or greedy for results. Let us show Sosthenes courtesy and
trust. We won't take advantage of him, or gloat over what has
happened. We will try to avoid quarrels, and concentrate on all
that we share with our Jewish brothers—not on what we think
they have done wrong in bringing us to Court. Perhaps that way
they will learn to rejoice with us in the truth. I worry sometimes
about our emphasis on prophecy, and on speaking with tongues.
All our knowledge and skill is incomplete, waiting to grow up,
you might say. All we can see now is a blurred reflection in a
mirror, but if we hold fast to the cross and the Gospel, we shall
one day see reality, whole and clear; and others will see it
through our faith in Jesus. We need faith—plenty of it. We need
hope—however hard the road is. But most of all we need what
we tried to show today—plain, simple love in action.

STEPHANAS' WIFE: (*Entering from the inner room.*) Paul, Sosthenes would like to talk to you.

PAUL: I will come at once. (*He goes out.*)

AQUILA: That man is a giant!

EPAINETUS: Just when things seem too bad to be true, he always
cuts through to the essentials, and you see it all differently.

(*A knock at the outer door.*)

PRISCILLA: I expect that is Crispus. (*She lets* CRISPUS *in.*)

SILAS: What news?

CRISPUS: Everything is quiet. I called on Nathanael, and he told
me the Synagogue people are very upset about Sosthenes.

TIMOTHY: Do they know where he is?

CRISPUS: Yes. Several of them saw us take him away, and they
followed us. They know we are trying to help, and I think they
are really grateful.

PRISCILLA: What is the next step, Crispus?

CRISPUS: Some friends of Sosthenes will be here in a few minutes,
to take him home if he is able to go.

PHOEBE: He should be ready, unless he is asleep. Who started the
riot?

CRISPUS: Apparently nobody knows. Sosthenes had a lot of enemies. Perhaps it just happened—with no one really planning it.

PHOEBE: When trouble arises, everyone turns on a Jew. Have you
eaten, Crispus?

CRISPUS: No, I'm famished.

STEPHANAS' WIFE: We kept some supper for you. Here. (*She brings it.*)

CRISPUS: Thank you! (*He sees meat on the plate.*) Oh, I—

AQUILA: Worried about the meat, Crispus?

CRISPUS: It's no use! I can't get the old ways out of my system! Every time I see food in the home of a Gentile Christian, the Law comes back and hits me.

TIMOTHY: That's natural, Crispus. I only wish you could have heard Paul just now. He was telling us—here he is! (PAUL *enters.*)

CRISPUS: Paul, I need a lesson in charity. I almost refused to eat meat, without inquiring where it was bought.

PAUL: How could you have any other reaction, Crispus? From Head of the Synagogue to membership of our hotchpotch of a Church is a big step! But the only rules which matter are those that your heart and conscience tell you to keep. That is what Jesus has taught me. All food is alike, except the bread and wine of the Lord's Supper. If we can teach ourselves to reverence those more, and forget our prejudices over other foods, we shall be finding the right priorities.

CRISPUS: It tastes good, Stephanas!

STEPHANAS: And you don't have to worry, Crispus. My wife doesn't buy from pagan temple shops!

AQUILA: Crispus was telling us that Sosthenes' friends will come to fetch him soon, Paul.

PAUL: I'm glad. He began the day hating us bitterly. From talking to him I have found out some of the strange things be believed about our Church. It's truly terrifying how two sets of people, both believing in God, can live in the same town and work up a fire of hatred and prejudice. But at least we have broken down part of that. There won't be such a wall between us any more. Sosthenes is a good man—a very loyal Jew. Perhaps one day it will be God's will that he should understand, and come to Jesus. I will go and tell him that his friends are coming.

SCENE SEVENTEEN: FAREWELL AT MILETUS

Bible reference: Acts 20, 15-38

CHARACTERS PAUL
His companions, listed in verse 3: SOPATER, ARISTARCHUS, SECUNDUS, GAIUS, TIMOTHY, TROPHIMUS, and LUKE
Christians from Ephesus (including AQUILA and PRISCILLA) and from Miletus

This is an improvised discussion. PAUL explains his eagerness to reach Jerusalem (verse 16) He asks for reports from the various cities represented by the people present

Look up Revelation, chapters 2 and 3. Assign different cities to students, and ask them to give reports on their "Church."

Paul and his companions report on the situation in Macedonia, including the Jewish plot mentioned in verse 3.

These reports call for imagination and knowledge. If the students have read the book carefully up to this point, it should be possible for them to make up convincing situations based on the text.

Then PAUL says goodbye. He should study verses 18-35 carefully, and give his own version of the speech.

Finally, he blesses them, and they exchange "The Peace" with great emotion. Paul clasps the hands of each of them, or embraces them, and says: "The peace of the Lord be always with you, Aquila," etc. and each one replies, "And also with you, Paul."

SCENE EIGHTEEN: THE WARNING OF AGABUS

Bible reference: Acts 21, 8-14. (Compare Acts 11, 27-30)

CHARACTERS: PAUL
LUKE
PHILIP
His WIFE and FOUR DAUGHTERS
AGABUS

NOTE: Philip was one of the seven Deacons. (See Acts 6, verse 5, and 8, verses 4-40). Agabus here acts very much like some of the Old Testament Prophets. (See Isaiah 20, verse 2; Jeremiah 13,

verse 1; Ezekiel 4, verse 1.) He performs a sign which is symbolic
of God's will for the future. This scene is not well known; but it
introduces fresh characters and a new type of situation.

All the characters except AGABUS *are sitting in* PHILIP*'s home.*

PAUL: My friends, it is wonderful to be here in your home. Whatever the future holds, I want you to know that this is a very
happy day for me.
PHILIP: And for us, Paul. Ever since the news came of your conversion at Damascus, I have longed to meet you.
PAUL: And before that you shrank from me—oh, Philip! I can't
forget that Stephen was one of your closest friends.
PHILIP: I don't forget it either, Paul; but Jesus used Stephen's
martyrdom to bring you among us, and none of us bear you any
ill will.
PAUL: Let us share Jesus between us tonight. I will tell you again
what happened to me at the gate of Damascus. Luke will tell us
of his calling, and how we left Troas together for Macedonia;
and let each of you speak of your experience of the Lord—for I
know that all of you are close to him, even the youngest of your
girls, Philip.
PHILIP: Melanippe? Yes, indeed she is close to Jesus. We will do
as you say, Paul. You are the youngest, Melanippe. Begin, and
tell us your witness! Each of us will share our favorite parts of
the Lord's message, or our own knowledge of his love.

> (*Improvise their stories. The* FOUR GIRLS *either tell stories
> from the Gospels, or experiences made up by the actors.*
> PHILIP*'s* WIFE *does the same.* PHILIP *tells of experiences based
> on the references given above. We do not know the story of*
> LUKE*'s conversion; but it is a good challenge for the actor to
> make it up.* PAUL *comes last, describing his conversion. As he
> is finishing,* AGABUS *knocks, and one of the* GIRLS *lets him
> in.*)

PHILIP: Come in, Agabus!
PAUL: Agabus! It must be at least seven years since I saw you last
at Antioch. How are you?
AGABUS: I am well, Paul, thank God. I have heard so much of
your journeys and sufferings.
PAUL: The joys have far outweighed the sufferings! This is Luke,

my friend and companion. Luke, Agabus is revered for his powers of prophecy.

LUKE: I have heard of you, Agabus; and how you predicted the famine.

AGABUS: And you and Barnabas took our gifts to Jerusalem. Ah, Paul! So much has happened since those days!

PHILIP: Great things, Agabus! And now Paul is on his way to Jerusalem.

AGABUS: Yes, I heard that. In fact, that is why I am here.

PAUL: To go with me?

AGABUS: No, Paul—though I would gladly do that. I am here to warn you that it is dangerous for you to go.

PAUL: What we do is always dangerous, Agabus.

AGABUS: That is true. But I have to tell you the vision which the Lord has sent to me. It happened two nights ago. Give me your belt, Paul!

PAUL: My belt? Why—

AGABUS: Give it to me! (AGABUS *takes the belt, and begins to bind his own hands and feet.*) I am only telling you the message of God. This is what the Holy Spirit says. "The man to whom this girdle belongs will be bound like this by the Jews in Jerusalem and handed over to the Gentiles."

PHILIP: Paul, if this is true—

LUKE: It is a warning. Ought you not to take notice of it?

PAUL: Thank you, Agabus. You did right to come here.

PHILIP: Will you leave Judaea, Paul?

PAUL: No, Philip. I will go to Jerusalem, as I have planned.

PHILIP: But Paul—

PAUL: Of course we must all pray tonight, and be sure that it is God's will for me to go. But I have no doubt about it in my heart. Don't cry, Melanippe! Or any of you! You know that Jesus turned his face toward Jerusalem, knowing full well what faced him there. None of you would hesitate to do the same, if you knew it to be right. And I don't think God means me to die there, as Jesus did. In all my years of preaching I have never yet seen Rome. I think he means me to go there still.

PHILIP: Of course you must go, if it is the will of the Lord. But you know your reputation, Paul! Sometimes you love to look for danger. Remember the Church's need comes first!

SCENE NINETEEN: DANGER AT JERUSALEM

Bible reference: Acts 21, 15-22, 9.

NOTE: This incident illustrates three important elements in Acts. (1) The violent hatred which some Jews felt for Paul. They thought that he was a traitor to his faith, because he had become a leader in a heretical sect, in which Gentiles were mixed with Jews. (2) Paul's courage, and his witness to the Gospel under stress of danger. (3) The determination of the Romans to see proper justice done. The book of Acts contains many examples of these things. Here they are brought together in an exciting story.

FIRST EPISODE

CHARACTERS: PAUL
FOUR JEWISH CHRISTIANS (verse 24)
A CROWD OF JEWS
CLAUDIUS LYSIAS, *Roman Commandant*
ROMAN SOLDIERS
A CENTURION

This episode is to be improvised. The Praetorium, headquarters of the Roman Army in Jerusalem, was next door to the Temple courtyard. Paul is walking across the courtyard, with the four Jewish Christians. They are talking together about going into the Temple, and finding the right official to notify about their vows and purification. PAUL talks about why he consented to this surprising action. He probably did it to conciliate hostile Jewish opinion in Jerusalem, where many people, even inside the Church, still thought of him as showing too little respect for the Law. Improvise this conversation. (Compare Peake, 798e-g.)

Several Jews in the crowd see him. They were "Jews of Asia," and had perhaps known him in one of the cities where there had been clashes earlier. They cry out:

"Look, there's Paul—Traitor!"

"Are you sure?"

"I'm certain."

"Who are those men with him?"

"They're Gentiles! I tell you, he has brought Gentiles into the Temple!"

"Drag him outside! Lynch him!"

There is a general rush toward Paul, and a struggle. One of Paul's companions runs to the steps of the Praetorium, shouting for help. The Commandant, with a Centurion and soldiers, runs down the steps. Paul is secured with chains, and lifted through the crowd to the steps. Imagine what everybody would say: the fury of the crowd, the orders given by the Commandant, etc.

SECOND EPISODE

CHARACTERS: The same as the first episode

With the crowd still yelling "Kill Him!" PAUL *is set down near the top of the steps by the soldiers.*

PAUL: Colonel, may I have a chance to—
CLAUDIUS: You speak Greek, do you? Aren't you Egyptian?
PAUL: Egyptian? What makes you think that?
CLAUDIUS: We were told to keep an eye out for an Egyptian terrorist. I thought you must be the one.
PAUL: (*Laughing.*) I've been called many things in my lifetime, but never that! You're quite wrong, Sir. I am a Jew, from Tarsus in Cilicia, a citizen of a great city
CLAUDIUS: Well, what do you want?
PAUL: These people also made a mistake. They thought I was breaking the Law by taking Gentiles into the Temple. If you let me speak to them, I think they will quiet down.
CLAUDIUS: All right. Go ahead! It will at least show me what all this is about. (*He yells to the crowd for silence.*) That's better! Now, all of you, keep quiet! I want to hear what this man has to say.

(PAUL *makes a speech based on Acts 22, 1-21. Read it, or improvise a scene built around it, with interruptions.*)

THIRD EPISODE

CHARACTERS: PAUL
CLAUDIUS LYSIAS, the Commandant
*REGULUS, a Centurion
SOLDIERS

SOLDIERS *push* PAUL *into a room at the top of the stairs.*

CLAUDIUS: Get him in here! Centurion, keep a section of your men out there on the steps! If anyone tries to come up, take him prisoner!

REGULUS: Yes, Sir! Calvus, form up Number Two Section half-way down the steps. Report to me here if you have any trouble.

(Some of the soldiers go out to the steps.)

REGULUS: What about the prisoner, Sir?

CLAUDIUS: Yes. We have to deal with him. You seem to be the cause of a lot of trouble, Jew. I'm not convinced that we've got to the bottom of it. Centurion, tie him up and lash him! Then he'll be more in the mood to give us some straight answers. I'm going back outside to review the situation.

REGULUS: Yes, Sir. (CLAUDIUS LYSIAS *goes out.* REGULUS *orders* SOLDIERS *to tie* PAUL *up for a flogging.*)

PAUL: Centurion, do you intend to lash a Roman citizen, without even a trial?

REGULUS: Don't give me that! Are you crazy, pretending to be a Roman? You could be flogged to death for that.

PAUL: You and your Commandant will be in bad trouble if you flog me. I want to avoid that if I can.

REGULUS: Are you serious? Here, Metellus, go and tell the Commandant he's needed here. At the double! (*A* SOLDIER *runs out.*) You'd better be speaking the truth, Sir, or I wouldn't like to be in your shoes!

CLAUDIUS: (*Entering.*) What is it, Centurion?

REGULUS: I think you should talk to this man, Sir, before we lash him.

PAUL: I have been telling my friend the Centurion that, as I am a Roman citizen, it would cause him and you embarrassment if you beat me without a trial, Colonel.

CLAUDIUS: You? A citizen?

PAUL: Naturally you will want to verify that. I have my diploma at my lodgings, and am registered at Tarsus.

CLAUDIUS: You don't exactly dress like a Roman. How could someone like you afford to buy citizenship?

PAUL: I was born a citizen, Colonel. My father was one of the duumviri at Tarsus before my birth.

CLAUDIUS: And it cost me three years' pay! Well, I have to believe you, of course. I'm sorry we handled you rather roughly—

PAUL: I have no objection to that, Colonel. You saved my life. But I do object to a Roman Officer ordering a flogging for any man without trial.

CLAUDIUS: Look, Sir, if you had to keep order in this place, you'd soon find that legal forms don't mean much. It's a nightmare coping with all the fanatics in Jerusalem! I'm sorry, I know you're a Jew, but—

PAUL: (*Remembering his own part in lynching* STEPHEN.) Yes, Colonel. I know what you mean. What do you want to do with me now?

CLAUDIUS: It's hard to know what to do with one of these religious cases. We'll have to hold you—for your own safety. Tomorrow I'll try to find out whether anyone means to charge you. Probably it will all blow over.

PAUL: It may—but I doubt it.

CLAUDIUS: Meanwhile I'll have a room prepared for you; and I'd like to send for corroboration of your citizenship.

PAUL: Thank you. It's not the first time I have owed my life to the Army. If Pontius Pilate had been a man like you—

CLAUDIUS: Pilate? Wasn't he Prefect here back in Tiberius' reign?

PAUL: Yes, Colonel, he was. Perhaps I shall have a chance to tell you about him one day. But you probably want to take me away from here.

CLAUDIUS: Yes, Sir. Please come this way. We'll put you on the side of the building away from the Temple.

FOURTH EPISODE

CHARACTERS: PAUL
                *JONATHAN, his nephew
                CLAUDIUS LYSIAS
                A SOLDIER

PAUL *is in a small room in the praetorium, writing at a table. A* SOLDIER *opens the door, and brings in* JONATHAN, *a boy of about sixteen.*)

SOLDIER: Visitor for you, Sir. He says it's urgent.

PAUL: Thank you, Metellus. Jonathan!

JONATHAN: Uncle Paul, I had to come! I never thought they'd let me in.

PAUL: Get your breath, and tell me what has happened.

SOLDIER: The Commandant is coming up, Sir, in a minute. He gave us orders to let the boy see you. I'll be outside the door.

PAUL: Thank you. (*The* SOLDIER *goes out.*) Now, Jonathan!

JONATHAN: There's a plot to kill you, Uncle. I heard about it from Phinehas Bar-Tolmai, whose father is in the Sanhedrin.

PAUL: What kind of a plot? I know there are plenty of people who hate what I have done—or what they think I have done.

JONATHAN: This is serious. I told James and some of the elders, and they agreed that I had the best chance to get in here and warn you—

(*The* SOLDIER *opens the door, stands at attention, and lets* CLAUDIUS LYSIAS *pass.*)

CLAUDIUS: All right. You may wait outside. What's the trouble, Paul?

PAUL: This is my sister's boy Jonathan, Colonel, a student here in Jerusalem. He was just telling me there is a plot to kill me.

CLAUDIUS: Tell us about it, Jonathan. You were quite right to come. Now try to give us the facts simply and briefly.

JONATHAN: Yes, Sir.

PAUL: I think Jonathan has a reliable story, Colonel. He has been sent here by the leaders of our Church.

CLAUDIUS: Go on, Jonathan.

JONAHAN: Well, Sir, what I heard was this. Forty Jews have taken an oath to kill my Uncle. They say they won't eat or drink till he's dead.

CLAUDIUS: How do they mean to try to reach him?

JONATHAN: They went to the High Priest this morning. They said that if the Council asks for Uncle Paul to be brought down for questioning tomorrow, they will get him somehow in the street.

CLAUDIUS: That part about the Council is true, Paul. The request from the High Priest came in an hour ago. Thank you, Jonathan. Don't tell anyone you have been here. We'll let you out at the back. And I promise you no Jewish gang is going to catch my troops unawares. Now run along! Get in touch with me if you have to; but what I want you to do is keep quiet about this.

PAUL: The Lord bless you, Jonathan! When I can do so, I will send you a message. Tell your mother I pray for her every day.

JONATHAN: I will, Uncle. God be with you—and with you, Sir! (*He goes out.*)

CLAUDIUS: A nice lad, Paul.

PAUL: What will you do?

CLAUDIUS: I didn't want to tell you in front of the boy. It's better that he shouldn't know, in case they catch him. You're leaving Jerusalem, Paul.

PAUL: By myself?

CLAUDIUS: Not on your life! If there's one thing I hate, it's a lynching mob. You're going to the Governor at Caesarea, and you're going to arrive with a whole skin, if it takes half of my troops to get you there!

PAUL: Thank you, Colonel. I am at your disposal at any time. I should like to say how much I appreciate your concern. In fact, there is only one thing I regret.

CLAUDIUS: What is that?

PAUL: That I have never had time to tell you about Pontius Pilate.

SCENE TWENTY: PAUL PREACHES TO A KING AND A GOVERNOR

Bible reference: Acts 25 and 26

Liturgical use: Epiphany season

CHARACTERS: FESTUS, *Governor of Judaea*
KING HEROD AGRIPPA
BERNICE, *his sister*
ROMAN OFFICERS
JEWISH LEADERS

NOTE: Festus was the newly appointed Governor of Judaea. Paul's accusers demanded that he should put Paul on trial. Festus consulted Agrippa II, whose Kingdom contained large areas of Judaea. Agrippa was Jewish, and Festus hoped that he would shed some light on a puzzling religious case which was causing strong feelings in Jerusalem. (Peake 796g).

This scene therefore shows Paul in a different setting. It was before Festus that he demanded to be sent to Rome, as a citizen, and tried in the Emperor's court.

FESTUS *escorts the* KING *and* BERNICE *into an audience chamber.* PAUL's *accusers stand on one side,* PAUL *on the other, between two* OFFICERS.

FESTUS: Your Majesty, will you sit here? And you, Princess, on this side. Please be seated, gentlemen. (*All sit.*)

AGRIPPA: Is this the prisoner Paul?

FESTUS: Yes, Sir. If I may, I will go over the facts briefly, for the benefit of those of you who are not familiar with the case. As I told you, Sir, the Jewish authorities all approached me as soon as I arrived in my Province, demanding that I put this man on trial. They wanted a death sentence, and they had plotted to kill him illegally. That shows you how strongly they feel. But Paul, quite within his rights, has refused to go on trial in Jerusalem. He has appealed to Caesar. That puts me in an awkward position, Sir, and I hope you can help me. I don't have any clear charges to send to Rome. I thought that a preliminary hearing today might clear the matter up.

AGRIPPA: I and my sister wish to hear the prisoner explain his position.

FESTUS: Paul, you have the King's permission to speak.

(PAUL *gives the speech from Acts 26, 2-23. He can read it, or make up his own version.*)

FESTUS: A great deal of that is crazy talk, Paul, in my opinion. Too much book-learning has sent you mad!

PAUL: Ask King Agrippa whether he thinks me mad. He knows the background of my story, and I can speak freely in front of him.

AGRIPPA: He's right, Festus. I can see how this Jesus movement arose out of Jewish beliefs; but I'm not surprised that the High Priest is upset over it!

PAUL: So you can see that I am very far from mad, Your Excellency. I am speaking the truth, plain and simple. All that I have told you has taken place quite openly, and I am sure that His Majesty the King understands the situation.

BERNICE: We have heard accounts of Jesus; but I had no idea how far the movement had developed.

FESTUS: If these Jewish representatives have their way, it won't develop much further!

PAUL: Nothing can prevent the spread of the Gospel. You can silence me, but you cannot muzzle the good news about Jesus.

AGRIPPA: It's a fascinating story, Paul.

PAUL: Fascinating? Yes, I suppose you can call it that, Sir. But the vital thing is that it is true. You know our Scriptures, and the message of the Prophets. If you accept what they say, then surely you can see—

AGRIPPA: Wait a minute, Paul! Festus, I think you had better take us away from this man. He's dangerous!

BERNICE: No, Agrippa! I want to hear more.

AGRIPPA: It isn't safe, my dear. With his eloquence, he'll be turning us into Christians if we stay here any longer.

PAUL: I wish to God I could turn you to Jesus, Your Majesty. I wish that both of you, and every man in this room, could share all that Jesus has given to me, and stand where I stand—except for these chains!

BERNICE: Why is he kept prisoner, Festus?

AGRIPPA: Yes, Governor. I'd like to know the answer to that. You surely don't call Paul's preaching a criminal offense.

FESTUS: No, Sir. As far as I can see, no formal charge against him would stick for a moment; though of course I felt bound to take seriously the very strong pressure put upon me by these influential accusers. Paul would have been discharged, if he had not appealed to Caesar. But once that appeal has been made, it can't be reversed.

AGRIPPA: A pity.

PAUL: No, Sir, not a pity. It will enable me to preach the good news at Rome.

BERNICE: You really believe in this, Paul, don't you?

PAUL: Princess, it is the only reality in my life. Jesus is my Savior, and yours. I pray that one day you will believe it also.

BERNICE: Are you sure we must go, Agrippa?

AGRIPPA: Yes, my dear. We can't afford to get ourselves involved in a hornet's nest like this.

FESTUS: Shall we go this way, Your Majesty?

SCENE TWENTY-ONE: SHIPWRECK

Bible reference: Acts 27

Liturgical use: Early in October, the time of the shipwreck

CHARACTERS: PAUL
        *TROPHIMUS, *Captain of the Ship*
        JULIUS, *Centurion in charge of the prisoners*
        *BALBUS, *Owner of the Ship*
        BOATSWAIN
        SAILORS and PRISONERS

NOTE: First read the whole chapter, to put this scene in context. The Alexandria cornships were the largest vessels in the Mediterranean. The Captains tried to avoid being at sea in them after mid-

September, as the weather then became very dangerous. The names of the Captain and Owner are made up.

Try first to build up a convincing atmosphere of panic and violent movement. Nobody has eaten anything for a long time, and the Ship has been drifting helplessly. Improvise conversation among the prisoners, who are tied and huddled down below, and the sailors.

PAUL, TROPHIMUS, JULIUS *and* BALBUS *are on deck. It is night-time. A* SAILOR *is taking a sounding.*

TROPHIMUS: What is the sounding?

SAILOR: Twenty fathoms, Sir.

BALBUS: Twenty! That means land not far off. We'll lose the Ship!

JULIUS: More important than the Ship, Balbus, are my two hundred and fifty prisoners.

TROPHIMUS: For God's sake stop arguing! What's the sounding now?

SAILOR: Fifteen, Sir.

TROPHIMUS: Drop the four stern anchors! Boatswain, do you hear me?

BOATSWAIN: Ay, ay, Sir. Stern party, drop the four stern anchors!

JULIUS: Will they hold us?

TROPHIMUS: They may, and they may not. Just leave me alone! I'm Captain of this ship, and if you give me a chance I shall try to get you ashore alive.

PAUL: We shall all get to shore alive.

BALBUS: What do you mean?

PAUL: I know we shall. God has assured me.

BALBUS: What's going on up there? In the bows!

TROPHIMUS: I can't see a thing.

BOATSWAIN: (*Running toward them.*) Sir, some of the Crew are lowering the boat. They pretended to drop the anchors, but—

JULIUS: Lowering the boat! You mean they're trying to sneak away?

PAUL: Stop them! Unless they stay on board, everyone may die.

TROPHIMUS: Boatswain, cut the boat loose!

BOATSWAIN: Ay, ay, Sir. (*He runs back to the bows.*)

BALBUS: That's our only boat, Trophimus. Why do you listen to this man?

TROPHIMUS: I listen to him because he has more guts and more common sense than all the rest of you put together. Thanks,

Paul! I think we've saved a mutiny. (BOATSWAIN *returns*.) Did you manage it?

BOATSWAIN: Yes, Sir. Just in time. I put two men under arrest.

JULIUS: (*Laughing*.) Two more prisoners! What worries me is that some of these brutes down below may make a break for it. I shall have to be ready to kill them if there's a danger of that.

PAUL: Do not touch them, Julius! We shall all reach the shore alive, and none of them can get away.

BALBUS: I suppose God told you that too!

PAUL: Yes. He has told me what we should do, and what will happen.

JULIUS: It seems a little calmer. Don't you have any clue as to where we are, Trophimus?

TROPHIMUS: After fourteen days drifting? I've told you, we can be anywhere South of Crete—Carthage, Cyrene, the Syrtes—

BALBUS: So what is the great Paul's plan?

TROPHIMUS: Yes, Paul. What do you suggest?

PAUL: I think we should distribute as much food as the men can eat. We're all weak from hunger, and this is a chance to eat before morning. If we have to swim for it, we shall need to build up our strength.

TROPHIMUS: You're right again. I'll go and see to it. Boatswain! (*He goes out toward the bow*.)

BALBUS: Of all the crazy situations I ever saw, this is the strangest! A prisoner giving orders to the three of us!

PAUL: They are not my orders. Jesus sent me here to save your lives.

BALBUS: Jesus? That's a new one. Who's he?

JULIUS: Paul has been telling me about Jesus ever since he was handed over to me in Caesarea. I tell you, I've never had a prisoner like this. I'd give a year of my pension to see him go free!

PAUL: And I would give a year of my life to see you accept Jesus in your heart, Julius. As for me, he means me to go to Rome and witness for him. What happens after that is in his hands.

BALBUS: Look! It's beginning to get light! (TROPHIMUS *returns with a tray of food and cups*.) Do you know where we are yet, Trophimus?

TROPHIMUS: No. But the lookout thinks there's a sandy bay southwest of us. Here, I've brought you some food.

JULIUS: Thank you, Trophimus.

PAUL: Have all the prisoners been given food?

TROPHIMUS: Don't worry! It's on the way to everyone. Your friend

Luke is helping to pass it round. We'll dump the rest overboard, and loose anchor an hour after dawn.

BALBUS: Can you save the ship?

TROPHIMUS: Not a hope, Balbus! If we stay out here another day, the anchors will drag, and we'll end up on those rocks. But the way the wind is now we might make it through the currents to that cove—you can see it now. If we don't, we all drown. If we do, we beach the ship and jump for it.

PAUL: I know that we shall all be safe. Don't worry about the prisoners, Julius! I shall go and break bread with them, and offer thanks to God. I shall tell them how you thought of killing them, but did not do so on my advice. And I promise you that they will not try to escape. When we come close to the shore, Luke and I will help those who are sick. Now eat and drink with thankful hearts, my friends! If we show no fear, the rest will follow us.

(PAUL *goes below.*)

BALBUS: I can't believe it! I hope I never have another voyage like this!

TROPHIMUS: I'm telling you, without Paul I think we'd all be dead. Who this Jesus is, I can't understand. But Paul—you can't help respecting a man like that.

JULIUS: He told me he has been near to death time after time, all because of this new religion. If I get to Rome alive, I shall go and learn all about it.

BALBUS: You'll forget the whole thing in a week, Julius! Religion is fine in a storm at sea; but if I get to Rome all I shall be interested in is my insurance money for the ship!

TROPHIMUS: You're a hard man, Balbus! Well, you'll know soon whether you collect your insurance or a tombstone. Boatswain! Assemble both watches, and raise the anchors! Hoist the foresail, and unlash the steering paddles!

BOATSWAIN: Ay, ay, Captain.

BALBUS: May the Gods protect us!

JULIUS: Time for a prayer, Balbus? I know I trust more in Paul and his prayers than in what little faith I have ever had in our gods.

BOATSWAIN: Both watches assemble on the after deck!

JULIUS: (*Under his breath.*) Now Jesus, if you are really God's Son, watch over us!

SCENE TWENTY-TWO: A PRISONER AT ROME

Bible reference: Acts 28, 16-31, and the Letter to Philemon

Liturgical use: General, at any season

CHARACTERS: PAUL
                    MARK
                    ONESIMUS
                    MARIUS, a Roman soldier

NOTE: It is uncertain what happened to Paul after his imprisonment in Rome. He may have remained a prisoner there until his death; or he may have been released, made some further journeys among the Churches, and returned for a second period of imprisonment. Luke ends his story with the picture of Paul living in Rome, a prisoner, but able to preach and write freely.

Onesimus was a slave who had run away from his master Philemon. Paul sent him back, with the short letter which appears in the New Testament. The name Onesimus means "Profitable" (compare Onassis—the same Greek root!) Paul makes more than one pun on this name in the Letter. You could call him Nicholas and change the puns into references to "nickels." Marius is an imaginary character.

PAUL *is sitting at a table with* MARK. MARIUS *stands by the door.* ONESIMUS *is preparing a meal. It is a plainly furnished room.*

PAUL: Is breakfast nearly ready, Onesimus?

ONESIMUS: Very nearly.

MARK: Do you need any help?

ONESIMUS: No, Mark. I can manage. It was a lot harder work at Philemon's!

PAUL: Marius, you must join us in a moment. It's our custom here for the guard to eat with us.

MARIUS: That's what they told me. It's not like the usual prison job, they said. And they're certainly right!

PAUL: (*Laughing.*) I'm glad, Marius. I *am* a prisoner, and I shan't try to run away. But we don't have to shed tears over it.

MARIUS: When will the Emperor's court hear your case?

MARK: If we knew that, we'd be wiser than the Emperor!

PAUL: We don't know, Marius, and we have to be patient. Now, Mark, what is going to happen today?

MARK: A group of Greek freedmen are coming to see you; and Rufus and Amplias later this afternoon. We hope that Tychicus will be here by evening. He got into Puteoli two days ago.

PAUL: Good! That will mean news from Ephesus. Meanwhile we can try to finish the letters to Laodicea and Colosse—and I have to write to Philemon about our runaway friend here.

ONESIMUS: Breakfast, Paul!

MARK: I'll clear the things off the table.

PAUL: Marius, you haven't really met our cook, have you? This is Onesimus, a slave of Philemon, from Colosse.

MARIUS: Colosse? Isn't that somewhere in Asia? You're a long way from your master, aren't you?

PAUL: We won't be ashamed, Onesimus. We'll tell Marius the problem. He ran away, Marius.

MARIUS: Ran away! (*He whistles in astonishment.*) That wasn't very smart!

PAUL: Not what you'd expect from an "Onesimus" either! But we're keeping him useful. And perhaps he can go back and live up to his name better than before.

MARIUS: If he goes back, he'll be lucky to get a chance to be useful!

ONESIMUS: I know that is what you'd expect, Marius. But I believe I can go back and tell Philemon that I'm sorry I ran away, and that I mean to be a better servant from now on.

MARIUS: And he'll believe you?

PAUL: Philemon is a kind of child of mine, Marius. I brought him to Jesus six years ago, with his wife Apphia and their son Archippus.

MARIUS: You keep talking about this Jesus. I know he has something to do with you being a prisoner.

PAUL: That's true. I am his prisoner, not the Emperor's. Later we'll tell you about it. But now I must begin my letters. Onesimus, why don't you take the dishes away, and then tell Marius how you found joy in the Lord? I will dictate to Mark the letter that you are to take home to Philemon.

> (*The scene can continue with improvisations.* ONESIMUS *talks to* MARIUS, *and tells him how he first met Christianity. He must make this up, as we know nothing about* ONESIMUS *outside this letter.* MARIUS *can talk about his upbringing, and re-*

ligion in the Roman Army. PAUL *dictates the letter to* PHILEMON *and he and* MARK *can also discuss some of the people and questions raised in the Letter to the Colossians, written at the same time.*)